Capitalism and Crises

Advance Praise for *Capitalism and Crises*

"Colin Mayer has been an influential voice in the debate about corporate purpose for many years. In this new book, he tackles the problem of how to rethink the entire capitalist system. His core argument – that we should seek to solve the problems of people and planet in a profitable way – is simple and profound. There are no easy fixes, but this important and carefully-argued book provides individuals, businesses and policymakers a practical route to progress."

- Julian Birkinshaw, Vice Dean and Professor of Strategy and Entrepreneurship, London Business School

"The refrain throughout this remarkable book is solving problems for others and not causing problems for others. That is a theme that will resonate with entrepreneurs in early-stage companies who in my observation are passionate about solving problems. Drawing on rich wisdom from a career of helping firms to define and realise their purpose, Colin Mayer moves the agenda from companies simply maximising shareholder value to companies promoting wider prosperity. Everyone who wants to understand this transition and participate in it should read this."

- Andrew Briggs, Emeritus Professor of Nanomaterials, University of Oxford

"In this ambitious and insightful book, Colin Mayer untangles some of capitalism's intrinsic problems and offers some detailed proposals to tackle them. Moreover, he introduces the relevance of moral principles back into economics and business and develops the organizational architecture for corporate purpose. The outcome is a very compelling framework on how companies can be governed and managed, how investors should broaden their responsibilities, and how governments can contribute to more prosperous societies. Colin Mayer's book makes a very unique and relevant contribution to the discussion on reinventing capitalism."

- Jordi Canals, IESE Foundation Professor of
Corporate Governance, IESE Business School

"Reviving Adam Smith's real legacy, this book is a tour de force of one of the most astute thinkers of our time. Colin Mayer's sophisticated and fascinating multi-disciplinary study harshly criticizes contemporary capitalism and develops the notion of problem-solving capitalism as an inspiring alternative. Combining learning and experience, integrity and courage, Mayer urges us to reform the way we conceptualize and regulate the financial system and, most fundamentally, the ownership and governance of firms. While his bold vision is radical, this insightful book shows that this ideal is also practical: firms can and should incur the full costs of the problems they create and profit only from the solutions they produce."

- Hanoch Dagan,
Professor of Law and Director, Berkeley Center for Private Law
Theory, University of California Berkeley Law School

"This book is the culmination of thinking over a brilliant career, and it comes just in time. It provides profound but practical ideas for addressing the underlying issues that are creating an ongoing set of crises. The most pressing and overarching one in the U.S. is a culture war based on extreme political polarization. Professor Mayer's book explains why this polarization exists and the transformation in capitalism he calls for should resonate on both the left and the right."

- Robert Eccles,
Visiting Professor of Management Practice, Said Business School,
University of Oxford and Retired Professor of Management Practice,
Harvard Business School

"This is a remarkable and profoundly insightful book on both the huge strengths of capitalism as a means of delivering what we want, but also its current massive failures. Based on a wealth of experience, the book is crystal clear in proposing how to transform the capitalist system so as to avoid such crises by a combination of systems thinking and a radical program of values-based action. This will promote human well-being and justice through a reformulated Golden Rule embodied in corporate law and governance. This important book is highly recommended."

- George Ellis, Emeritus Professor of Complex Systems
in the Department of Mathematics
and Applied Mathematics at the University of Cape Town

"Mayer provides a compelling journey that documents the baleful consequences when business pursues profit as an end to itself rather than as a means to address societal and ecological problems. He goes on to offer a roadmap to escape from this trap, including a welcome emphasis on the responsibility of the educational system to help shape a socially productive rather than destructive business system."

- Geoffrey Jones, Isidor Straus Professor of
Business History, Harvard Business School

"We are failing to address the now existential problems of people and planet - our economies and our businesses are not currently designed to address these problems. Colin Mayer's book is an important contribution to the debate about how to ensure that this design problem is addressed. It should also be a salutary reminder to all of us of the urgency to do so."

- Colm Kelly,
Global Leader Corporate Sustainability, PwC International Ltd

"As Adam Smith was the Father of Capitalism in the 18th Century, Colin Mayer is the Grandson in the 21st Century, restoring Capitalism to its central and essential role in society today and in the future. *Capitalism and Crises* is the third book in the trilogy that is the foundation for the future study of Capitalism and for the adoption of laws and approved practices. It provides a clear, actionable, and timely roadmap for management teams and boards of directors to take into account their impacts on employees, the environment, customers, suppliers, and local and national communities. Meticulously researched, *Capitalism and Crises* is essential reading for business leaders and investment stewards seeking creative solutions for confronting the pressing corporate and societal questions of our time."

> \- Martin Lipton, Founding Partner, Wachtell, Lipton, Rosen & Katz

"In *Capitalism and Crisis*, Professor Mayer has provided a master class in why we must, and how we can, reform our capitalist system. By suggesting a reformulation of the "Golden Rule" itself, he guides the reader to a new framework for the role of business in society. He provides provocative, inspiring, and motivational ideas. This book is for anyone interested in true system change."

> \- Lynn Forester de Rothschild, Chief Executive of E.L. Rothschild LLC

Capitalism and Crises

How to Fix Them

Colin Mayer

OXFORD
UNIVERSITY PRESS

Great Clarendon Street, Oxford, OX2 6DP,
United Kingdom

Oxford University Press is a department of the University of Oxford.
It furthers the University's objective of excellence in research, scholarship,
and education by publishing worldwide. Oxford is a registered trade mark of
Oxford University Press in the UK and in certain other countries

© Colin Mayer 2024

The moral rights of the author have been asserted

All rights reserved. No part of this publication may be reproduced, stored in
a retrieval system, or transmitted, in any form or by any means, without the
prior permission in writing of Oxford University Press, or as expressly permitted
by law, by licence or under terms agreed with the appropriate reprographics
rights organization. Enquiries concerning reproduction outside the scope of the
above should be sent to the Rights Department, Oxford University Press, at the
address above

You must not circulate this work in any other form
and you must impose this same condition on any acquirer

Published in the United States of America by Oxford University Press
198 Madison Avenue, New York, NY 10016, United States of America

British Library Cataloguing in Publication Data

Data available

Library of Congress Control Number: 2023936000

ISBN 978–0–19–888794–2

DOI: 10.1093/oso/9780198887942.001.0001

Printed and bound by
CPI Group (UK) Ltd, Croydon, CR0 4YY

Links to third party websites are provided by Oxford in good faith and
for information only. Oxford disclaims any responsibility for the materials
contained in any third party website referenced in this work.

To my parents,

Who experienced the worst of crises,

And the best of times.

As the whistle blew and a guard closed the doors of the train, a young girl looked out at the figure of a woman on the platform waving to her. She waved back, trying to hold back her tears.

The train glided out of the station and passed through beautiful green fields, pastures, forests, hills, and terraced vineyards. At one point in the journey, the young girl rummaged in her handbag and found a thin silver necklace that she had been given for her 14th birthday and loved to wear. It was of little value, but she concluded that there was only one thing she could do.

She got up from her seat, made her way down the passage to the toilet, dropped the necklace in it, and watched as her early life was flushed away.

The train was nearing the border. She returned to her seat and her heart began to throb as she heard the customs officers coming down the train. The door of the carriage opened. A young official asked for her passport and inspected her bag. There was a slight tear in the lining and the official asked whether this was an accident. She mustered a weak smile. The official smiled back and returned her passport.

A few minutes later the train ground to a halt. They had crossed the border into Holland.

The girl was my mother. The woman at the station was my grand-mother. The year was 1939. The girl was fleeing from Nazi Germany to refuge in Holland.

She was one of the lucky to escape.

Preface

As I write this book, the world is in crisis. No, scrap that—the world is in multiple crises. There is war in Europe, a drought, floods, a pandemic, an energy crisis, a food crisis, a climate crisis, and a crisis in our democratic and political systems. There was a financial crisis; there is now inflation and recession. No doubt by the time you read this there will be others.

Crises are increasing in frequency and growing in intensity. Their frequency and intensity will continue to increase until we solve the problem.

The problem is our capitalist system. It is a source of remarkable prosperity, growth, employment, and poverty alleviation. But it is also a cause of terrible suffering, disasters, inequality, environmental degradation, and social exclusion. And they are getting worse.

This book is about solving the problem. It is the third in a trilogy that I have written on what's wrong. The first (*Firm Commitment*) was about the problem; the second (*Prosperity*) was about the solution. This is about the transformation—the fundamental change in our capitalist system needed to fix it.

The first book identified the absence of trust and commitment in a capitalist, market-driven system as the problem, the second purpose as the solution. This is about how to get us from where we are to where we need to be—the fundamental transformation from lack of trust and commitment to purpose.

The first two books laid the foundations for what has gone wrong, why, and what is needed—not a revolution but a reformation, learning from the future as well as the past—crafting our future in the way in which we wish it to be, not being a slave to the past but a respecter of it.

The first book was about one of the most important institutions in our lives—business. The second broadened the horizon to economies and the law. This book extends the horizon to all our institutions and organizations—economic, legal, political, public, social, as well as commercial—and emphasizes that there are common approaches to bringing about the transformation required of all of them.

Key to appreciating this is to recognize our institutions and organizations as systems—as systems that need fundamental change to reboot them. This is not about meddling on the side-line with a few policy instruments, changing one or two things here and there. It requires a coherent, consistent set of policies to coordinate the necessary changes.

Equally, it is not about discarding or weakening what is good and what works. It is about strengthening and reforming existing structures so that they are fit for purpose for the twenty-first century.

They are not fit for purpose at present, suited to a minority, leaving the rest poor, disadvantaged, inadequate, excluded, and aggrieved. Our capitalist system has been the source of immense and unsustainable dissatisfaction that threatens our politics, societies, economies, and environment. We need to fix it fast.

That will not happen so long as it is not in people's interest for it to happen. If it doesn't make money for business and investors, then it is pie in the sky and wishful thinking. However much we may believe in the goodness of leaders, investors, communities, and societies, if it is not profitable, it is not possible. In fixing the system, we need to be realistic about what it takes to fix it properly.

Profit should be recognized for what it is—the driver of one of the most important institutions in our capitalist system—business. It is the reason why business exists, what it is there to do, its reason for being, namely its purpose. Business exists to make money. Profit powers progress and progress produces prosperity.

But profit also produces problems of petrifying proportions and capitalism has become a cause of continuous and increasingly uncontrollable crises. Profit has been both a blessing and a curse and it has become increasingly a curse as the problems it creates have intensified. Why?

The answer is that profits come from causing as well as solving problems. Profits are earned at the expense as well as to the benefit of the environment, our health, homes, neighbourhoods, communities, and societies. They should not be. They should come from solving our problems, not creating them.

Business exists to make money and the purpose of business is to profit but the question that we have failed to ask is: where does that money come from—what is the source of that profit? If it comes from solving problems of others that is all to the good, if it doesn't then it isn't.

Profits should be the product of solving not producing problems and the purpose of business is to profit from producing solutions not problems for others. In other words, the purpose of business is to produce profitable solutions for the problems of people and planet, not profiting from producing problems for either.[1] Profits then come, as they should do, from producing solutions not problems.

The importance of this is overwhelming. It is not just about saving our planet or protecting our health and wellbeing. More fundamentally it is about aligning our minds with our motives. The pursuit of profit has made our motives misaligned with our emotions of what it means to be human, and the morality of money has become an oxymoron. It need not and it must not be if capitalism is to be a cure not a cause of catastrophes.

Once profit is recognized for what it is, namely the product of solving the problems of others, then far from being misaligned, our emotional and reasoned motives are aligned with each other and with the world around us. Profit derives from the resolution not the creation of problems and with that comes the power to harness global resources for the benefit of all, including the world itself.

There is another reason why this is so important. It is critical for the functioning of markets and economies. So long as people can profit at the expense of others then they will. Those who don't will look stupid, naïve, sanctimonious, and self-righteous.

The corrosiveness of unjust profit should not be underestimated because profiting at others' expense undermines those who do not wish to profit in that way. It contaminates competition and causes it to do exactly the opposite of what economics suggests it does—promote human wellbeing.

Some believe it impossible to have the nice bits of capitalism without the nasty—innovation without destruction; efficiency without redundancy; profit without problems. That misses the point. So long as the nasty is permissible, the nice will be impossible. The drive to innovation, efficiency, and profit is intensified not diminished by a focus on solutions without problems.

Preventing profiting from problems makes profiting from solutions the only course of action. It moves our minds as well as money not just to profit but to where profit is just. It creates justice as well as respects it. It is empowering, enabling, and enriching as well as caring, communal, and considerate.

Furthermore, while profit is naturally associated with business, it is relevant to all aspects of our lives, economies, governments, and societies. We should not accept that current generations profit at the expense of future ones, a country or region benefits to the detriment of another, one person or group prospers at a cost to another, or humanity flourishes from the extinction of the natural world.

These are examples of 'unjust enrichment'—one party gaining at the expense of another. As capitalism has grown and powered ever greater prosperity, it has simultaneously intensified the scale of unjust enrichment that has occurred at the expense of individuals, communities, societies, and the natural world. We should be protected from this and instead be enriched where we enrich.

But this is not just or predominantly about distribution of income and wealth between rich and poor. It is about contribution as well as distribution. It is about growth, development, prosperity, and flourishing; innovation, investment, finance, and risk taking. It is about promoting our individual and collective contributions to these because currently our capitalist system is doing exactly the opposite.

How can this be if profit is the engine of growth? The answer is that by mismeasuring profit we are misallocating all our resources—not just existing ones but also future and unforeseen ones. In principle our economic system is self-equilibrating in identifying profitable investment opportunities wherever they may be hiding—'leaving no money on the table' as it is often described.

Where opportunities are greatest so too is funding and the taps of capitalist finance flow to where their needs and benefits are largest. And if social needs exceed private benefits and markets fail to supply what is required, don't worry the benevolent hand of government will rush in to fill the vacuum that private capital leaves behind.

If only. Unfortunately, that is exactly the opposite of what happens. Finance does not flow to developing or impoverished people, places, countries, or regions of the world. It is allergic to them and instead attracted by the developed and rich. Why? Because that is where the money is, and the purchasing power lies. It is not just grossly unfair but incredibly inefficient.

'But that is not the role of the private sector—that is the role of government and public sectors' is the predictable retort of those who fundamentally do not believe in government but rush to its defence when it is convenient to do so. In principle, it is the role of government to fill the vacuum, but in practice it does not.

Governments are no less and, in some respects, more prone to the same pressures as the private sector to go where the money is. They are by no means fully liberated from the constraints of funding that restrict their less enlightened private counterparts—'living within your means' is the analogy that former UK Prime Minister Margaret Thatcher drew in justifying fiscal austerity in the 1980s.[2]

The problem is that we have fundamentally misconceived the whole system—private and public—both are driven by the wrong measure. I have called it profit because it is easy to grasp the inequity of profiting at the expense of others. But it applies to all forms of income—personal and corporate; public and private; individual and social; national and international. All of them are grossly mismeasured because we do not subtract the income that derives from producing detriments from that which comes from creating benefits.

To take an obvious example, much of our expenditure and income from pharmaceuticals and public health is simply reversing the damage done by expenditure and income from alcohol, cars, cigarettes, social media, and pollution. We are counting as income and wellbeing what derives from exactly the opposite.

But even that does not capture the real underlying cause of the problem. It comes from a confusion of cause and effect. We should not be pursuing the money but pursuing solutions to problems. We should be searching out where there are problems that you, me, our families, friends, communities, nations, and natural world face and we should solve them. We should all be doing that to our full capabilities.

And we should all be assisted and equipped in doing that because that is why we exist. As Plato in 387 BC Greece and then Cicero in 44 BC Rome reminded us, we exist to help others to be able to help others and, in the process, to earn and profit from doing so.[3] But income and profit are not the motive or the purpose of our existence. They derive from it.

That is at the heart of why our capitalist system is going so awry. If we pursue money then we inevitably leave out the vast body of the world, let alone the entire natural world, which does not have it. And don't believe that it is just a matter of time—that all will be well in the long run. Those at the bottom of the pile need fear not because the trickle down of the treacle will eventually be within their grasp. Only it won't.

It is not simply a problem that 'in the long run we are all dead' or even that 'we will all be dead in the short run', which on current trajectories we will be, but that in the short or long run the poor will remain poor, the deprived places will remain deprived, the rich will get richer, and the natural world won't be on the map.

The system is not self-equilibrating. It is exactly the opposite so long as money is the objective, and wellbeing is derivative of its competitive pursuit, because those who haven't got it are increasingly excluded from the game. Turn the objective round to promoting their wellbeing and money being the outcome and then the excluded are included by a combination of technological, business, social, and public innovations making it possible for them to be so.

That is why I talk about problem-solving and creation not just social wellbeing and welfare. We must be actively productive in addressing defects, not just reactively distributive in redressing them.

This comes from an appreciation that our problems derive from a deficiency in the fundamental moral foundations of not just Western civilizations and capitalism but indeed many civilizations around the world, namely the Golden Rule—'do unto others as you would have them do unto you'. Enlightened as it appears, its consequences have been exactly the opposite. It has created polarization not unification, self-interest not common interest, a cult of individualism not communitarianism.

The reason is that it is self-referential. It tells us to recognize the world beyond ourselves and to act according to the interests of others, but to do so through the lens of our own not their eyes. It imposes our not their preferences and priorities on our conduct towards them. I do to them what, were I them, I would wish them to do to me.

In contrast a reformulated Golden Rule of 'do unto others as they would have done unto them' requires us to regard and act towards others in a form that recognizes and respects them for who and what they really are and want to be—benefit yourselves from doing to others what truly benefits them. It is more demanding on us (and that may explain why it was not expressed that way) but its application is transformational in how we live our lives and run our institutions and organizations.

Where did we go wrong? The answer is right at the beginning. The capitalist equivalent of the Messiah came to Earth in the guise of Adam Smith. He delivered us our capitalist learnings. But we only read half of them. It was as if we forgot to turn over the tablet of stone and failed to read what was on the other side.

It was what I did in the first exam I ever took at school. The last question on the exam page was a list of abbreviations, e.g., 'e.g.', which I was expected to explain. I could do all of them except the last one which was 'PTO'. I had no idea what it meant, so I didn't, failed to turn over the page, omitted half of the exam, and failed it!

Well, we have done the same with Adam Smith, only in reverse order. We have avidly consumed his second book, *The Wealth of Nations*, while conveniently forgetting its predecessor *The Theory of Moral Sentiments*. So, we have willingly accepted the story that 'get rich quick' helps to promote markets that temper our avaricious greed but failed to attend the previous lesson on the moral preconditions that are required for this to work, and without which markets far from being benign become perniciously malign.

With the emergence of capitalism came the division between left and right in politics and in particular the distinction between public and private ownership of the means of production.[4] For the left, the obvious resolution to the problem of public interest was public ownership. For the right, the obvious problem with public ownership was private interest. For those in the middle, no one was interested in owning their problems.

And there is the nub of the problem. Ownership is not about owning the means of production—the assets—but owning the problems those assets are there to solve. No one owns most of the assets used in production and no one at present takes ownership of the problems they create.

We shouldn't start with the ownership of assets and fix the problems that causes. Instead, we should start from the ownership of problems and then determine the assets needed to fix them. That, amongst other thing, corrects the failure of macroeconomic austerity to invest in the human capability and physical capacity required to address inequality in opportunity and income.

This book describes how to achieve the required transformation of our world by recognizing the reason why we exist and what that implies for all aspects of our lives and institutions. Is it feasible and practical or wishful thinking to expect this to happen? Not only is it possible it is simply good management, sound policy, and best practice in private, public, and philanthropic sectors.

It does not require a change in corporate law. It is the basis on which corporate law in some parts of the world can be interpreted and corporate success can generally be assessed. It is precisely the way in which at least one country, Denmark, with one of the highest levels of income per capita, lowest levels of inequality, and highest indices of happiness in the world is run.

This is not wishful thinking, but it is thinking that starts from what we want and works back to how to get there. Don't just take what is as given and immutable. We have created our capitalist system and we have the potential to mould it in the form in which we wish and need it to be.

That is exactly what this book does. *Firm Commitment* identified lack of commitment and trust as the problems to be solved, *Prosperity* purpose and prosperity as the solutions. This book is about problem-solving and profits to fix capitalism and its crises. It begins by describing where we are, how we got here and the problems that have arisen as a result. It sets out the principles that should determine where we are aiming and want to be.

It then turns to how to go from here to there, and the systems change—the laws, ownership, governance, measures, performance, finance, and investment—required to get us there. It provides a coherent and practical programme of reform which takes what we have and describes what should change to deliver what we need and want. If we can do this then far from the cataclysmic collapse that many fear, the twenty-first century will deliver unimaginable rewards for the many not the few, for the future as well as the present.

The book has been guided by the circumstances and experiences of the last few years as the coronavirus pandemic subsides, the Russia–Ukraine war rages, the climate crisis grows ever more alarming, and governments of Western democracies become even more dysfunctional. What these events reveal is an intense vacuum of the global leadership the world so desperately needs.

We have created a system that promotes self- over common interest, ideology over pragmatism, profit over purpose, nation states over global concerns. We have lost sight of where we are going, how we should get there, and how collectively and collaboratively we can address the immense and growing problems we face.

Towards the end of writing this book, I underwent two cataract eye operations. The remarkable feature of such operations is their power to transform how one sees the world. But so too can ideas, and while eyes last no longer than their owners, ideas can endure for ever. Come with me as I explain how a few simple ideas may yet help us to restore our faith in humanity and its capitalist system.

Colin Mayer
Oxford
31 January 2023

Acknowledgements

As with the previous books, this one draws on an immense amount of research and research programmes. Many of those mentioned in *Firm Commitment* and *Prosperity* have continued to play an important role in this one. In particular, I have drawn extensively on work done on the Future of the Corporation programme at the British Academy; the Ownership Project at the Said Business School at the University of Oxford; the Rethinking Performance programme at the Said Business School; the Mars Inc./ Said Business School programme on Mutuality in Business (the Economics of Mutuality); the Enacting Purpose Initiative at the Said Business School; the Regeneration of Left-Behind Places and the Foundations of Values and Value programme at the Blavatnik School of Government at the University of Oxford; the Purposeful Company programme in London; and the Scottish Government Business Purpose Commission—all programmes that I have led or co-led over the past eight years.

I have also drawn on my experience as an Ordinary Member of the Competition Appeal Tribunal in London; a founder and director of Aurora Energy Research Ltd and Oxera Economic Consultancy Ltd, now some of the largest and most significant companies in their fields; a member of the International Advisory Committee of the Securities and Exchange Board of India (SEBI); a member of the UK Government Natural Capital Committee, a Trustee of the Oxford Playhouse; the first Professor and then Dean of the Said Business School at Oxford; a founder, fellow and board member of the European Corporate Governance Institute (ECGI) and the Global Corporate Governance Colloquium (GCGC); a fellow and director of the Financial Economics programme at the Centre for Economic Policy Research (CEPR) in London; and a professorial fellow and Sub-Warden of Wadham College, Oxford.

I would like to thank Amar Bhide, Andrew Briggs, Ruth Chang, Paul Collier, Luis Correia, Robert Eccles, Fuat Ecer, George Ellis,

Markus Gabriel, Thomas Hellmann, Cameron Hepburn, John Hicklin, Will Hutton, Martin Lipton, Annette Mayer, Hannah Mayer, Anette Mikes, Andrew Mountfield, Andrea Polo, Dennis Snower, Leo Strine, David Tuckett, Peter Tufano, Ira Unell, David Vines, Rupert Younger, and two anonymous referees for very helpful comments on drafts of the book. I would like to thank Adam Swallow, Commissioning Editor for Business and Economics at Oxford University Press (OUP), for his continuing support and assistance with the publication of this third volume in the series, and Phoebe Aldridge, Project Editor for Social and Behavioural Sciences at OUP, for steering it through the production process. I would also like to thank the Blavatnik School of Government in Oxford for hosting me as a visiting professor while I wrote this book.

I am very grateful for the numerous research funds that financed the research which lies behind the book. I would particularly like to mention the funders of the British Academy Programme on the Future of the Corporation; the funders of the Enacting Purpose Initiative at the Said Business School; the ESRC funding of the NIESR Rebuilding Macroeconomics, Decentralized Reciprocity Programme; the European Union's Horizon 2020 Research and Innovation Programme, Marie Skłodowska-Curie grant; the Ford Foundation funding of the Ownership Programme at the Said Business School; Mars Inc./Economics of Mutuality Foundation funding of the Mutuality in Business Programme at the Said Business School; the New Institute Hamburg funding of the Foundations of Values and Value Programme at the Blavatnik School of Government; Oxford Martin School funding of the Regeneration of Left-Behind Places Programme at the Blavatnik School of Government; and funding from consortium members of the Oxford Rethinking Performance Initiative at the Said Business School. I am also grateful for the advice of the advisory and steering committees of the British Academy Future of the Corporation programme, the Oxford Enacting Purpose Initiative, and the Ownership Programme.

I have benefited immeasurably from all the friends and colleagues with whom I have worked over many years, in particular, in addition to the ones mentioned above, John Armour, Richard

Barker, Lilian Barratt, Ian Bateman, Marco Becht, Bill Blair, Isabella Bunn, Clare Chapman, Jennifer Corbett, Paul Davies, Alex Edmans, Jeremy Edwards, Luca Enriques, Teppo Felin, John Feddersen, Julian Franks, Leo Goldschmidt, Jeff Gordon, Tom Gosling, Dieter Helm, Cecilia Heyes, John Hood, Jay Jakub, Tim Jenkinson, John Kay, Valerie Keller, Robin Knowles, Bridget Kustin, Mary Johnstone Louis, Georgina Mace, Philip McCann, Hideaki Miyajima, Sudhir Rama Murthy, Denis Noble, Ryo Ogawa, Paul Polman, Henry Richards, Bruno Roche, Kate Roll, Peter Roth, Jacob Schumacher, Tom Simpson, Judith Stroehle, Steen Thomsen, Gareth Williams, Kathy Willis, and Amir Amel Zadeh. I am also grateful for invitations from organizers of literally hundreds of summits, conferences, lectures, seminars, workshops, and webinars around the world to present, discuss, and test the ideas in this book.

The main burden of writing a book is obviously borne by one's family and I am extremely grateful for their, and especially Annette's, unfailing support during the process. While we work to live, we don't just live to work. I have said that this is my final book on the subject, so this must be the last word.

Contents

Introduction

Economics is not just about the relation between ends and scarce means but also what lies between them in avoiding detriment and fulfilling potential.

Capitalism

Capitalism is a remarkable system. It delivers the food we eat, the clothes we wear, the houses we inhabit, the entertainment we enjoy, with no conductor, director, or leader at the centre to coordinate or control the process. In fact, it does it far better than any individual could because no one possesses the knowledge or information required to achieve that feat. It is as if billiard balls randomly bumping into each other suddenly align themselves of their own accord in producing beautiful patterns and arrangements that not even the most advanced computers could replicate. Capitalism is not only magical; it is the twenty-first-century sun king we have all come to worship and to whom we should give thanks for each night before we go to sleep.

How does it achieve this? The answer is through an incredible system of conversion. It converts our individual self-interests into a collective good. What do I mean by this? Well, let me illustrate by insulting you. You know you are selfish. You might think that you are a saint in looking after others, your families, your friends, the sick, and the elderly, but let's face it, you do those things because they make you feel and look good. Sure, you are better than people who do not gain any pleasure from helping others but your interest in other people is only as good as the pleasure you gain from it.

You might legitimately quibble with my bleak picture of your 'goodness' but stick with it for a moment. What capitalism does is not dig deep into your psyche and determine whether you really are a saint or a sinner in saintly disguise. It does not care in the slightest whether you are simply selfish—in fact, in some respects it rejoices if you are—because it likes tackling tough problems.

However selfish you are, it converts your selfishness into a collective good. Why? Because the more your greed and selfishness mean you want something, the more you are willing to pay for it; and the more you are willing to pay, the more someone is willing to provide it; and the more they are willing to provide, the more they will pay people to produce and finance it.

There in a nutshell we have the essence of capitalism and free markets. No one needs to tell you how to behave or what you should produce or whom you should employ or finance. A series of chain reactions set off a process that automatically delivers the desired outcomes.[1] It creates a self-igniting bonfire of virtues from a cesspit of vices.

Alongside this remarkable productive capacity, capitalism has one further and some believe even more important characteristic, and that is free choice. It grants us what is sometimes termed 'agency' in determining our course of action and conduct. The absence of a central planner, conductor, or director means that there is no one dictating our lives. We can determine what we do, purchase, consume, invest, squander, and save. In other words, it grants us the freedom that once liberated us from serfdom and oppression and delivered us self-determination from evil demagogues.[2]

Not bad—capitalism converts selfishness into the common good and oppression into freedom. No wonder any attack on capitalism is regarded as a fundamental threat to our liberties, rights, and interests, and provokes knee-jerk hostility. It is to be defended as much as democracy, human rights, health, and happiness—no ifs or buts. Even a mild questioning of the merits of capitalism risks your being tarred with the brush of communism or socialism—a central planner wolf disguised in capitalists' sheep clothes—the most dangerous of them all.

But as with many zealots, the capitalism creationists undermine the very principles of freedom and liberty for which they stand. They deny the right to contemplate another world. It is not that capitalism is without immense merits, and it is not that the alternatives of socialism and communism are not without tremendous defects and dangers. It is just that the denial of the capitalism creationists shuts their eyes to the possibility that capitalism may have its own deficiencies, let alone that there could be an alternative that does not entail the horrors of central planning. Is there anything wrong with capitalism?[3]

Competition

Let's go back to your pursuit of what you want and how a market-based system responds by delivering it—at a price. What price? The answer is the right price—a price that equals the cost of producing and delivering what you want. How do we know it is the right price? The answer is that if it was anything less than the cost of producing what you want then no one would provide it and, if it was any more, not only would someone be eager to produce it, but everyone would because it is profitable to do so. In other words, there will be competition to meet your selfish demands that will push down the price to precisely the cost of meeting them.

It is not just that the market delivers you choice, it provides it through competition that ensures it is delivered at a fair price that equals the cost. That is the real ingenuity of the market—all those calculations of determining costs and prices are done by every consumer and supplier acting entirely independently without any external intervention—Adam Smith's 'invisible hand'.[4]

Competition is therefore 'a', if not 'the', key to the story. It is not just miraculous that all the billiard balls align themselves of their own accord. Even more impressively, if there were only a few of them then they would not create the remarkable patterns we observe. Without competition, the great calculating machine of the market will not compute the right prices or charge you the correct amount for satisfying your selfish demands.

Capitalism without competition is like Picasso without a paintbrush—a poor reflection of its real image. All that government must therefore do is to set 'the rules of the game' by which competing firms play and ensure that they abide by the rules. Where the rules are violated then offending firms should be penalized. Beyond that, government is regarded by market advocates as a spoiler not a helper, an impeder not a facilitator.[5] But for others that is not the end of the story.

Trust and Trust Busters

Every year for the past 39 years, Ipsos-Mori, the market research company, has been undertaking a survey of which professions people trust to tell the truth. Each year they ask one thousand people the same question: 'Now I will read you a list of different types of people. For each would you tell me if you generally trust them to tell the truth, or not?' It is one of the largest, longest running, and most careful surveys of trust undertaken anywhere in the world.

At the top of the professions that people trust the most, I am pleased to say, alongside doctors, nurses, and teachers come university professors! We might have no power, pay, or prestige, but at least people trust us to do nothing, earn nothing, and take no credit for it. Near the bottom come business leaders, just ahead of estate agents (realtors), professional footballers, and journalists. And rock bottom come—yes you have guessed it—politicians, alongside advertising executives. Business leaders are ranked below trade union officials and 'the man and woman in the street'.

People's mistrust of business leaders is not just a reflection of their mistrust of bankers—indeed business leaders come below bankers in the survey. Nor is it just a temporary phenomenon or simply a reaction to recent crises. It has been true for nearly all the 39 years of the survey. Mistrust of business leaders is profound, pervasive, and persistent.[6]

To most people, this is entirely understandable—business is about the grubby job of making money and one cannot, therefore, expect it to be anything other than a disreputable activity. It is at the opposite extreme of the noble pursuits of saving people's lives, teaching the next generation, or researching major scientific discoveries.

No one exemplifies that contrast better than the archetypal 'robber baron' of nineteenth-century United States, Cornelius Vanderbilt, who amongst many other achievements commissioned construction of New York's remarkable Grand Central Station between 1869 and 1871. Beneath Vanderbilt's commercial successes lay a rapacious desire to accumulate wealth, which Mark Twain eloquently described in an open letter to him in 1869:

> You have got seventy millions and you need five hundred millions, and are really suffering for it. Your poverty is something appalling. I tell you truly that I do not believe I could live twenty-four hours with the awful weight of four hundred and thirty millions of abject want crushing down upon me. I should die under it. My soul is so wrought upon by your helpless pauperism that if you came to me now, I would freely put ten cents in your tin cup, if you carry one, and say, 'God pity you, poor unfortunate.'[7]

However, it was not Vanderbilt's wealth or the aggressive means by which it was acquired that really disturbed Twain but the idolatry that it inspired in the popular mind:

> You seem to be the idol of only a crawling swarm of small souls, who love to glorify your most flagrant unworthiness in print or praise your vast possessions worshippingly; or sing of your unimportant private habits and sayings and doings, as if your millions gave them dignity.

It was the unquestioning popular acceptance of accumulation of unimaginable fortunes by such robber barons as Carnegie, Mellon, Rockefeller, as well as Vanderbilt, that Mark Twain found particularly perplexing.

What lay behind this then and remains true to this day in many parts of the US was a belief that the robber barons' fortunes were the source of America's greatness as they pushed back the frontiers of the Wild West, and it was part of the American dream that boys like

Vanderbilt, who quit school at the age of 11 to work on his father's ferry in New York harbour, could grow to become one of the wealthiest people in the world through dogged dedication, determination, and discipline. No matter the brutality and cruelty that was often involved, the single-minded pursuit of wealth was a fundamental human right of liberty and freedom.

The motto 'Go West, young man'[8] and make your fortune remains the dream today of many an aspiring entrepreneur heading to Silicon Valley, and it is a 'right' that has over the last 60 years been reinforced by the assertion that the desire to amass fortunes is not only a noble ambition but the *only* legitimate aim of those seeking to build their corporate empires. They are neither equipped nor authorized to do anything with their investors' money other than to make more of it. They should not be lured by the enticing songs of the sirens of do-gooding onto the rocks of financial destruction.

Government

Such was the success of the robber barons that their companies grew into empires—Andrew Carnegie's Steel Company into the US Steel Corporation, Andrew Mellon's T. Mellon & Sons into the Mellon National Bank, and John D. Rockefeller's Standard Oil of Ohio into the Standard Oil Company.[9] But as they grew, they encountered a newly emerging obstacle that would come to dominate business in the twentieth century—government. A raft of legislation was introduced in the US between the end of the nineteenth century and the outbreak of the First World War to control the newly emerging monopolies.[10] The Sherman Antitrust Act of 1890 resulted in the dismemberment of Rockefeller's Standard Oil in 1911, a failed case being brought against US Steel in 1920, and the break-up of AT&T into a long-distance carrier and seven 'Baby Bells' 60 years later in 1982. In 2020, some of the US's largest and most successful corporations—Amazon, Apple, Facebook, and Google—are faced with the prospect of having to confront lengthy competition policy investigations over the coming years.

Competition policy is not the only area where business finds itself up against the government—another is regulation. The 2010s were the decade of financial, especially bank, regulation as regulators sought to correct the staggering abuses revealed by the financial crisis. The 2020s have started off as the decade of environmental regulation and in particular carbon emissions, as global warming is recognized as an existential threat. Companies are increasingly expected to report on their 'carbon footprint' and demonstrate how they will reduce it over the coming decades. Financial institutions that invest our savings in companies are expected to record the carbon emissions and 'global warming' associated with their investments and how they intend to diminish them. Banks will be required to account for their financial exposure to environmental risks of companies to which they lend and insurance companies for the climate risks of policies they insure.

All of this is placing limitations on the ability of companies and investors to pursue unrestrained profits and growth. Capitalism in the twentieth and twenty-first centuries is therefore characterized by corporations voraciously seeking profits and growth until they confront the boundaries imposed by anti-trust policy and regulation, at which point they slam on the brakes, change behaviour, or get broken up. Put another way, we look to business to drive growth, prosperity, and employment by whatever means it deems necessary and then to government to rein in business through competition policy and regulation when it lurches out of control.

Does this combination of avaricious pursuit of profits and wealth, restrained by the power of the state, work? The simple answer is no—it never has, and it is increasingly failing to do so. There are four reasons for this. The first is market failure; the second government failure; the third regulatory failure; and the fourth human failure.

The Limits to Markets and Governments

There are good reasons why, as companies grow, markets fail. As companies expand from small, local businesses into large, national, and international businesses, they command vast arrays of resources and people. They establish processes and procedures that codify and standardize activities and allow them to operate at low cost nationally and globally. They become 'natural' monopolies, dominating markets in which they operate, establishing webs of relations with their customers and suppliers, and evolving from basic organizations into complex systems that are costly for others to replicate or displace.

Take Facebook (or Meta, as it is now known) and Google (or Alphabet, as it is now known) as examples. They have little in the way of physical plants but large systems and processes for collecting, storing, and processing data to connect people with knowledge, analysis, and each other. They are natural global monopolies, not in the traditional multinational sense of having large physical plants scattered around the world, but in dominating markets where customers benefit from being globally connected. It is their complex webs of people and information, not their physical infrastructure, that competitors cannot replicate or displace.

Their 'systems nature' also makes it difficult for governments to correct their market failures. Unwinding complex systems is painful, expensive, and damaging for customers. The AT&T case started in 1974 and took seven years to complete. The case brought by the Department of Justice against IBM in 1969 lasted 13 years, by which time half of IBM's products to which the investigation related no longer existed.

An alternative to draconian anti-trust dismemberment of firms is more restrained regulation. Problems of competition in digital and telecom services can sometimes be addressed by what are termed 'access' and 'interoperability' agreements. These give other service providers access to dominant firms' systems on 'fair price' terms. More generally, regulation seeks to restrain the prices that monopoly providers charge to levels that are commensurate with their costs of supply.

A vast industry of regulation has emerged over the past four decades. The UK was at the forefront of developing what is termed 'price-cap' regulation by which companies in the utility sectors, such as energy, transport, and water, have the prices that they can charge their consumers capped by regulators. I saw this first-hand when I was advising on the early development of some of these regulatory tools, particularly in the water sector, and later in adjudicating disputes between regulators and companies as a member of the UK Competition Appeal Tribunal.

The principles of regulation are straightforward, but the practice of implementation is complex and fraught with difficulties. To take the above example of fair access and interoperability agreements, these require regulators to determine the costs at which firms have access to a dominant firm's systems. But as previously mentioned, these corporate systems are large and complex organizations. Identifying the costs most relevant to access to a specific part of a firm is almost impossible, if not meaningless.

These problems of regulation have recently been intensified by three developments. The first is that, as Facebook and Google illustrate, companies are progressively relying less and less on physical assets such as plants and machinery and more and more on what are termed 'intangible assets', namely human intellect, research, and development, and their reputations.[11,12] Costing and valuing these are particularly difficult tasks.

Second, regulatory rules are largely determined at national levels whereas dominant firms are international without, as in the case of Facebook and Google, necessarily having a strong physical presence in countries where they operate. Therefore, attempts by one country's regulator to bear down on its dominant firms simply encourage them to shift their activities elsewhere. This problem of what is termed 'regulatory arbitrage', by which companies play off different countries' regulators against each other, is like 'profit shifting' between tax authorities to avoid paying corporate taxes.

Third, the stylized description of regulators setting the rules of the game and companies playing by the rules in maximizing their profits is completely unrealistic. Companies do whatever they can to get round the rules and, if anything, turn them to their competitive advantage by raising the costs that regulation poses to potential entrants. They do this by using their substantial political influence, financial resources, and, in some countries, bribery and corruption to subvert the regulatory process, assisted by armies of consultants, communication companies, lawyers, and lobbyists.

While these are all serious limitations on the ability of regulation to control companies which in many cases have more resources and greater revenues than national governments, there is a still more serious threat to regulation in the future—non-human intelligence. At present we associate the new field of artificial intelligence with the ability of computers to process vast amounts of data and information faster than human minds and to undertake routine physical tasks more efficiently and accurately than human hands. But the emerging forms of artificial intelligence are beginning to incorporate a new feature that is far more troublesome—machine learning.[13] What this means is that machines are moving beyond algorithms that undertake tasks in ways pre-determined by their human programmers to systems optimizing how they perform those tasks. Like humans, they are learning how to do things better.

A fascinating recent paper[14] demonstrates how this is beginning to have profound implications for the functioning of our capitalist systems. It examines what artificial intelligence machines do when they are programmed to maximize profits in a context in which they are competing against each other in a market. It finds that the machines quickly learn to price at levels that are closer to the monopoly than the competitive price. The reason for this is illustrated by what happens if one of them cuts their prices to gain a greater share of the market. One might expect that others would follow suit and that a price war would break out leading to a collapse in prices towards the competitive price. In fact, the machines quickly learn that this is damaging for all of them and that they can generate greater profits by raising their prices back towards the monopoly price.

What is particularly striking about this is that the behaviour of firms in this context occurs without there being any communication between them. The machines individually learn from observing the impact of price changes on their own profits what collectively generates the greatest profits for all of them. Competition policy that sought evidence of intent on the part of parties to collude would not find it from the normal source of communication between them. There has been no communication, just self-learning about how to fulfil the objective of maximizing profits for each firm.

Regulation is not likely to fare any better. From the perspective of artificial intelligence firms, a regulator is just another artificial intelligence machine against which to compete. If regulators can only determine competitive prices from observed costs, then artificial intelligence firms have incentives to find ways of 'colluding' in relation to their reported costs as well as the prices they charge customers without revealing any evidence of collusion. Artificial intelligence with machine learning will therefore significantly aggravate the failure of both markets and regulation to control company abuses.

It is therefore not only in military conflict that humans will be forced to grant artificial intelligence unrestrained licence to self-learn. It will occur wherever there are financial, survival, or other incentives to outcompete or outperform others. That is where the risk of humans losing control moves from the realm of science fiction to social fact. A recent example is the contest between chatbots and counter-bots to perform the superhuman task of replicating and distinguishing human and human-like communications.

But there is one respect in which artificial intelligence cannot and will not outperform humans and that is in terms of its humanity.[15] It can almost certainly be programmed to outperform us in terms of its inhumanity but understanding what it is to be human is not where its strengths lie. This is sometimes described in terms of its lack of 'common sense'.

There are two notions of common sense. The first is the Aristotelian one of unification of the senses of the individual, for example, their emotion and reason. The second is the sense of the community (*communis sensus*, as Cicero described it)—the 'collective' as against the individual brain.[16] The latter derives from the connectiveness that the human brain can achieve, which intermediation of artificial intelligence undermines rather than strengthens.

The failure of artificial intelligence on this score reflects in part its technology—its reliance on silicon as against water-based molecules[17]—but more substantially its inability to understand in any meaningful way the human condition. Programming to profit where this comes from human detriment is straightforward but restricting it to where it is enhancing human wellbeing is and will remain beyond its capability. We only need to recognize the problems we encounter in putting ourselves in the minds of our offspring, let alone our cats and insects, to realize that it is not just superior knowledge and intelligence that is the source of our empathy and understanding.

The central problem with the profit motive in this regard is that it undermines independent, objective, empathetic judgements to be made about actions that can have conflicting and potentially devastating effects on others.[18] A capitalist system that confers strong incentives of self-interest to pursue profits resolutely and aggressively exposes other parties to significant risks of abuse that neither competition policy nor regulation can possibly restrain.

Underlying this is a failure of government more generally. The public sector has the advantage that in principle it promotes the overall wellbeing of society rather than, as in the case of the private sector, just a small segment of it. However, in being accountable to everybody it suffers from no effective governance by anyone. The citizens of a nation are incapable of undertaking any more than the most cursory assessment of the performance of their representatives and leaders. In contrast, concentrated owners and shareholders of firms have strong financial incentives to ensure that their agents, the directors of a firm, uphold their interests.

Appropriately designed, the governance of business may therefore outperform that of government. Government has worthy objectives to benefit society but inadequate means to achieve them. Business can have strong forms of accountability but exclusionary objectives. The attempt to layer the former on top of the latter merely reveals the deficiencies of Plato's guardians charged with overseeing self-interested producers.[19] That is one of the reasons why, while business leaders come low in such polls as Ipsos-Mori in the UK, politicians come even lower.

Instead of expecting government to remedy the deficiencies of business, perhaps we should recognize the defects of a system that divides economies and nation states into single-mindedly, self-interested businesses, and socially interested, weakly governed governments. We need a system that encourages business to have an intrinsic interest in the common good, not just rely on it being imposed from above by fictional, socially minded guardian angels in the guise of governments and regulators. We need a capitalist system that is designed to work not fail, which is exactly what the originator of the current capitalism system taught us to do.

Adam Smith

In *The Theory of Moral Sentiments*, Adam Smith stated that:

> The wise and virtuous man is at all times willing that his own private interest should be sacrificed to the public interest of his own particular order or society. He is at all times willing, too, that the interest of this order or society should be sacrificed to the greater interest of the state or sovereignty, of which it is only a subordinate part. He should, therefore, be equally willing that all those inferior interests should be sacrificed to the greater interest of the universe, to the interest of that great society of all sensible and intelligent beings, of which God himself is the immediate administrator and director.[20]

Could this possibly be the same Adam Smith who much more famously wrote in *An Enquiry into the Nature and Causes of the Wealth of Nations*: 'it is not from the benevolence of the butcher, the brewer, or the baker that we expect our dinner, but from their regard to their own self-interest. We address ourselves not to their humanity but to their self-love, and never talk to them of our own necessities, but of their advantages'?[21]

The answer is it is and, far from reflecting schizophrenia on the part of Smith, it reveals a collective mental aberration on our part to fail to recognize the former as the moral foundations of the latter. *The Theory of Moral Sentiments* is arguably one of the most important books of the Age of Enlightenment.[22] It provides the moral meaning of Adam Smith's merits of markets.

It is sometimes suggested that, in the rush to adopt the latter, we forgot the former. But that is perhaps a rather naïve account of the fallibility of human nature. There is a very good reason why *The Theory of Moral Sentiments* was forgotten and that is, in comparison with *The Wealth of Nations*, it is quite unworldly. While *The Wealth of Nations* is practical and accessible, *The Theory of Moral Sentiments* can seem esoteric and idealistic.

Furthermore, developments in intellectual thought during the nineteenth century appeared to render *The Theory of Moral Sentiments* largely irrelevant. The first development was the emergence of the concept of utilitarianism and the consequentialist notion that economic success can be evaluated in terms of its contribution to human happiness and social wellbeing.[23] So long as we progressed in the direction of increasing the wellbeing of the greatest number all was well and we were on our way to the attainment of individual and collective nirvana. That measure of success, together with the guidance that *The Wealth of Nations* provided on the role of markets and competition in achieving it, was sufficient to guide economies effortlessly towards their desired goals.

Where for some reason that was not the case, and markets and competition failed to attain beneficial outcomes, then there was a second set of ideas that were emerging around the role of government which suggested an alternative remedy. If economics alone could not direct our natural self-interests towards the fulfilment of our collective as well as individual wellbeing, then a political resolution was required through the intervention of government, law, and regulation. The economic liberalism of competitive markets and public policy was the basis of an emerging twentieth-century consensus.[24]

But there was a final step that rendered Smith's *Theory of Moral Sentiments* not only irrelevant but positively undesirable. The growth of big business in the nineteenth and twentieth centuries imposed a massive demand for funding, especially from manufacturing industry, which created a new industry of its own—finance. Capital markets became an ancillary of business, demanding that businesses not only compete one against another in selling what their customers want but also in raising finance from their investors. They had to satisfy investors' demands for financial reward as well as their customer demands for material benefit.

Furthermore, as the providers as well as the owners of capital required by businesses, investors were the pipers that called the tune to which the captains of industry had to dance. Anything else was an infringement of the primary obligations and responsibilities of those captains as they steered their corporate vessels through perilous competitive waters. Not only are we the lazy, greedy, and selfish individuals of *homo economicus*[25] but, were we not, we would suffer the fate that Bernard Mandeville described in his *Fable of the Bees* 70 years before Smith's *Wealth of Nations*—namely the collapse of a thriving hive of bees into 'a hollow Tree, Blest with Content and Honesty' when 'Honesty fills all their Hearts'.[26]

As a result, any duties other than to succeed, survive, and satisfy shareholders were not only impractical but immoral. They were beyond the legitimate rights of sticking to the knitting to which those charged with running businesses were required to adhere. In particular, the second half of the twentieth century became Mandeville's 'Golden Age … free, For Acorns, as for Honesty'—a period when making money became the sole moral motive of business.

Of course, the twenty-first century has been the one when we recognized the consequences. But, and this is a central message of the book, we have not identified the solutions. We are still heading in the wrong direction and indeed the remedies that have been suggested to date are making matters worse not better. A combination of recognizing our goodness as social as well as selfish beings, the long term as against the short term, an 'enlightened' view of shareholder interests, the wellbeing as well as wealth of shareholders, stakeholder as well as shareholder interests, sustainability, measurement, international standards, and regulation are thought sufficient to fix the problem.

They are not and they will never be. They miss the point of what is fundamentally at fault and why we will not create the wealth of nations without a theory of moral sentiments. The fault is that, without perfect markets and moral sentiments, not only does competition fail to deliver desired outcomes, it does the opposite: it promotes highly undesirable outcomes.[27] It encourages 'runs to the bottom' not the top where everyone competes to extract as much as possible from everyone else, and the regulator is just another victim of that opportunism. Far from the spontaneous emergence of harmonious patterns, capitalism creates dissonance and distortion, not only in distributional fairness but also, as Chapter 10 demonstrates, economic efficiency, and macroeconomic performance.

What this book does is provide the glue that cements the wealth of nations with our moral sentiments in a form in which, as Adam Smith intended, they are conjoined at the head as well as the hip— conjoined even in the absence of our innate goodness, competition, or regulation in the presence of *homo economicus,* market, and government failure. It is not that social connectedness, competition, and regulation are unimportant—they are vital, but they are not sufficient in the absence of the institutions of capitalism that bind them together.

The Book

Part I of the book discusses the nature of our capitalist system and how it is currently conceived. It describes how this derives from a bottom-up view of the world based on our individual conduct and how that view is being challenged from a top-down perspective of the system itself. It suggests that there are deficiencies in both and that we need to retain the benefits of individual choice while acknowledging the contribution to the system required of individuals and organizations. It sets out how that can be achieved based on a view of the values that underpin our individual behaviour.

It then turns to the challenges our capitalist system faces in addressing the mounting crises we are confronting and argues that they are manifestation of the failures of the system itself. At present these are not being addressed, and they will not be so long as we do not appreciate the underlying systemic problems that need to be fixed. That involves recognizing that notions of something being legal and profitable are no longer sufficient for them to be acceptable. We need to determine the ethical basis for what is both legally and profitably acceptable.

Part II moves on to develop an ethical framework within which capitalism can be positioned. What are the criteria against which we should judge success and failure, and what should we be striving to achieve? The fundamental principle of the book, which is termed 'the Moral Law', is based on a reformulation of the Golden Rule. This suggests that not profiting at the expense of others is a critical condition for the operation of competition and markets as well as the avoidance of unjust enrichment.

The Moral Law must be a central fulcrum of legal systems and the rule of law around the world for economies and markets to function effectively. Corporate law should enable business to commit to profiting from producing solutions to problems as well as avoiding profiting from creating them. While it is possible to interpret some countries' corporate law this way, that is not universally the case. This reflects a failure of existing law to prevent profiting from detriments. To achieve that, corporate purposes of profiting from solving problems without creating them should be the basis on which corporate law establishes the duties of directors.

Part III turns to two key aspects of the nature of problem-solving organizations—who owns them and how they are governed. It describes how organizations need to own the problems they are seeking to solve and structure their forms of ownership accordingly. The multiplicity of problem-solving objectives of organizations has given rise to a wide variation in forms of ownership around the world, some better suited to effective achievement of profitable problem solving than others. In particular, the widespread co-existence of dominant and dispersed shareholders reflects the different functions they perform in owning and stewarding delivery of corporate purposes.

Leadership has a critical role to play in defining, inspiring, and implementing corporate purposes. But ownership of problem-solving does not just reside at the top of organizations. It must be established throughout to ensure that problem-solving is deeply embedded in the culture and values of all managers and employees. That allows processes of problem-solving to be delegated to those with a deep appreciation and understanding of the specific nature of the problems to be addressed and the methods, procedures, experimentation, evaluation, and learning required to solve them.

Part IV considers how to measure the performance of organizations against the problems they exist to solve. It describes how this should be done at national and international levels to protect the environment and ensure the long-term survival of human society. Some widely adopted forms of measurement pose serious risks to nature if they are not combined with appropriate methods of ensuring its conservation. Preservation of natural and social capital has significant implications for measurement of aggregate national income as well as that of individual organizations.

Critical to this is accounting for profit. At present profit fails to incorporate the true costs of rectifying, remedying, and compensating for detriments. This creates misallocation of resources within as well as across organizations. Appropriately formulated management accounts are used to incentivize those working within them to deliver profitable solutions for the problems of others. This requires identification of the contribution that different parts of an organization make to its overall objectives and the partnerships that are needed with outside organizations to ensure problem-solving is commercially viable and profitable.

Part V turns to the financing of problem-solving organizations and in particular the provision of risk-sharing equity capital. It describes how this comes from a combination of business, banks, private equity, and financial institutions. It is critical for the start-up and mentoring of entrepreneurship and social enterprise in the poorest parts of the world, the development and networking of small and medium-sized enterprises in left-behind places and depressed regions, and the funding, stewardship, and ownership of the largest international businesses. Through financing, mentoring, networking, and stewardship, investors contribute to both the delivery of profitable problem-solving organizations and the avoidance of profiting from problem creation.

While law and regulation can prevent profitable production of problems, they cannot produce unprofitable solutions. That requires public policy to make unprofitable solutions profitable. Partnerships between problem-solving business, investors, governments, and educational institutions forge common purposes around shared prosperity across communities, nations, and the natural world. They are central to the promotion of growth, productivity, and investment and in addressing problems of regional disparities, inequality, social exclusion, and the delivery of essential goods and services. There is shared prosperity when common purpose is established between problem-solving private, public, and social organizations, and immense economic, social, and political damage done when it is not.

Recommendations

The book argues that:

> We should reformulate the Golden Rule around doing unto others as they would have done unto them.
> This should be reflected in corporate purposes of producing profitable solutions for the problems of people and planet, not profiting from producing problems for either.
> Corporations should determine their purposes conditional on not profiting from harming others.
> Directors can then retain a singular duty to their shareholders not to multiple stakeholders.

This requires that:

> Corporate purpose should be placed at the heart of corporate law around the world.
>
> Appropriate interpretation of existing legislation in some jurisdictions may already provide courts of law with the basis for doing this. Elsewhere, new legislation will need to be enacted.
>
> Dominant shareholders should take ownership of the problems their companies exist to solve and promote their profitable resolution without detriments.
>
> Leaders should bring clarity and commitment to their organization's purposes, values, and culture, and delegate authority and resources to those responsible for their implementation.

Measurement and finance are critical:

> Corporate profit and national income should account for costs of sustaining the wellbeing of those outside as well as within their formal legal boundaries, including in the natural world.
>
> Organizations should incur the costs of rectifying and remedying the problems they create and account for them in both their internal management and external reporting.
>
> International standards should set principles of accounting and reporting for corporate purpose; accountants and auditors should assure adherence to them.
>
> Institutional investors should provide adequate risk-bearing, predominantly equity capital for delivery of problem-solving purposes and steward their profitable delivery.

Public and private sectors should work together:

> Leaders of public and private sector organizations should forge common purposes to create shared prosperity inclusive of left-behind people, places, and nations.
>
> Central governments, financial institutions, and organizations should delegate authority and finance to those best placed to deliver shared prosperity.

Regulators should align the purposes of dominant corporations and essential service providers with the interests of their customers, communities, societies, and environment.

Universities and other educational institutions should provide leaders and employees with the knowledge and skills required to support their purpose-driven organizations.

Part I begins by identifying the problems we have inherited and need to resolve.

PART I

THE PROBLEM

Capitalism is one of many systems in our lives. From an economics perspective, it is regarded as driven from the bottom-up by the individuals who comprise it. A top-down view looks at it from the perspective of the overall system in relation to society and the natural world.

The bottom-up notion is associated with free will and the pursuit of individual objectives, and the top-down with socially imposed values, particularly from institutions and governments. Other disciplines such as biology, physics, and psychology are the subject of similar debates about reductionism and raise questions about the existence of free will.

Both upward and downward concepts of capitalism have their limitations and it is a mistake to restrict consideration to one or the other. We should embrace both individual and collective choice in a values-based, problem-solving approach to the purpose of capitalism.

The integrity of systems depends on the values that underlie their purposes. Problem-solving purposes create value by contributing to the performance of others. Value creation is the source of profit that resources and rewards contributors to the system. Alongside this, equity involves sharing as well as owning rewards, care derives from relationships between individuals not just contractual concerns for the wellbeing of others, and citizenship is a collaborative contribution to a common purpose of shared prosperity.

Embracing upward and downward causation requires system-based policies regarding all of law, regulation, ownership, governance, measurement, performance, finance, and investment.

The failures of our capitalist system have manifested themselves in increasingly frequent and intense crises. This is what we are currently experiencing. The crises have revealed several aspects of the properties and deficiencies of capitalism: the ability of problem-solving companies to turn crises into opportunities; the need for greater clarity and commitment to problem-solving purposes; the influence of societal pressures on the behaviour of companies; and the challenges created by conflicting societal demands.

Conflicts have arisen between climate change, environmental impacts, and the affordability of energy; innovation in public health, for example in relation to the development of vaccines to tackle COVID-19, and their global accessibility; and decisions by companies to withdraw from or remain in politically unacceptable countries.

The most successful businesses in the world tackle the biggest challenges. At present, they do so in a form that causes as well as solves problems. For example, addictive, unhealthy, polluting products remain highly profitable, competition to develop artificial intelligence poses serious threats to humanity, and problems of inequality and social exclusion have intensified as an ever-stronger drive to generate profit encourages companies to concentrate on affluent customers.

At present profits derive from the creation of problems as well as the delivery of solutions. While business needs to be profitable to be able to function and flourish, profits should come from the resolution not the creation of problems for others. It is moral for business to be profitable but what is profitable is not necessarily moral.

1
The System

By Systemes; I understand any numbers of men joyned in one Interest, or one Businesse.

Thomas Hobbes (1651), *Leviathan*, ii. xxii. 115

Systems

Systems, Thomas Hobbes wrote in 1651, can 'be compared to the homogeneous parts of man's body: the lawful being comparable to the muscles; the unlawful ones to warts, boils, and abscesses, caused by the unnatural flowing together of bad bodily fluids'.[1]

We are victims and products of the system. We rail against 'it'—the capitalist system, the ecosystem, the educational system, the health system, the biological system, the transport system, the social system, the financial system, the evolutionary system, and the energy system. We are part of the system, contribute to it, and affected by the system in every part of our lives. We design, engineer, maintain, degrade, and rebuild systems. They are based on science, engineering, life sciences, physical sciences, mathematics, and computer systems.

Yet we do not understand systems, we feel powerless in the face of them and alienated from them. They are out there, impenetrable and yet all pervasive. We talk of systems 'change', systems 'leadership', but have no idea what they mean or how to bring them about. They are 'buzz' words because we cannot conceptualize and conceive of systems. They are the source of the failures of economics, the misperception of business, the collapse of governments, and the reason for our sense of isolation and alienation. The common properties of systems are their scale, complexity, and dynamic rather than static characteristic.

The origin of the word system is the Greek σύστημα (sústēma, 'organized whole, body'), from σύν (sún, 'with, together') + ἵστημι (hístēmi, 'I stand'). In other words, it means to stand together in an organized whole or body in contrast to individual, independent entities. That is an important notion of a system. A system has properties that are derived but distinct from its constituent elements in isolation.[2] It is about standing together in an organized whole or body. It requires integrity in the sense of integrating across diverse elements and organisms in determining a coherent whole, as well as the qualities of honesty and strong moral principles. In other words, it is about creating a community that stands and acts together for a common benefit—the Commonwealth as Hobbes described it.

In contemplating questions about the design, development, and delivery of systems, we need to draw on not just the life, physical, and social sciences in describing what a system does and how it does it, but also the humanities in considering why systems are created, why they exist, and what they do. Every part of our intellectual understanding and knowledge is therefore relevant to systems.

Reductionism ad Absurdum

Underpinning current notions of systems is something very different—one of the most pervasive and influential concepts in existence—reductionism—the idea that everything can and should be reduced to its constituent parts. It is a concept that prevails in physics, psychology, biology, and economics to name but a few disciplines. It presumes that things are no more than combinations of atoms; intelligence is collections of neurons; living organisms are products of genetic codes and economies groups of individuals. It does not see or permit there to be any features, properties, thoughts, development, or activity that derives from anything other than an aggregation of the constituent parts of an object, mind, body, or economy.[3]

The success of reductionism derives from it being both simple and comprehensive. It has profound implications for how we view and understand the world. It means that the world is deterministic in the sense that we can explain and predict it from its component parts; that we have no agency or freewill to think, do, or say anything other than what has been pre-determined by our DNA and neurons; and there is no notion of the wellbeing of communities and societies beyond that of the individuals who comprise them. It is a bleak barren landscape of pre-programmed organisms, behaving like automatons without self-determination of their own course of action and no recognition of their communal beyond their individual interests.

The power of reductionism is particularly great when combined with the feature of economics which I previously described, namely, competition. In the presence of limited resources, as organisms multiply, they, like competing firms, face fights for survival. Only the fittest survive in the context of, what Charles Darwin described in evolution, as the natural selection of those organisms that are best adapted to defend themselves against their competitors and predators.

Systems in physics, psychology, biology, and economics possess properties that are no more than an aggregation of their component parts. In one sense that is self-evident but in another it is not very insightful because it is purely descriptive of what different things and entities do, not why they exist or why they are created. Reductionism may be descriptive of what the world is but does not necessarily need to be. We could just be collections of atoms, neurons, DNA, and individuals bumping around and fighting for our survival in a self-interested fashion. On the other hand, we might overlay this reductionist description with systems that not only possesses properties that are distinct from their components but are also products of higher-order influences.

Some people instinctively recoil from such notions of higher-order influences because they associate them with the sacred. Other people choose to interpret them in this way, but there is no reason why that must be. Systems may be created and brought into existence not through a supernatural process but because they are simply thought to be desirable and beneficial. The potential to create them may arise from newly emergent technologies or the availability of component parts that did not previously exist. Alternatively, they may be brought into existence to solve a problem that has recently emerged and for which a new systems innovation is required. In other words, new systems are created to serve the purpose of solving a new problem or providing a new solution to an old problem.

From the point of view of those in the system, their creators may appear to have divine properties or capabilities, but they may be no more than organisms, plants, humans, and societies with problems to solve and the capacity to solve them. Does this therefore mean, after all, that systems are just products of atoms, neurons, DNA, and individuals, as reductionism suggested? No, because what underpins their creation and existence is a reason for their being, namely a purpose, a purpose of addressing a problem that individually they cannot solve but collectively can.

Purpose

There is a purpose that underpins all that we do in our daily lives, our working lives, our recreation, and our families. What is your purpose? Why do you exist? What are you there to do? Those are not the types of questions that you are conventionally asked to address in books on the economy and business. How do you increase your happiness or your wellbeing, how do you improve your wealth and financial condition? These are much more common and familiar themes than the reason for your existence.

The very fact that few economics and business books pose these questions reveals a problem. We presume we know the answer—we exist to be happy, well, wealthy, and prosperous. Everything relates to us as individuals. I am interested in myself, my family, my friends, my local community, and possibly my town, and it stops there. I sit at the pinnacle of my world and everything and everyone else fall away rapidly in my vision the further they are physically and emotionally from me.

It is a law of nature and to suggest any other human response is unnatural. We cannot seriously engage with any other than our nearest and dearest. Talk about a higher purpose, the reason for our existence or the greater good is highfalutin, pretentious claptrap. It is very presumptuous of me even to suggest that you might have an interest in such stuff.

But hold on. Is the reason for your existence, your life and creation so esoteric and nebulous as to be unworthy of further consideration? Or is it so fundamental as to be a prerequisite for understanding everything else that you do, say, and think? Economics has presumed that the answer to the question of your existence is you. Your utility, your happiness, is what economists believe drives everything you do. Your happiness might derive at least in part from helping others, but you only help others to the extent that you derive pleasure from so doing.

That simple idea has for the past two centuries driven thinking about individuals, societies, economies, politics, governments, and nations. We characterize the world as populated by people who are individually and collectively motivated by their self-interest, and in doing so, we make it so. This leads one immediately to conclude that one must motivate people to do anything that incorporates the interests of others. Their instinct is not to look after others, and one therefore must encourage them to do so by making it sufficiently rewarding.

This book argues that this is fundamentally incorrect. It is a confusion of cause and effect. It is not so much that we are naturally social rather than selfish, though we may be—'socially hardwired' as it is sometimes described—but more that we can be encouraged to be so, not just by incentives or coercion, but through an appreciation of our collective as well as our individual wellbeing.[4] We benefit from contributing to a collective purpose because by so doing we can achieve more than we individually are capable of.

Purpose is about solving problems—the problems that you and I, our families and friends, our communities, and societies, and the natural as well as human world face now and in the future. That is why we exist. That is why we bring others into existence—to bring joy, happiness, and fulfilment to us and others. This notion of solving the problems of others is internally consistent because, in assisting others, we in turn are assisted by others fulfilling their purposes and helping us. It is the mutually self-supporting system by which the world functions and develops. We exist individually and collectively to assist others to exist.

It is not only the reason for our creation but also that of inert objects, concepts, and institutions. Everything we do, we say, we produce, we create is designed with a purpose to assist us and others with solving the problems we and they face, and the more we do so, the more we create. Higher-level system purposes are enriching in broadening the range of possible outcomes and alternatives beyond what lower-level organisms and processes can achieve on their own.

But it would be naïve and simply wrong to think that this is always the case. We create harm as well as good. We damage as well as assist one another. We destroy as well as build. We are motivated by selfish as well as kindred spirits by placing ourselves, our children, and our families at the top of the pinnacle and relegating others far below. We are careless, negligent, and ignorant as well as ill-intentioned.

Furthermore, high-level purposes risk being constrictive and authoritarian rather than liberating and enabling. They impose the beliefs and wishes of some on others. They threaten the freedom of competition and markets described in the introduction. They undermine the ability of individuals to pursue their own objectives unconstrained by the views of others. Far from being enriching, purposes can be impoverishing.

We must recognize the failures as well as the benefits of purpose. Instead of dogmatically propagating conflicting ideologies regarding individual liberties versus collective wellbeing, we should recognize the merits of both reductionist bottom-up and teleological (purpose driven) top-down perspectives. It is not a matter of 'either, or'. It is 'both, and' or, as it has been described in a biological context, 'no-privileged level'.[5] We must sustain the benefits of both bottom-up markets and competition, and top-down systems and purposes.

The question is: how can we achieve this? Surely the imposition of a top-down purpose undermines the independence of lower-level purposes. That is precisely the conundrum that this book seeks to resolve. I will argue that correctly specified, higher order purposes confer greater not less agency on individuals and organisms below. They can enhance our ability to choose and free us from the deterministic conditions that are imposed on us from below by our inherited genetic traits. This requires an appreciation of the values that underpin purposes and the criteria by which their performance is judged.

Integrity

On 20 September 2015, Martin Winterkorn, the chief executive of VW, the German car manufacturer, publicly admitted that the company had cheated on US emission tests to make its vehicles appear less polluting.[6] What was particularly disturbing about the case was that VW had used a mechanism known as 'a defeat device' that causes a vehicle to behave differently during an emission test than on the road. Prior to the VW revelation, the notion of a defeat device was not familiar to people outside the industry, but it was quite familiar within the industry.

A defeat device has two components—a monitor that determines if an emission test is in progress and a modify component that alters the vehicle behaviour when under test conditions. Between 1991 and 1995, General Motors used the fact that, if the air conditioning units in its Cadillacs were to be turned on, then that ruled out the possibility of a test being in progress, in which case the modify component switched to the higher engine performance, more polluting mode.[7]

The defeat device in VW vehicles used a component supplied by Bosch, known as electronic diesel control unit 17, which resulted in Bosch agreeing in February 2017 to a $328m civil settlement for claims against it in the US.[8] It might reasonably be suggested that the employment of devices in vehicles to evade environmental testing procedures designed to protect the health and wellbeing of customers, societies, and the natural world reflects a certain lack of integrity.

Integrity means two related but distinct things. First, it means the condition of being whole, unified, and undivided, and second, the quality of being honest and of strong moral principles. For a system to function efficiently and effectively it requires the former, namely that the component parts complement each other in creating a whole that is greater than the sum of the parts. That is the mechanics and engineering of a system to ensure that the parts are there and interact in such a fashion as to create a unified, undivided whole.

But there is a second feature it needs to demonstrate if it is to solve problems of others, not create them, and that is it must demonstrate strong moral features of honesty and conviction in so doing. A defeat device in cars may satisfy integrity in terms of contributing to their engineering and financial performance but in forms that clearly violate the second condition of solving problems honestly rather than creating them dishonestly.

The mechanism by which a system demonstrates a commitment to purpose is, first, to have the internal features, structures, and components to deliver the purpose and, secondly, the principles and values associated with adherence to purpose.[9] It is the combination that gives a system integrity in both senses of the word. That combination was a feature of the complete, well-functioning competitive markets and capitalism that I described previously and the reason why they could convert individual self-interests of us as individuals into collective mutual benefit.

The self-interest of individual components becomes directed towards fulfilment of the purpose of the system by virtue of the components having a combined value that is greater than the sum of their parts.[10] The achievement of that value involves aligning the values of the components with fulfilment of the system purpose. In the case of capitalist systems, the market ensures that all necessary components are present by establishing prices that are sufficient to elicit the desired production, and the price mechanism aligns individual values of providers with their customers' values.

A well-functioning market system therefore demonstrates integrity in both senses of the word. But it is not the only system that does. Any system that assembles the necessary components and aligns their interests with those of the system purpose fulfils that condition. Furthermore, ironically because other systems can do what markets do and sometimes do it better, markets fail.

For example, Facebook and Google have created internal global systems that dominate competitive markets because of the benefits that users derive from being able to interact with each other on one platform. As they grow to become global monopolies then other firms find it impossible to compete with them. They have replicated the features of markets more successfully than markets.

While in the presence of complete competitive markets, capitalist systems demonstrate integrity, the success of its central feature—firms pursuing ever greater profits—leads inexorably to the failure of competition and therefore the disintegration of integrity of capitalism. One cannot have a system of integrity that both relies on competition and encourages pursuit of monopolies. It is inherently contradictory.

One form in which it is suggested that this dilemma may be resolved is through the 'creative destruction' that Joseph Schumpeter described of new firms—entrepreneurial innovators—entering the domains of large, established firms and chipping away at their self-sustaining systems until they collapse.[11] Kodak and Nokia are often cited as examples of companies that failed to recognize the changing nature of technology in their businesses of photographic films and telecoms respectively and suffered death or near-death experiences as other companies incorporated cameras and computers in their mobile phones.

But does substituting one dominant firm, for example Apple, for another, for example Kodak, really solve the problem? More significantly, does Schumpeterian creative destruction not demonstrate the power of purposeful problem-solving entrepreneurial firms rather than the advantage of profit-focused competition? Corporate purpose is much more in evidence in start-ups than in established firms that frequently lose sight of their fundamental reasons for being.

Knowing that the destination of the most successful firms is and always has been exploitative monopolies and the failure of unrestrained markets throughout history, then we should re-examine whether the premise that the purpose of business is solely to pursue profits is correct.

The inevitable failure of competition to align the private objectives of profit-seeking companies with the public interest implies that the objectives of firms must be consistent with what we wish them to be even in the absence of competition. We should encourage companies to do what we want them to do, not what we don't want them to do and then rely on markets to put things right.

In other words, we should recognize that the integrity of markets relies on the integrity of their participants. They cannot perform the remarkable transformation I described at the beginning of converting individual self-interests into collective interests once participants reach a scale of monopolizing their markets. You are not the problem, even if you are entirely self-interested, because you are, I am afraid to say, too small to count. But the Amazons, Apples, Facebooks, and Googles of this world certainly are not. They require purposes that we—their customers, societies, employees, and suppliers—need.

Their incentives must be brought into line with ours, not through relying on either competition, which may simply not exist, or regulation, which is a poor substitute for it, but through their intrinsic interests being aligned with ours. It should be part of their inherent motivation. In other words, we should ensure that the purpose of companies naturally drives them towards solving our problems through the profits they earn and that the profits they earn derive from the problems they solve not the problems they create.

Profit

The word profit comes from the Latin '*prōfectus,* progress, success', which comes from '*prōficere* to advance'.[12] In other words, profit is best understood as progression and advancement towards the achievement of a goal or objective. Today, profit is understood as being about money, specifically the surplus that a company earns over and above the costs that it incurs in running its activities. The original notion of profit is of progression and advancement; the current one is of financial benefit.

Profit in the contemporary sense is the notion of personal benefit or financial gain. It is what we derive from doing something over and above the costs that we incur from doing it. This may be from financial reward but not necessarily. It could equally come from personal satisfaction of all the human attributes of greed and lust, jealousy and pride that drive us, as well as kindness and consideration, care, and concern. It may be from virtue or victimhood, sainthood, or sin.

So, we need purpose to be about more than just solving problems profitably. We need to be clear about what is a profit. To ensure that purposes do benefit others we need to restrict the domain of profit. We need to exclude what is earned or accumulated at the expense of others. A profit is not a profit if it is earned by producing problems for others. The profits that VW earned from incorporating defeat devices in its vehicles were clearly not profits in any meaningful sense.

That one simple rider fundamentally changes the nature of the world in which we live because it aligns purpose with intent and intent with purpose. Purpose then has two components. First, it is about producing profitable solutions for the problems of people and planet; and, secondly, and particularly pertinently for this discussion, it is not profiting from producing problems for people or planet.

That second part has a profound effect on the first part because it legitimizes all purposes since only those that are not undertaken to the detriment of others will be rewarded by a profit. So, in seeking a profit, firms and their investors will only pursue purposes that do not cause detriments to others. The significance of that is it means a purpose does not need to be imposed. We are at liberty to choose the problems we are solving provided that in the process we do not profit from producing problems that remain uncorrected.

Underpinning the failures of companies, economies, societies, and nations around the world and over history is a misconception and mismeasurement of profit. We have simply misstated what a profit is, or more precisely what it is not. That simple definitional and accounting mistake has been the basis of incorrectly specified law, regulation, ownership, governance, finance, and investment. It has been the source of incredible growth and prosperity, and disastrous failures and crises. Put it right and one corrects many of the failures of corporate, economic, and financial systems, and promotes a just and fair as well as a prosperous society.

The party most affected by changing the notion of profit is those to whom it is paid—the investors in a firm and, in particular, the shareholders, the holders of shares in the firm's equity. But there again that change also puts the notion of equity more in line with what we conventionally might understand by the term.

Equity

The origin of the word equity is *aequitas*, meaning justice, equality, and fairness, 'reasonableness and moderation in the exercise of one's rights, and the disposition to avoid insisting on them too rigorously'.[13] It is about the fair and just treatment of different parties, about the distribution of wealth not simply its creation and growth. In other words, it relates to fairness as well as value, to what we believe and value as humans, as well as the monetary worth we accumulate.

The double meaning of equity is paralleled in that of a share and a shareholder. A shareholding is the holding of a share but also the sharing of a holding. The first is passive and individualistic. It is reflected in the notion of equity as ownership—ownership of a share of a company, equivalent to that of ownership of any other form of property.

The second is active and communal. It derives from the association in common law countries of equity with trusteeship—the holding of someone's property on behalf of another party. The former is therefore concerned with the interests of the holder of the share, whereas the latter relates to the sharing of the benefits of a holding with the parties to a company.

Our understanding of equity has come to be increasingly dominated by the first interpretation. Equity is there to serve the interests of the owners—the shareholders. They are the beneficiaries and the role of intermediary institutions holding their equity is to manage their investments for their benefit and their benefit alone. Likewise, the board of directors of firms are agents of the shareholders, there to pursue the success of the company for the financial benefit of its shareholders.

The second interpretation is very different. A shareholding is the conveying of property, financial capital, from shareholders to the company in which they are invested for the benefit of multiple parties to the firm. The role of financial intermediaries in that regard is two-sided to the company in which they are investing as well as the shareholders whose money they are investing. Similarly, the function of a board of directors of a company is not simply as agents of shareholders but also as trustees of the interests of the different parties to the firm, such as its customers and employees.

Ironically, we have come to associate the private sector with provision of economic and productive efficiency, and the public sector and the state with distribution and 'equity', when the original notion of equity in common law was in relation to distribution and fairness. That concept of equity persists today in some of the largest and most successful companies in the world, including those listed on stock markets. These companies are owned by trusts or foundations and are called 'industrial foundations' or, as they prefer to be known, 'enterprise foundations'.

Bosch, IKEA, Rolex, Tata, and the Wallenberg companies (the 'Wallenberg Sphere', which includes Electrolux, Ericsson, Stora Enso, the oldest shareholder company in the world) are owned by foundations. Denmark is the country with the best-known foundation owned companies, for example, Carlsberg, Moller Maersk, and Novo Nordisk. In many cases, the companies are listed and actively traded on stock markets but with the dominant owners being the foundations.

In this second interpretation, the role of both intermediaries and boards is analogous to the two-sided relation of trustees to those depositing money in the trust (the settlor) and those benefiting from the trust (the beneficiaries). The duties of directors and managers of intermediary institutions and companies are not just to their shareholders but to the firms themselves and those who participate in and are affected by them.

This distinction bears on the nature of the duties of directors. The two duties that are most frequently emphasized are those of loyalty and care. In the traditional interpretation of equity, the loyalty and care that directors owe are to their shareholders. In the alternative interpretation, the directors' duty of loyalty remains solely to their shareholders, but their duty of care extends to the company and its stakeholders more generally. In this case, the concept of care is closer to how we conventionally understand it.

Care

Care is central to human emotions, feeling, and thinking. It is the essence of what it is to be human—to care for the wellbeing of others; to provide care for them; and to act with care in relation to them. It embodies everything from virtues to obligations and responsibilities.

Care is not just an abstract theoretical concept—it is of profound practical significance. It is commonly associated with notions of dependency on others and our natural human instinct to respond by providing care to those who depend on us. It has become one of the fastest growing industries as cohesive nuclear family units and communities disintegrate and traditional support from them diminishes. In its place has come the professionalization of care for the young, sick, and elderly by 'care workers' and a formalization of the procedures by which it is dispensed and evaluated.

The formalization of care derives not only from the dependency of others on us but the impact we have on them. As organizations grow in scale and significance, they have increasing potential to deliver both positive benefits and negative detriments, and those charged with running them have ever more extensive duties of care to promote the former and avoid the latter. This is reflected in the intensified regulation that we impose on the conduct of individuals and institutions.

Care is therefore associated with both solving and avoiding creating other people's problems. But the need to professionalize and formalize the procedures by which it is delivered reflects a fundamental failure of modern economic, political, and social systems to preserve and promote it. Care should be triggered by human emotions of empathy for those in need of it, and not rely on rules and regulations, monitoring and oversight to ensure its delivery.

Care transforms our individual self-interests into other-regarding interests and the selfish into the selfless. As a matter of course, it should therefore underpin everything we do as individuals, organizations, corporations, nation states, and societies. But it doesn't and it is increasingly failing to do so as we observe growing fragmentation of our nations and international order as well as families and communities.

With care, economies and communities promote inclusive growth that incorporates the interests of those who are otherwise excluded or left behind. It makes participation and access an intrinsic part of the development of economies and communities stemming from an innate desire on the part of those who enjoy the fruits of success to extend it to those who do not.

We are not taking adequate care of care. We are not protecting and nurturing this most important of human qualities as we emphasize rationality over emotions and value over values. We idolize hard and measurable financial value and scorn soft and subjective values. As we race for economic and financial value, we are denigrating care and the values associated with it.

Instead, we are subcontracting the provision of care to those who are professionally trained to provide it. That in turn raises questions of the legitimacy of the rest of us to offer it and creates a vicious cycle of separation between those who are charged with delivering it and others who feel increasingly alienated from expressing it.

We are substituting emotion-driven care with market transactions in which care is delivered through contract rather than an intrinsic concern for the wellbeing of others. That points to two distinct policies for promoting care: market transactions supplemented by government provision or the enhancement of social settings that stimulate our inherent sense of care for others. Focusing on the former risks discouraging the latter.

Care should be incorporated as a core value of institutions and organizations from the outset. We should look to all of them to specify and justify their values and include care among them. The HRM of human resource management should be replaced by humane relations matter. We should call upon nation states across the world to embed in their constitutions the principle that they, their citizens, corporations, organizations, and institutions exist to 'care for the wellbeing of others, especially those who most depend upon it'.

According to UK and US, a director must discharge their duties with a degree of care that might reasonably be expected of them.[14] As a consequence, 'directors have a duty "to exercise oversight" and to monitor the corporation's operational viability, legal compliance, and financial performance. A board's "utter failure to attempt to assure a reasonable information and reporting system exists" is an act of bad faith in breach of the duty of loyalty'.[15]

We should interpret this as implying that directors have a duty to ensure that their organizations care for all those with whom they engage and impact. Directors of car manufacturers have a duty to ensure that their vehicles do not employ defeat devices, not simply because they violate laws or regulations, nor merely because deliberate deceit is manifestly dishonest, but because by so doing they are inflicting harm on others. And their shareholders should care not just about their own wellbeing but that of everyone affected by their investments, not tolerating deceit, dishonesty, or lack of integrity in any guise or disguise. They need to do this in the context of understanding their role of promoting not only their own purposes as directors and owners but their common purposes as citizens of the world.

Citizenship

We live in a selfish world, in a world that is appearing to become more selfish, in a world that is dominated by increasing polarization and populism, isolationism and protectionism. We are retreating into ourselves, and the pandemic accelerated that process by making isolation not just a psychological phenomenon but a medical one as well.

As this happens then the politics of consensus that we thought was becoming universal disintegrates, as reflected for example in the so-called Washington consensus around liberalism, free trade, markets, and governments to correct market failures.[16] In its place, comes the politics of dissent which feeds on individual senses of grievance and distrust that we are being exploited and disadvantaged and that only those who recognize our individual self-interests and grievances can and should be trusted. Feelings of persecution breed grievance and vengeance that are mirrored and reinforced in the politics of illiberalism and extremism.

Why is this happening? The answer is that we have developed a system of economics and politics that has promoted it. As the influence of religion and the monarch in politics waned during the period of the enlightenment, that of the individual grew in significance. This first took the form of a social contract between citizens and the monarch or state, as described by Thomas Hobbes and John Locke, and then the form of utilitarianism, as developed by David Hume, Jeremy Bentham, and John Stuart Mill, in which social preferences were simply the sum of those of individuals.

At the same time, economics was emerging as a distinct discipline around the idea of markets as being a source of economic prosperity and a way of achieving the maximization of social preferences as reflected in those of individuals. What then was beginning to develop in both politics and economics was the primacy of the individual.

However, the significance of this was initially constrained by the limitation on the resources and the economic influence that individuals could exercise, first in an agrarian context and then in industrialization that was predominantly restricted to that of small-scale family-owned business. But that all changed with the rise of manufacturing industry, then service industries, in particular financial services, and the emergence of multinational enterprises, technology companies, information-based networks, and platform business models. Suddenly we observed, as in the case of Vanderbilt, the accumulation of huge amounts of wealth and economic power in the hands of those owning and running business.

But that merely reflected the underlying philosophy of business and was widely felt to be in the interests of society. The sole interest of owners and managers in making money was the source of prosperity and wealth. This was particularly true for a small segment of the shareholding and property-owning classes.

Two things initially sustained the acceptability of this. The first was the role of the state in distributing wealth through taxes and subsidies as reflected for example in the New Deal in the US and then the welfare state in the UK and elsewhere, and secondly a combination of competition and regulation that constrained the worst abuses of the corporate sector. But both began to fall apart as the limits of the state to redistribute and of competition and regulation to restrain big business became all too evident.

This came to a head in the financial crisis of 2008 when the degree of exploitation and manipulation was laid bare for all to see, and the inability of governments and regulators to punish misdemeanours and correct injustices was exposed. That failure has been repeated elsewhere in such instances as the VW diesel scandal which revealed neither governments nor regulators capable of preventing widespread adoption of deliberate deception by the car industry over an extended period.

The consequence has been growing distrust and mistrust not just in business and finance but in all the surrounding architecture of privilege and entitlement. The notion of meritocracy and reward for ability and effort became seen not as the great leveller of opportunity for all but the privilege of inheritance, upbringing, and education.[17]

All that has happened since in terms of financialization, globalization, inequality, racial discrimination, regional disparities, urban degeneration, environmental degradation, the destruction of nature, the social divisions caused by the pandemic, and now the threat to humanity posed by artificial intelligence has only served to reinforce this. The ascendancy of the individual has reached its natural apogee. The economics of profits has replaced people and the politics of 'me' has replaced 'we'.

In both cases, as Alasdair MacIntyre and Michael Sandel amongst many others have noted and Adam Smith originally warned us about in *The Theory of Moral Sentiments*, we have lost sight of the notion of common purpose—the 'cum panis' of breaking bread together in the company—and of common unity in the community and the state.[18] We have basically eliminated the notion of either business or the state as being anything other than pass-through vehicles to reflect the ultimate interests and utility of individual citizens in the state and shareholders in business.

Instead of being entities for forging a sense of common purpose to which all subscribe and from which all benefit, companies reinforce the influence of the shareholder over the stakeholder and governments of the majority over the minority. Our institutions of both business and government accentuate the notion of individualism over citizenship and the promotion of individual over common purpose.

We need to rediscover citizenship rapidly if the fabric of communities, nations, environment, and nature is not to disintegrate. This is a pivotal moment at which we must reverse the polarization of our society by recognizing our common purpose as citizens of the world for the benefit of the many not the few, for the future as well as the present.

Implementation

This book describes how to put purpose, integrity, profit, equity, care, and citizenship at the heart of our economic, social, and political systems as part of their governing architecture. The creation of a common purpose should drive the design of these governance arrangements in public, not-for-profit, charitable, social as well as commercial enterprises. The next chapter describes how if this were done, it would resolve the greatest challenges that the world currently faces.

There are four pairs of policies that are associated with the governing architecture: law and regulation; ownership and governance; measurement and performance; and finance and investment. At present, corporate law is currently conceived as being about the duties of directors to their shareholders and how businesses should be run to promote their success for the benefit of their shareholders. Regulation is about the rules of the game by which businesses should conduct their activities and promote their success in the interests of their shareholders.

Ownership is concerned with the rights of shareholders and how they should exercise those rights. Corporate governance is concerned with the alignment of the interests of management with those of their shareholders and addressing problems that arise from a lack of alignment through, for example, monitoring and incentive arrangements.

Measurement is about accounting for the physical and financial assets and liabilities of a firm, such as its buildings, plant, and machinery. Performance is evaluated in relation to the profits of a firm measured net of the cost of maintaining its physical assets, and remuneration of executives and management of firms is determined by its profitability.

Finance is concerned with promoting the interests of investors and protecting the interests of minority shareholders. Investment is undertaken to maximize the value of shareholders' equity.

This is a coherent, consistent description of the nature of the economic system around the interests of shareholders—their legal rights, and their regulatory limits; their ownership, and governance rights; measurement of their assets and their performance; the returns on their investments and management to maximize their value.

In contrast, what is suggested here is that an equally coherent and consistent system should be structured around a common purpose to promote economic success for the benefit of individuals, society, and the natural world at large. To do this, the law should be about the duties of directors to determine and promote the purpose of the company. Regulation should be concerned not just with the rules of the game but the alignment of the purposes of the firm with social considerations in those firms that perform particularly important public functions.

Ownership is not just about the rights of shareholders but their duties to uphold the purpose of their businesses and ensure that they abide by their principles and values. Governance is concerned not just with aligning managerial interests with those of their shareholders but with the leadership and management that delivers the company's purposes.

Measurement is concerned with accounting not solely for financial and material assets and liabilities, but also with human, social, and natural assets outside as well as within the legal boundaries of the firm. Performance should reflect the success of companies in delivering on their purposes and measure profits in relation to upholding the interests of all the parties on which they impact.

Finance is about promoting equity and the success of the company in funding its investments and protecting it against risks of failure; and those investments should be directed towards promoting common purposes of companies undertaken in partnership with other organizations in the public, not-for-profit as well as the corporate sector.

This too is a coherent and consistent description of law being about promoting corporate purposes and regulation aligning them with social objectives where appropriate; ownership is about establishing principles and values around purpose; governance is about the leadership and management of purpose; measurement is about the effect of companies on their relevant parties; performance is about their success in delivering their purposes; and finance is about funding the investments that then help to deliver purposes.

The eight chapters of Parts II to V of the book describe the principles and policies that are required to enact problem-solving not creating capitalism. But before that, the next chapter will describe how the wrong model of capitalism has got us to the point of collapse we currently face.

2
The Challenge

*You are here to enrich the world and you impoverish yourself
if you forget that errand.*

Woodrow Wilson

COVID-19 and Pandemics

It was just after 7 a.m. on Wednesday, 30 December 2020 when
news came through that the Oxford vaccine for COVID-19 had been
approved. 'A game changer'; 'a profoundly important moment'; 'a
ray of light in the fog of gloom' were some of the ways in which the
announcement was greeted. Why? Why should the discovery of the
third vaccine and the second to be approved in the UK meet with
such rapturous applause? It is not the winner of the silver or bronze
medals who usually receives all the acclaim.

There was a bit of an element of national pride that this vaccine
had been developed in the UK by a British university, Oxford, and
a British–Swedish company AstraZeneca. But there was more to it
than that. There were two features of the vaccine that differentiated it
from the others—firstly it could be stored in regular fridges and did
not require particularly low temperature refrigeration. It was therefore capable of being distributed and delivered faster than the other
vaccines.

But there was a second feature that has had profound implications on its global impact. It was much cheaper—approximately
one-eighth of the price of one of the others[1] and as a statement from
Oxford University made clear 'a key element of Oxford's partnership
with AstraZeneca is the joint commitment to provide the vaccine

on a not-for-profit basis for the duration of the pandemic across the world, and in perpetuity to low- and middle-income countries'.[2]

The origins of that partnership between AstraZeneca and Oxford University date back to the start of the pandemic in Europe. It was in the early hours of Saturday, 11 January 2020, that Professor Teresa Lamb received the information in her email she had been waiting for. It was the genetic code for the new coronavirus, provided by scientists in China. She worked day and night that weekend on the information so that by the following Monday she had constructed the template for the coronavirus vaccine.

On 17 April 2020, the UK announced the establishment of a vaccine task force with AstraZeneca as a founding corporate member[3] and shortly thereafter Oxford University initiated the first human trials of a coronavirus vaccine in Europe.[4] On 29 April, AstraZeneca announced that it was partnering with Oxford University to develop the vaccine.

Announcing the partnership, Pascal Soriot, the CEO of AstraZeneca, said that the fact AstraZeneca was UK-based made Oxford University a natural partner. 'Being British-based we are in regular contact with British academia', he said. 'We had discussions with the vaccine group in Oxford, we looked at the vaccine, we thought it had a good chance of working. [It is] one of the best, if not the best, vaccine teams in the world.'[5]

But it nearly wasn't so. Six years earlier in 2014, AstraZeneca almost ceased to be a UK-based pharmaceutical company when it was subject to a hostile bid by the US pharmaceutical company and the producer of the first approved vaccine in the UK, Pfizer. It was only the AstraZeneca board's resolute rejection of the bid and the consequent threat to Pfizer's tax inversion benefits that led to its withdrawal, to the profound irritation of many of AstraZeneca's largest institutional investors, who stood to make large financial gains on the takeover.[6]

This illustrates two things—first the importance of partnerships between business and universities in promoting R&D and distributing its benefits. Second, the importance of ownership of companies and where they are run for promoting such partnerships. But there is a third element that was equally important. The Oxford vaccine is not cheaper because it cost less to develop.

On the contrary, it was significantly more expensive than the other two. The vast bulk of its funding came from private sources but around £1.5bn is estimated to have come from the government and £0.5bn from philanthropic sources. In total governments are estimated to have invested £6.5bn in vaccine development around the world.[7]

What this shows is the complexity of the process of organizing major initiatives such as vaccine development. They involve partnerships between businesses, universities, governments, NGOs, and charities. But matters do not stop there.

Once the vaccines have been produced then there is the formidable task of getting hold of and distributing them, a particularly serious problem for low and middle-income countries. A large proportion of the pre-order purchases were made by developed countries leaving others exposed to serious shortfalls.[8] The coordination required was not just cross-sector within countries but global across countries.

The COVID vaccine story is illustrative of the critical but largely undiscussed aspect of the modern world—its governance—not just its governments or its corporate governance but the governance of every aspect of its organizations and institutions in the private, public, not-for-profit, individually and collectively, domestically and internationally.

Opportunity in Adversity

COVID-19 propelled purpose to the top of the corporate and policy agenda. This might be surprising because, unlike many of our other problems, the origins of coronavirus, while not entirely clear, were almost certainly unrelated to business. But its impact on business was devastating—propelling economies into one of their deepest recessions since the Great Depression.

Out of crises come opportunities and rarely had such an opportunity for business been created before. It was an opportunity for business to restore its trust and respect. The vital contribution and role of business in our lives is not always as fully acknowledged and recognized as it should be, but this was a time when it could be seen to stand square with individuals, societies, nation states, the natural world, and the global economy.

How could it do this when it was facing such serious challenges that its very existence in many cases was in doubt? How could it survive when its markets had imploded and, in many cases, disappeared entirely? What could an airline without passengers, and a theatre, cinema, bar, and restaurant without audiences and customers, possibly do? How could orchestras and football teams function that could not meet let alone play or perform in front of others? What could they do other than close their premises, lay people off, cut costs, and shut down their supply chains? What was the use of talking about trust and respect when businesses didn't have customers or clients?

The answer was two things. The first was equity. The companies that were best placed to survive within their industries and sectors were those that had the equity base and liquidity to do so. Then more than ever they needed reserves on which to draw to cushion the costs they incurred. Those with high levels of debt that had distributed their reserves in dividends, paid cash to their shareholders to buy back their shares or rewarded their executives exorbitantly were the ones that were most at risk.

But even some of those companies came to appreciate the power of equity markets to tide them over hard times. Calls on raising equity from investors are usually associated with stock market booms, not busts when equity is cheap. However, the great merit of public equity markets is that they price equity at a level that reflects investors' beliefs about the value of a company's prospective earnings. The investor community was expected to stand behind companies that depended on it by accepting new equity issues and dividend cuts that were required to see businesses through their existential threat.

The second answer was corporate purpose. What is the relevance of corporate purpose when corporate survival was in question? The answer was 'more than ever' if one recognizes that the purpose of business is to produce profitable solutions to the problems of people and planet, not profiting from producing problems for either. Never had the notion of purpose been more relevant.

What at that time was the purpose of an airline without customers, a theatre without audiences, a restaurant without clients, a bar that was closed? The answer was the value proposition—namely the value it could create for its investors in the long term—on the back of which it could seek to raise equity finance. What solutions to customers' needs to travel, to be entertained, to eat and drink could, and should, businesses have been providing once the virus subsided and some semblance of normality returned?

How could business not only restore but enhance its relevance and value when customer preferences unquestionably had altered because of the pandemic?[9] Building trust and confidence was more critical than ever. What and whose problems needed to be solved, how and when those problems could be solved, why a particular business was especially well placed to solve them, were the critical questions that needed to be answered for a business to have a credible value proposition and be able to raise the equity capital it required.

And in the process of answering those questions, businesses needed to demonstrate how they would avoid creating problems for their employees, communities or environment. The crisis brought to the fore the importance and plight of those working on zero-hour contracts in precarious forms of employment. As the First World War fundamentally altered people's attitudes towards the suffragette movement, so COVID-19 transformed people's views about employment, the nature of work, exploited workers, supply chains, natural resources, and the environment.

This was therefore businesses' moment but only if both business and investors realized what it took to turn tragedy into triumph. It required foresight, honesty, and money to seize the moment. While governments were needed to provide the immediate resources to rescue businesses and economies, business and investors had to recognize their mutual obligation to support their stakeholders—their employees, customers, pensioners, and communities. The banks squandered public support for their bailout after the financial crisis by not immediately embracing their social licences to operate; business had to avoid making the same mistake again if they were to deflect demands for their regulation and nationalization.

People's pensions were on the line through their investments but so too were their livelihoods and survival through their employment. It was companies' purposes and the values associated with them that guided the tough decisions and trade-offs which needed to be made about raising prices, cutting dividends, laying people off or closing operations. It was ultimately business and financial markets, as well as governments, which determined whether what emerged from the pandemic panic of 2020/21 were cinders or solutions.

Until COVID-19 struck, the talk had been about business becoming bigger than nation states. With COVID-19, the tables were turned, and business was at the mercy of governments to bail it out. The talk then became of the growth of government and the shrinkage of the private sector. This is the wrong debate. It was fatuous to think that business could substitute for government. It was equally misguided to think that government could rescue economies without business. It is not a competition. It is about cooperation.

During a pandemic, nations are at war, not against a foreign enemy but a global enemy. They need all the resources they can mobilize from both the private and public sector to defeat the virus. Part of the solution was public health management—testing, tracing, vaccines, isolation, and lockdown[10] and part was a massive public expenditure programme to support businesses with loans, grants, tax breaks, and subsidies for the employed and self-employed.

That was a vital part of solving the problem. But it was only one part. It was a top-down strategy that benefited from central government coordination. But there was another part that involved exactly the opposite—decentralized experimentation where many minds tried different approaches. That was where business came in. It was a call to arms of business in all its manifestations—global multinationals, social enterprises, small and medium-sized companies, and entrepreneurial start-ups. What they could do that government could not was to provide the ideas, processes, management, and financing to innovate, test, and invest.

The development of the Oxford-AstraZeneca vaccine was illustrative of that. So was the rapid ramping up of the production of penicillin during WW2. 'For corporations, the absence of restrictive patents eliminated traditional barriers to sharing resources. As early as 1942, industrial groups entered into agreements to exchange information and specimens with one another. The first to do so were Merck and Squibb, joined a year later by Pfizer.'[11]

As George Merck, President and Chairman of Merck between 1925 and 1957, said, 'We try to remember that medicine is for the patient. We try never to forget that medicine is for the people. It is not for the profits. The profits follow, and if we have remembered that they have never failed to appear. The better we have remembered it, the larger they have been.'[12]

Merck's words were as true then as they were in 2020. During a pandemic, we need a collective endeavour around a common purpose of containing and extinguishing viruses, where business, government, investors, and stakeholders around the world recognize their mutual dependence on each other. A purpose of solving problems helps business to focus on and identify what problems it can solve, whose problems, how it can solve them, when, and why it is well suited to solving them.

Disasters, disturbances, downturns, and depressions create new problems that must be solved. Out of those problems come new opportunities for business to solve them and turn them into commercially viable and profitable innovations that their investors can fund. In the process, businesses need to mobilize their stakeholders—their customers, employees, suppliers, and communities and investors—to support them in this endeavour and they need to support their stakeholders in the process.

In the early stages of the pandemic in June 2020, the *Financial Times* published an analysis of which companies prospered from COVID-19 and on 1 January 2021 it published an update.[13] In the June 2020 survey it noted that: 'in a dismal year for most companies, a minority have shone—pharmaceutical groups boosted by their hunt for a COVID-19 vaccine; technology giants buoyed by the trend for working from home; and retailers offering lockdown necessities online'.

The January 2021 survey updated the ranking based on an analysis of dollar equity market value added, that is, by how much companies had increased their equity market value during the pandemic. What emerged was that companies and sectors that used their ability to solve new problems and needs that emerged from the pandemic were the ones that prospered the most in terms of increasing their equity market values—Apple, Amazon, Tesla, Microsoft, Alphabet, Tencent, and so on.

Those that were in exploitative industries or failed to capitalize on changing consumer and societal behaviour and preferences performed the worst—ExxonMobil, Wells Fargo, Royal Dutch Shell, AT&T, Chevron, and Boeing. Not only were the best supporting their customers, employees, societies, and suppliers they were also benefiting their investors. The worst undermined both their stakeholders and their shareholders.

Energy companies were in general in this latter category at that time. And those that responded the least or the slowest in transitioning from oil and gas into renewable energy—ExxonMobil, Shell, Chevron, and BP—performed the worst within their sector. But there was something else that was impacting their performance.

The Environment, Climate Change, and Energy

On 26 May 2021, a seismic shock befell the oil sector, or to be precise two of its largest companies—ExxonMobil and Shell.

ExxonMobil's purpose at the time was 'to be the world's premier petroleum and chemical manufacturing company', which 'must continuously achieve superior financial and operating results while adhering to high ethical standards'. Its commitment to remain dependent on fossil fuels saw its return on capital employed fall from an average of around 35% during 2001–2010 to around 6%

from 2015 to 2019 and its stock market value drop by around three-quarters from a peak of $505 billion in 2007 to a low-point of $139 billion in 2020. ExxonMobil lost its 92 years' position in the Dow Jones Industrial Average in 2020 and Standard & Poor's downgraded its credit rating twice over the previous five years.

To reverse this decline, a previously unknown institutional investor called Engine No. 1 amassed a small stake of less than 0.02% of ExxonMobil's stock market value. With that stake and in the face of vociferous opposition from ExxonMobil, on that day in May 2021, Engine No. 1 successfully elected three new members to its board of directors.[14]

The same day as ExxonMobil's annual meeting, the Hague District Court ruled on a lawsuit brought by seven climate activist groups collectively referred to as 'Milieudefensie et al.' against the Shell group. The court ordered Shell to reduce its CO_2 emissions by 45% in 2030 compared to 2019 levels, through the Shell group's corporate policy.

Although Shell expressed its disappointment in the ruling and said it would appeal, the difference between the two companies was stark. Shell's purpose was stated to be to 'power progress together with more and cleaner energy solutions'. In 2020, the company committed to become a net-zero emissions energy business by 2050 and in 2021 it was the first energy company to offer investors an advisory vote on its energy transition strategy. It also linked executive compensation to its target of reducing its Net Carbon Footprint. Nevertheless, a group of climate activists argued that the company was not doing enough, and the Court agreed.

Shell faced a challenge that many companies will confront—a shift in where society draws the line between problem-solving sustainable solutions and problem producing unsustainable detriments. The Hague Court concluded that the company was not doing enough to demonstrate that it was the former.

The company argued that the 'reduction obligation' would put it at a competitive disadvantage but the Court did not find this compelling. It acknowledged that 'the reduction obligation requires a change in policy' that 'could curb the potential growth of the

Shell Group' but it went on to state that 'the interest served with the reduction obligation outweighs the Shell's group's commercial interests'.[15]

In other words, what Shell regarded as a profitable solution, the Court viewed as unsustainable business behaviour. By taking this position, the Court raised the bar for Shell on how it needed to adapt its strategy to fulfil a purpose of profiting from producing solutions not problems. Should Shell not find ways to meet these higher sustainability standards profitably, then it too could be the victim of an activist institutional investor campaign to help it do so. If, on the other hand, Shell rose to the occasion, the bar would rise for all other oil and gas companies. In other words, competition of the future will relate to levels of sustainability as well as profitability—runs to the top for the environment and shareholders.

But it is not just companies that are feeling the heat of climate change. At the UN Climate Change Conference (COP26) in Glasgow in November 2021, it was not governments that made the most impressive or credible commitments but a party that had never featured so prominently before—financial institutions. At the conference, Mark Carney, UN Special Envoy for Climate Action and Finance and former Governor of the Bank of England launched the Glasgow Financial Alliance for Net Zero (GFANZ), which stated that 'financial sector commitments to net zero now exceed $130 trillion, a 25-fold increase under the UK and Italian Presidency'.[16]

In a foreword to the report, Mark Carney said that: 'GFANZ now represents over 450 major financial institutions from across 45 countries, controlling assets of over $130 trillion. Members represent every segment of the financial-sector value chain—asset owners, insurers, asset managers, banks, investment consultants, exchanges, rating agencies, audit firms, and other key financial service providers. Member commitments are aligned with the science on climate change and anchored in the United Nations Framework Convention on Climate Change's (UNFCCC) Race to Zero net zero criteria, including the requirements to set near-term decarbonization targets, release plans to support their longer-term pledges and report progress annually. These commitments will demonstrate the determination of financial institutions to help the world decarbonise. In all aspects, GFANZ will be grounded in and guided by science, including through the GFANZ Advisory Panel of technical experts.'[17]

Increasingly institutional investors are therefore expected to report the contribution of their corporate investments not just to the financial returns of their investors (i.e., how many millions of dollars they are earning for their investors) but also to global warming (i.e., whether they are associated with global warming of 1, 1.5, 2, or 3 degrees above pre-industrialized times over the coming decades) and their path to net zero. Companies and investors are therefore under mounting pressure to diminish the extent to which their own investments and supply chains are contributing to global warming.

This falls into the second aspect of a corporate purpose—namely not profiting from producing problems for people or planet. To the extent that companies and investors are earning income from engaging in activities and investments that are exacerbating global warming, they are profiting from producing problems. They are not reporting the true costs of mitigating or remedying the problems they are creating and thereby overstating their profits. They should therefore set clear targets for diminishing their carbon emissions in their operations and portfolios and account for the costs incurred in meeting those targets. To go further and provide profitable solutions, companies should account for costs of reversing their past as well as current carbon emissions and become net positive not just net zero in the future, extracting carbon from the atmosphere, as Microsoft has pledged to do.[18]

Impressive though this all sounds, practice fell well short of promise. The subsequent energy crisis in 2022 created by rising oil and gas prices and the Russia–Ukraine war, yielded massive profits for fossil fuel companies as the oil and gas taps were rapidly turned back on and renewables were put on the back burner. By the time of COP27 in November 2022, promises made by GFANZ a year earlier at COP26 had come up against the hard-nosed reality of their financial implications for investors and proved unsustainable in the face of anti-trust and political threats.[19]

And as for that seismic shock in May 2021 when little Engine No. 1 successfully slung three members onto the board of Exxon Mobil, it certainly had earth-shattering results—both in terms of the near doubling of its share price, and the drilling and CO_2 emitted in producing it. But the energy crisis revealed a still more serious problem of a rapid transition to renewables and that was the conflict it created with another political imperative—inclusion.

Inequality, Social Exclusion, and Unaffordability

Renewable energy sources that are unaffordable by low-income or deprived households or are inaccessible to populations in remote, rural, or developing economies are no solution. They are just a transition but not a just transition. They are part of a process by which inequality and social exclusion are steadily exacerbated by a shift of business to high income and wealthy customers in relatively affluent regions of developed economies. Solutions to climate change that intensify unaffordability and exclusion are merely solving one problem by creating another. Companies should not profit until they have solved both.

Accessibility and affordability are increasingly being recognized as a pervasive problem. I discussed this above in relation to the pandemic and access to COVID vaccines but there are many more traditional and widely recognized cases. 'Approximately 80% of the 463 million adults worldwide with diabetes live in low-income and middle-income countries' but 'fewer than one in ten people with diabetes in low- and middle-income countries receive coverage of guideline-based comprehensive diabetes treatment.'[20] In other words, diabetes is predominantly a low- and middle-income country problem, and treatment is mainly a high-income country privilege. As with so many of the world's problems, needs are greatest where solutions are scarcest. Citizens of low- and middle-income countries face the double jeopardy of high incidence and low resolution of diabetes.

One company that is seeking to address this problem is the Danish pharmaceutical company, Novo Nordisk, which produces insulin, used in the treatment of type 2 diabetes. Its original purpose was simply to produce insulin but on realizing that it was failing to reach the people and places that were most in need of its product, it began to reconsider its purpose. It concluded that it was to help people treat type 2 diabetes, which might involve them taking insulin, but not necessarily.

So, it started working with hospitals, doctors, and universities in identifying the best forms of treatment for type 2 diabetes in different parts of the world. It then recognized that it could further help to eradicate type 2 diabetes not just through treatment but prevention. So, it started to work with governments, local authorities, and health workers around the world in identifying changes in lifestyles and nutrition that might assist people in avoiding getting type 2 diabetes at all.

You might think that this is all very worthy and noble, but did it not undermine Novo Nordisk's basic business model of selling insulin? The answer is no. On the contrary, its business has flourished on the back of the discovery of its true purpose. The reason is that in the process of establishing relations with hospital, doctors, governments, and health workers around the world, it became a trusted supplier of medical products and advice.

This brings out three important points. The first is the need to bring clarity to a company's purpose and provide specificity to the nature of the problems that it is seeking to solve and for whom and how it will deliver the solutions. The second is the need to build relations with other parties, such as professional, public, and social organizations as well as other businesses in delivering solutions to significant social problems. The third is that if a company can do that and commit to the realization of its purpose then it creates one of the most valuable assets a firm can possess—trust—to be recognized as being trustworthy and thereby a trusted provider of goods and services.

These mutual benefits for firms and societies rely on a commitment to a sufficiently long-horizon investment. Novo Nordisk was assisted in this by the nature of its ownership. It is a listed company and actively traded on the Danish and New York stock exchanges. But it also has a dominant shareholder—the Novo Nordisk Foundation—which owns just over a quarter of the shares in Novo Nordisk and controls just over three-quarter of the votes through a dual-class structure that prevents the Foundation from selling its shares in return for granting it disproportionate voting rights. This ownership structure provides the company with stable ownership that allows it to commit to the eradication of diabetes around the world over the long term and access liquid stock markets for long-term equity finance.

But let's now test out the power of profitable problem-solving purpose on a group of companies for which it blatantly cannot possibly work—the 'sin stocks'.

Sin and Salvation

How can a cigarette manufacturer, an alcohol producer, a gambling company, or an arms manufacturer possibly have a meaningful purpose? They are inherently evil and therefore beyond salvation.

A fossil fuel firm might seek redemption by transforming itself into an energy company by credibly committing to solving the world's energy problems by providing affordable and accessible renewable sources of energy. But what about cigarette manufacturers producing addictive, unhealthy, environmentally polluting products that kill and disable? Is there a legitimate purpose for them?

Some are trying to reinvent themselves as 'smoke free' using substitute products such as e-cigarettes that do not burn tobacco. But while these may be lesser evils than their predecessors, they are hardly angelic. What is the positive rather than just the less damaging purpose they can fulfil?

The function that cigarettes, alcohol, gambling, and fast-food snack companies seek to perform is to provide low-cost ways for us to enjoy and feed ourselves, relax, and socially interact. However, in doing that they cause addiction, pollution, ill-health, and death.

They are profiting from producing problems as well as solutions. In reinventing themselves, they need to find cheap ways for us to gain enjoyment, nourishment, relaxation, and social interaction that are non-addictive, non-polluting, healthy, and safe.

But if some people are perfectly willing to take the risks of ill-health, death, or addiction, why should they be prevented from doing so? Why should one infringe people's liberties to determine for themselves what is in their interest? Why should we tolerate the nanny state of others telling us what is in our best interests?

The answer is we should not. But at the same time, companies should not profit from the costs that they impose on health services, support services, and the environment because of the ill-effects of their products. Companies should incur the costs of cleaning up the mess that their products create. Otherwise, they are profiting at the expense of the rest of us, especially as taxpayers and providers of public services.

The freedom of some should not come at the expense of the ability of others to avoid the consequences of worsened health services, support services, and the environment. The inherent problem is not just the production of problems or detriments but that their costs are not fully borne by those who create them as either producers or customers. Profits from producing sin are overstated and therefore sin stocks are overvalued and sin is overabundant. Correct the true costs and profits of sin, and it will be sanctified by the market.

But what about another source of sin—conflict?

Conflict

The conflict between Russia and Ukraine that is in progress as I write this has raised the issue of companies' withdrawal from Russia. The Russian invasion of Ukraine presented companies operating in Russia with difficult decisions about whether to continue their operations or withdraw. The case for withdrawal is that by continuing to operate in Russia, companies may be directly or implicitly supporting a country that has invaded another, inflicting substantial human, emotional, and physical damage and destruction on people and property. The boards of companies have in many cases faced considerable pressure from their customers, employees, citizens, and governments to react to the crisis by severing or curtailing their links with Russia.

On the other side of the coin, companies may inflict significant harm on their employees and customers in Russia, many of whom might well be innocent bystanders or opposed to the invasion. Furthermore, the markets in Russia may be of considerable significance for companies and exiting from them could come at considerable cost to their employees and investors. The issue that arises is, how should companies respond to these conflicting interests and pressures?

The Yale Chief Executive Leadership Institute has been tracking the response of 1,200 public and private companies around the world with operations in Russia. They classified the responses of companies from 'withdrawal' involving a 'clean break' from Russia through 'scaling back', suspending a significant portion but not all their business in Russia, to 'digging in', defying demands to exit and largely continuing business as usual.

They studied 593 publicly listed companies in detail to evaluate how the stock market reacted to their withdrawal.[21] They found that 367 of the companies withdrew completely or significantly suspended their operations, 161 largely continued their businesses or 'dug in', and the remaining 65 fell in the middle, partially scaling back.

Although the costs of ceasing operations could be very significant in terms of disposal of assets, loss of custom, interruptions to supply chains and restructuring costs, the authors found that the stock market returns of the companies that made the greatest commitments to withdraw were the most positive, or the least negative, from the date of the invasion on 24 February 2022.

The authors then examined the influence of the region of the world from which the companies came and recorded more positive share price reactions to complete withdrawal than any other decision for all companies in their study, irrespective of whether they came from

North America, Europe, or Asia. They looked at the influence of the size and sector of a company and reported stronger share price reactions to withdrawal than digging in across nearly all size groups and sectors.

In addition to stock markets, the researchers looked at the response of credit and derivative markets. They found that increases in probabilities of default on corporate bonds between February and April 2022 were greatest for companies that dug in or largely continued their operations relative to those that completely or mostly withdrew. This was found to apply to companies based in different regions of the world and operating in different sectors of the economy.

So, what the researchers report is that, despite the costs involved in ceasing operations in Russia, the greater the degree of withdrawal of companies from Russia, the more positive was the market response. Far from there being a trade-off between ethical concerns about remaining in Russia and the financial consequences of withdrawing, ethical principles and financial incentives pointed in the same direction of encouraging decisions to withdraw.

What might be giving rise to the results? Several factors might be at play. First, there may be concerns on the part of investors about the reputational consequences of being invested in companies that remain in Russia. Second, there might be a risk of repercussions for their operations in their domestic markets and elsewhere in the world from their continuing presence in Russia. Third, there might be a fear of the exposure of their operations, assets, and personnel to retaliation in Russia.

Another study provides some answers to these questions. It reports, firstly, that those companies which withdrew from Russia had comparatively little revenue exposure to Russia and, secondly, they were subject to particularly intense boycott campaigns as reflected in Tweets that went viral, referring to the company, and the words 'boycott' and 'Russia or Ukraine'. In other words, it was relatively easy for these companies to withdraw from Russia and the reputational damage from remaining was perceived to be particularly great.

The implication is that the companies that withdrew were the ones for which the costs were comparatively low and the reputational risks from failing to do so were greatest. Withdrawal decisions were therefore predominantly determined by profitability effects and anticipated stock market responses rather than wider ethical considerations.

Furthermore, the study found that Tweet boycott campaigns were particularly targeted against large companies and larger companies were more likely to withdraw from Russia than small ones. And indeed, there are particularly important lessons to be learnt from the largest companies in the world.

The Trillion Dollar Companies

There are about half a dozen companies in the world with a stock market valuation of approximately a trillion dollars. What marks them out is a relentless focus on a purpose of solving challenging problems: Amazon, in allowing us to search, order, and deliver virtually any consumer product in the world to our homes in a matter of days; Apple, delivering computing power greater than that which put men on the Moon in the hands of people's iPhones, tablets and PCs; Facebook/Meta, social networking the world; Alphabet/Google making the internet, information and knowledge globally accessible; Microsoft, developing artificial intelligence and cloud computing; and Tesla building electric cars and rockets.

Each has had its inspirational (some might say fanatical) founders and leaders—Jeff Bezos, Amazon; Steve Jobs (now Tim Cook), Apple; Mark Zuckerberg, Facebook/Meta; Larry Page and Sergei Brin, Alphabet/Google; Bill Gates (now Satya Nadella), Microsoft; and Elon Musk, Tesla. A capitalist system must allow leaders to flourish and solve really challenging corporate problems in the way in which Henry Ford did at the beginning of the twentieth century in developing the Model T and mass car production.

But they have also come in for criticism—Amazon in terms of how it treated its employees; Apple in sourcing and exploiting natural resources; Facebook/Meta in its use of people's data; Google/Alphabet in abusing its dominant position; Microsoft in exercising insufficient restraint in competing to develop artificial intelligence that poses immense threats as well benefits for humanity. Their massive equity market valuations have therefore in the past in part derived not from just solving but also creating problems.

To that extent, their profits and valuations are overstated. In most cases they have recognized and responded by changing their businesses practices or incurring the remedial expenditures required to correct the problems. Where they have delayed or failed to do so, as in the case of Facebook's initial reaction to concerns about its use of data, then their market values have consequently suffered.

What this demonstrates is that far from being a diversion from the real business of making money, solving the world's greatest problems is the business that really makes money. The failure of less successful companies is not an excessive focus on addressing problems but a lack of ambition or ability to solve the world's biggest challenges and use technology and innovative business techniques to do that profitably. On the other hand, the greatest risk faced by the most successful companies is a failure to recognize where their success and profits come at the expense of others.

Judgement

A combination of COVID, vaccine development, climate, and the war in Ukraine demonstrated the power of problem-solving purpose to make a profit and a virtue out of problems. They point to the role of equity finance in funding problem-solving purposes and the growing interest of institutional and activist investors in the financial benefits that derive from purpose. They emphasize the importance of clarity about the problems companies are there to solve and the credibility of their commitments to solve them.

This has come in response to intensified societal pressures on companies to take account of the impacts of their activities on the environment, inequality, and inclusion. But it poses significant challenges for firms when there are inherent conflicts in those pressures between, for example, cleaner and affordable energy, or innovative cures for health and their accessibility in the poorest parts of the world. Where problem-solving and profit are aligned then the right course of action is comparatively easy to identify as was the case for some companies withdrawing from Russia but not for others.

At the end of the day, it is clear from recent experience where corporate and institutional priorities lie—where the money is. If it isn't the most profitable course of action, then it won't happen. In one respect that is quite right because business is not philanthropy and problem-solving must be profitable. Profit as such is not the problem. The problem is the provenance of profit. Does it come from problem solving, which is the source of the wellbeing of others, or from problem creation which is their affliction?

The presumption is that what is profitable is right. It is immoral for companies not to be profitable and what is profitable is moral. That it is immoral for companies not to be profitable is justified by the need for business to generate financial benefits for their shareholders. But the converse is not true. The persistence and profitability of sin stocks are just one illustration of the fact that what is profitable is not by any means always moral. Companies profit from creating problems for others. It is right that business should be profitable but what is profitable is not necessarily right.

The crises of the last few years have increased awareness of the potential financial benefits of doing the right thing and the risks of doing the wrong thing. They have closed avenues of exploitation and forced change. The financial crisis resulted in reform of banking systems. COVID-19 propelled new ways of working and recruiting staff. The energy crisis drove energy efficiency and savings. War in Europe and political tensions in Asia uprooted supply chains and promoted security of supply. Artificial intelligence threatens the operation and survival of educational institutions and businesses.

Crises cause change, but they don't solve problems. On the contrary, crises beget crises. They have not stopped financial benefit deriving from doing wrong as well as right. We need to determine minimum levels of standards that apply universally if markets are to function, humanity is to thrive, and the planet is to survive.

PART II

THE DUTY

Companies span everything from the psychopathic to the brilliant but blemished. At present we attempt to constrain the conduct of companies through regulation. While regulation has been essential, it has not been sufficient to align the interest of companies with those of society.

A growing preoccupation of companies with their share prices has intensified the problem. It has deepened the divergence between the interests of those owning and running companies from those of the rest of society. The generation of profit is not itself a problem. Instead, it is the provenance of profit which is the issue and the fact that profit originates from producing as well as solving problems.

Underpinning this is the current self-referential formulation of the Golden Rule: 'Do unto others as you would have them do unto you.' It should be reformulated as a genuinely other-regarding rule: 'Do unto others as they would have done unto them.'

A corollary of this is the Moral Law of profiting from producing solutions not problems for others. The Moral Law enhances trustworthiness and promotes relations based on trust. It extends concepts of unjust enrichment and account of profit, and it should be the basis of corporate law.

Corporate law is permissive in allowing companies to adopt their desired purposes. Corporate purposes conform with the interests of society if the Moral Law applies. Corporate law should be permissive of purposes that do conform and proscriptive of purposes that do not.

The Moral Law is not at present explicitly included in corporate law. It may be possible to interpret the 'enlightened shareholder value' nature of UK company law in this way. But it cannot be associated with US corporate law, even in its stakeholder-oriented forms as exist in some states of the US.

The reason why there is ambiguity in the interpretation of UK company law and omission from US corporate law is a failure of the laws of either country to establish a clear basis on which to prevent firms profiting from detriments. The Moral Law should be universally incorporated in corporate and company law.

This can be done through including corporate purposes of profiting from solutions not problems in law. These establish appropriate director duties. They retain the sole accountability of directors to shareholders, but they also align interests of companies and shareholders with other parties. They internalize negative externalities, and they permit, but do not require, adoption of positive purposes.

The principles that apply to business are equally relevant to other corporate forms. They pertain to philanthropic, public, and social as well as business corporations. They provide a framework for adjudication over cases of corporate legal responsibility. These should relate to corporate structures and conduct as well as performance, particularly regarding the ownership, governance, measurement, and financial arrangements of companies.

3
The Moral Law

We are not rich by what we possess but by what we can do without.

Attributed to Immanuel Kant

There is a view that corporations are psychopathic.[1] Their single-minded pursuit of profit makes them exploitative, manipulative, and corrosive. They exploit their power and wealth to extract benefits, favours, and privileges at the expense of others. They manipulate governments to dilute regulation, avoid taxes, diminish competition, and distort public procurement. They corrode our moral values, our ethical principles, and our human instincts of care and concern for others.

This has been particularly in evidence in the financial sector, most prominently during and after the global financial crisis of 2008 and more recently in Danske Bank and Wells Fargo, but there are many examples elsewhere, of which Arthur Anderson, Carillion, Enron, FTX, Purdue Pharma, VW, Wirecard, and WorldCom are some high-profile cases. However, it is not the pathological that prove the normal. Many people contend that the vast proportion of businesses are run by people who are honest, upright, hardworking, and ethical.

And they are right. Most businesspeople are like you and me—normal, honest, family loving, community spirited, socially aware, environmentally concerned people. It is not in general the character of the individuals that is at fault but the system that forces them to take on guises in their workplaces that they would not dream of adopting in their domestic surroundings.

And it is not the extremes that really afflict us. It is the routine— the fact that companies routinely entice us to switch suppliers of banking, energy, insurance, and telecom services and then slowly and covertly raise prices and reduce rewards, relying on our inertia not to switch again. We tire of energy suppliers failing to provide adequate provisions for the rising cost of energy in offering fixed price contracts to consumers and then needing to be bailed out by governments when they fail. We are outraged by water companies profiteering from dumping untreated sewage into rivers, lakes, and sea; oil and gas companies buying back their shares when investment is desperately needed in renewable sources; and food companies reaping record profits when much of the world faces starvation because they have nothing to reap.

Of course, we can rationalize these actions as making commercial sense. But that is precisely the problem—commercial sense does not correspond with common sense. All too often, companies' interests blatantly do not align with our interests as customers, employees, suppliers, and communities. It is wearying, depressing, and enraging.

Even the real global success stories—the world's trillion dollar companies to which I just referred—with mission, vision, and purpose statements of Amazon 'to be earth's most customer-centric company', Apple 'to bring the best personal computing products and support to students, educators, designers, scientists, engineers, businesspersons and consumers in over 140 countries around the world', Facebook 'to give people the power to build community and bring the world closer together', Google 'to organize the world's information and make it universally accessible and useful', Microsoft 'to empower every person and every organization on the planet to achieve more', and Tesla 'to accelerate the world's transition to sustainable energy'—are as I mentioned tainted by the way in they have treated data, employees, the environment, inequality, natural resources, social inclusion, social networks or their dominant market positions. As is so often the case, their idealistic foundations to inform the world and connect people eventually give way to realistic concerns to increase wealth and collect payments. It is not surprising that several of them have fallen out of favour and the trillion-dollar class.

Companies therefore range between the psychopathic to the brilliant but blemished, with most being tolerable but inconsiderate. What is going wrong? Some would respond by arguing that it is a problem of government.[2] We are letting companies get away with being exploitative, manipulative, corrosive, harmful, and inconsiderate because we are failing to regulate and constrain their conduct sufficiently. We need tougher and more rigorously enforced regulation to prevent abuses and detriments.

We have had nearly two centuries of experimenting with regulation from the factory acts of the nineteenth century, through the anti-trust acts of the early twentieth century to the explosion of regulation at the end of the twentieth century through the twenty-first century's response to the global financial crisis. Not only has the problem not gone away but it has got worse. Concerns about the environment, inequality, social exclusion, data usage, and dominant market positions of the global giants have intensified. How long do we need to go on repeating taking the same failed prescription until we accept that it is not adequate? Something else is needed and that is a recognition of the much more fundamental nature of the problem—profit.

One of the most significant developments of the last few decades has been to summarize the performance of business in a single measure—their share price. It is the single driver of the largest businesses around the world. Where companies are private and not listed on stock markets, it is measured by their profits. Share prices and profits are embedded in business practice and financial investment. They are clear, precise, observable, and actionable—actioned by linking them to every aspect of incentives of organizations—remuneration, promotion, firing, and hiring.

The last 60 years have seen the progressive intensification of share-price and profit- driven incentives. Stock options, fair value, and mark to market accounting, financialization, hostile takeovers, and hedge fund activism. We have reduced the world to a single measure of performance. But this preoccupation with the beauty, simplicity, and clarity of share prices and profits has not been without its drawbacks. It is driving the world to a point of climatic collapse and social fragmentation. And we are seeing the consequences of that all around us.

What is wrong with this single measure? The answer is simple: profits and share prices do not measure what they purport to report. They don't measure either the profit or the value that a company creates. They don't take account of the value of the benefits that a company creates for the people and environment around them or the destruction they cause.

How can we record a profit where a company has earned it from destroying part of a rainforest, cutting down an ancient woodland, accelerating the extinction of species, employing people at below living wages, selling addictive products, or avoiding paying their fair share of taxes? Those are not profits any more than the earnings of a burglar taking someone else's property.

It is theft but its only distinction from theft is that we have legalized it. Not only have we legalized it, but we have also encouraged and immortalized it by incentivizing it and honouring the wealth that is accumulated from it. Like a patient pre-occupied with their temperature, we have created an addiction not just to the addictive products that are the source of share price increases but to the share prices themselves. Furthermore, we have gone on to suggest that anything else is a muddle, confusion, impractical, and inefficient—a distraction from the simplicity of share prices and profits.

But in a sense, it is worse than theft because, were it simply theft, then it could be dealt with under criminal law. If it was simply a wrong done unto another arising from, for example negligence, then it could be addressed through tort law. If it was a breach of contract, it would be covered by contract law. The problem is it is about a gain of one party that might not have come from theft, negligence, or breach of contract but simply the effect they have had on another party—the smoke or noise that has drifted from a factory to the neighbouring community or the impact that a social media company has on the mental wellbeing of children. It is therefore an externality in the sense that it is a cost not borne by the producer.

The externality could arise from profiting at the expense of future not existing property or wellbeing of others. It could reflect deprivation of what someone might legitimately expect in the future, a profit earned at the expense of others' legitimate expectations, including the collective expectations of society as well as individuals. It could be a profit resulting from a breach of trust or an explicit or implicit commitment to some future benefit.

How could we have possibly got to this point? I could give an economic answer and say that it is the beauty of the economic models that has driven a false belief in the power of competitive markets, the efficiency of finance, and the ability of regulation to constrain bad behaviour. I could give a sociological answer and talk about the power of vested interests in preserving the status quo where a small elite benefits at the expense of others and the natural world. I could give a historical explanation in terms of our enthusiasm for Adam Smith's *Wealth of Nations* while forgetting his *Theory of Moral Sentiments*.

But there is a more fundamental reason. We have forgotten why we are creating and running businesses. It is not to profit. It is to solve problems. To solve problems that you, I, societies, and the natural world face. And in the process to produce profits. And profits are essential. They are the lifeblood of business. Without them we do not have the investors that are needed to resource the solving of problems at scale. But profits are not the purpose; they are the product of purposes of solving problems.

It is a simple confusion of cause and effect. Solving problems is the cause; profits are the effect. We need to incur the full costs of avoiding, mitigating, remedying, and compensating for the problems that we cause. But even this is not enough. It is no longer enough to avoid causing problems. The crises have become too great. People are looking to business to proactively solve problems.

It is no longer just about being net zero, it is about being net positive.[3] It is not just the costs of avoiding detriments and problems that companies need to incur but the costs of solving problems. That is what defines a just profit of a company and shared value as well as share value. It is the basis of the moral law of business and economics.

The Case for the Moral Law

The moral law derives from our purpose, our reason why we exist and are created—to solve each other's problems, to do so profitably and not to profit from producing problems. The importance of this is not only that it suggests a reason for our existence or a basis for our conduct in terms of solving problems but also a definition of profit. It is what is sometimes described as a positive statement, not in the sense of the opposite of negative, but of being descriptive or factual, not normative, values-based, or judgemental of someone or something.

It is a statement that a profit does not derive from producing problems, and only problems that are solved profitably are valid. It therefore follows that we should only observe profits being associated with solutions to problems, not creation of problems. We should not be recording profits where problems are being created and should only be reporting them where solutions to problems are found.

The moral law is that we should only profit from producing solutions to problems of others and not profit from imposing detriments on others. Why is this a moral law, not just an assertion or rule? A moral law is an absolute statement of right action derived from divine ordinance or the truth of reason.[4] In this case the law has been derived from the rule of reason rather than religion. It does not require divine intervention to establish its basis. Instead, it derives from reasoning around right conduct.

Why is the notion of profiting only from producing solutions for others a rule of reason? Consider the contrary, that profit can derive from producing problems instead of or as well as solutions. In that case we would be rewarding and incentivizing those who are inflicting damage on at least one other party without remedying, rectifying, or compensating for the detriment they are causing.

The implication is that they would be benefitting at least in part from the losses of others.

Such an outcome might be justified in so far as the benefits that some parties derive outweigh the losses of others. But those who are creating or inflicting the detriments, as well as benefits, are not able to judge the merits of so doing. They are parties who are conflicted by their self-interest.

It is only where profits are restricted to the creation of benefits not detriments that we can be sure that we are promoting desirable outcomes. In all other cases, judgements are required that involve balancing the interests of different parties, and the merits of so doing cannot be objectively ascertained by those who stand to profit from them. Impartial judgements require that they be made in the absence of self-interest—by Plato's guardians as against his workers who can and should be rewarded for the profit of their labours.[5]

This inverts the argument that is sometimes made against businesses making value judgements that they are supposedly not authorized or elected to do. It suggests that, on the contrary, companies are not empowered to make decisions of balancing a benefit that one party derives from its activities against the detriments incurred by another in determining the net profit. They only have the legitimate authority to do so where they incur the full costs of rectifying, remedying, or compensating for remedying any detriments they are causing. A net profit is only an actual profit where it is net of the costs of reversing the harm that is associated with it.

Why does this justify a moral law and not just a law of the land or international law? The answer is that without a moral law of not profiting from producing problems that is universally applicable in all circumstances, then liberties will be constrained, and markets will not function as effectively or efficiently as they should. In the absence of the moral law applying to all activities then the moral, who abide by the principle, will be undermined by the immoral, who do not. Fair and free competition will not be possible, there will not be a 'level playing field' and bad conduct will drive out good.

With the moral law then markets and competition can and should be promoted and flourish because the pursuit of profit will be associated with unequivocally beneficial outcomes over which externally imposed judgements will not be required. Good conduct will be intrinsic to all and not dependent on its external imposition by others, namely the Plato's guardians.

Far from undermining the pursuit of commercial activities, the moral law promotes and facilitates them. It removes the constraints that currently afflict and undermine the free functioning of competition and markets. It provides a basis for commerce that is both meritorious and rewarding for its own sake without the intervention of others.

While it promotes the operation of competitive markets by establishing a level playing field, the economic benefits of the moral law do not depend on markets. By avoiding private benefit from public detriment, it aligns incentives with social wellbeing in all transactions, non-market as well as market.[6] It establishes a framework for the development of non-markets in the absence of markets as well as the correction of market failures.[7]

The case of media is particularly pertinent in this regard. It is one where business models have resulted in exploitation of people's personal data, data commons, breaches of security, dissemination of divisive opinions, and vulnerability of adults and children. However, at the same time, it raises critical issues regarding freedom of information and free speech. According to the moral law, owners and directors of the relevant print, broadcasting and social media companies and platforms should be responsible for ensuring they do not profit from inflicting detriments on others.

This is not an infringement of freedom of information or free speech. On the contrary, it promotes multiple organizational forms including for-profit, not-for-profit, public benefit corporations, and utilities operating under public licence to deliver it. What it requires is that the profit motive not operate against either the private or public interest and it places the onus on owners and directors of media companies to ensure that this is the case by determining appropriate corporate forms and governance arrangements to achieve it.

Why has the moral law not been recognized or universally adopted to date? The answer is that the insidious decline and debasing of society that derives from the profitable exploitation of others is not immediately evident and only fully exposed by crises. We are encountering multiple crises now and the urgency of recognizing the inherent conflict of our current notion of profit has become acute.

The moral law raises many obvious and important questions:

- What is the relation of the moral law to legislation and regulation?
- Who determines whether there are detriments from which companies should not profit?
- To whom should companies be accountable for ensuring this does not happen?
- Who has the responsibility for ensuring it does not happen?
- How should companies credibly commit to avoiding this?
- How should the moral law be reflected in accounting principles and measurement of profit?

These are fascinating issues the resolution of which lies at the heart of changing business to regain the confidence and trust of societies. We will explore them in the remainder of the book but at this point it is worth emphasizing that the moral law does not come from accountancy. It is not driven by how we account for profits. It is not determined by a concept of how business should be conducted, namely by purposeful businesses that solve problems. It is not even by any means restricted to business.

Instead, it comes from our reason for being—the reason why we are created and exist—to protect, preserve, maintain, and sustain the being of others, and organize ourselves, societies, and institutions to enhance their wellbeing. We should recognize our problem-solving purpose as determining what are legitimate sources of profit and methods of measuring it.

Let's start by looking at the relationship between the moral law and trust.

Trust

There are two concepts of trust. The first is what is termed strategic trust. It derives from the economic notion of trust as being 'a game' between different people.[8] Suppose you and I are both entirely selfish and only do things that are in our own interest. Why should I ever trust you to do anything that is in my interest if I know that you are purely selfish? The answer is that it might be in your interest to act in my interest if you know that, in return, I will do something that is in your interest.

Will you do that? The answer is yes so long as you believe that I will go on acting in your interest. Correspondingly, I will believe you will act in my interest so long as I believe that you recognize I will go on acting in your interest. We are in what is termed a 'repeated game' with each other by which we could both act in each other's as well as our own interest or we could both act contrary to each other's interests. We reach a mutually beneficial outcome, even though we are entirely self-interested, if we believe that the other person will go on behaving in the mutually beneficial way.

Let's take a simple example. You and I are working together on a common ongoing project and let's assume that we are not only selfish but we are also lazy and greedy. We don't like working but we do like earning money. That is basically how economics conceptualizes mankind, so we are merely examples of *homo economicus*—admirable people like you and me who are selfish, lazy, and greedy.

If neither of us can observe whether we are putting our fair share of work into the project, then we could both take the naturally selfish and lazy approach of leaving it up to the other to do the work and take our half of the income that is earned. If we both act in this way then we both end up doing nothing and earning nothing,

Recognizing that this is a problem we might both instead choose to work hard and earn sufficiently more than we would if only one of us were working hard to compensate both of us for the hard work we are putting in. Will we do this? The answer is yes so long as we believe that the other will go on working hard because we know that if we stop so will they and neither of us will earn enough to compensate for the effort of working.

We trust each other to work because we know it is in our collective interest to do so. But there is a problem with this. Suppose that I know you will have to retire in, say, three years. In two years, I will recognize that you will stop working next year anyway, so I might as well stop working then and enjoy my half of the earnings you produce without having to do anything myself. But anticipating this, you will stop in two years as well. But then anticipating in year one that this will happen in year two, we will both stop in year one and we will never opt to work hard and trust each other to do so.

In other words, a notion of trust that is based on repeated games is at best fragile insofar as it unravels as soon as there is an inkling on the part of one person that another might not cooperate. At worst, as this example illustrates, trust that is strategic in nature and relies on relationships continuing into the indefinite future is implausible and simply will not be sustained.

This brings out that trust is inherently desirable insofar as, where it exists, it is mutually beneficial. However, trust cannot be sustained in circumstances where individuals are inherently self-interested in the absence of powerful sanctions to adhere to it. It is only self-sustaining where individuals are inherently trustworthy and can legitimately be deemed to be trustworthy to justify the trust that we place in them.

As we will describe throughout the book, a key economic determinant and signal of trustworthiness is investment—an upfront commitment to an irreversible expenditure that takes time to be repaid. It not only takes time it also takes reciprocity—a willingness of the other party to make an equivalent irreversible investment commitment.

This reveals that it takes two to trust. A common complaint of modern financial markets is the 'short-termism' of investors in preferring safe, liquid, short-term over risky, illiquid, long-term investments. However, berating investors for their short-sightedness may have its counterpart in the unwillingness of customers to commit to purchase over the long term—what is sometimes termed 'customer loyalty'—from the companies to which investors are supposed to commit.

This suggests that far from being a fragile repeated game from which one or other party invariably withdraws, trust is a relationship in which both parties reveal their hands and their trustworthiness upfront. It also demonstrates that trustworthiness is not simply a psychological character trait of an individual but also a very tangible economic undertaking—an expenditure of money that cannot be withdrawn at will.

That does not mean that psychology is irrelevant. On the contrary, there is another aspect which can be described as moral trust. In the economic view of trust, individuals are inherently self-interested. They are not interested in others except to the extent that the behaviour of others impacts on them. In contrast, in a moral context we are conscious and concerned about the impact of our behaviour on the interests of others and act according to rules that reflect their interests.

An illustration of this is the Golden Rule, which in its Christian form is normally expressed as 'do unto others as you would have them do unto you'. If the Golden Rule was a universal law that applied to both of us in the context of our collaborative project, then I would know that you will act in the way in which you would like me to act—namely to work hard—and you know that I will do the same and so we will both choose to work hard. We solve what is termed 'the collective action' problem of failing to act in our collective interest by adopting a universal law of conduct by which it is our moral obligation to act in each other's and thereby the collective interest.

However, while the Golden Rule is widely advocated and deeply embedded in ethical and religious education, it is not without its deficiencies. 'Do unto others as you would have them do unto you' is inherently self-regarding if not self-interested. It reflects a consciousness of others beyond their impact on one's own interests, but it does so through the lenses of one's own eyes. It advocates conduct towards others from the perspective of what we wish them to do to us, not necessarily what they wish to be done to them. It perceives what others desire from what we desire and thereby imputes our preferences to them.[9]

That was not a problem in the above example of the joint project because I was implicitly presuming that we had similar preferences regarding leisure and money. But supposing you attach far more importance to money than me. You will then work hard and think me reprehensible for not doing the same. I will do nothing and think you despicably greedy. Our different preferences accentuate our divisions by attaching a moral as well as practical significance to them.

Instead, if the Golden Rule was reformulated as 'do unto others as they would have done unto them' then you will work less hard in recognition of the lower value I attach to money than you, and I will be more inclined to work because I know how much you appreciate the money. The outcome reflects our divergent but collective interests.

The distinction is important because arguably the Golden Rule as currently conceptualized has been the source of divisiveness, discrimination, and intolerance. Suppose that there are two types of people in the world—A and B. A people have preferences that are very different from B people. A people do unto other A and B people what they would have done unto themselves. A people are happy with this and B people deeply unhappy. B people do the converse and make A people unhappy. Call A and B male and female, old and young, white and black, and one has the basis of the identity politics and polarization that has afflicted societies around the world. Far from being a source of integration and tolerance, the apparently moral based Golden Rule can be the cause of disintegration and fragmentation.[10]

A reformulated Golden Rule around 'do unto others as they would have done unto them' achieves the opposite. A people do unto A what they wish and unto B what they wish. B people do likewise. Both groups seek understanding and tolerance. But that is precisely why it has not happened, and the current form of the Golden Rule prevails. It is much easier to impute your own preferences to others than it is to have to go the lengths of genuinely understanding and appreciating the preference and interests of others, particularly if their background, race, cast, religion, gender, age, location, and upbringing are different from one's own. It takes a real effort and degree of empathy to achieve that level of knowledge and understanding. It is so much easier to apply stereotypes particularly if one's moral and religious education appear to justify them.

The traditional Golden Rule is not only divisive for society; it is disastrous for the planet. 'Do unto others as you would have them do unto you' is meaningless in the context of nature and, in its anthropocentric formulation, leaves nature completely out of the equation. As a result, according to the Rule, we can benefit by exploiting nature to the point where it undermines our quality of life and existence. In contrast, 'do unto others as they would have done unto them' encompasses all of nature and therefore requires us to promote planetary as well as human wellbeing and flourishing.[11]

The traditional formulation of the Golden Rule and its impediments to cross-cultural understanding have one particularly serious consequence. Let us call group A the rich and B the poor. Group A does unto B what they would like B to do unto them—yield as high a return on their wealth as possible. They pay as little as possible to B to get them to work as hard as possible to earn as much as possible to produce goods that are sold to A and B at as high a price as possible. B for their part do unto A what they would like A to do unto them— demand as high a wage as possible for doing as little as possible to purchase goods as cheaply as possible. The wealthy feel entitled, the wretched feel expropriated. The inherent conflict of capitalism has a moral not just a material foundation.

In contrast, in the reformulated Golden Rule group A seeks to pay as a high a wage to B for doing as little as possible to purchase goods as cheaply as possible and group B seeks to work as hard as possible for as low a wage as possible to sell goods at as high a price as possible to A and B. The wealthy and the wretched feel rewarded and respected. The conflict of capitalism becomes cooperation, and morality the foundation of materiality.

The practical realization of this is for both A and B to produce profitable solutions for each other, not profiting from producing problems for either. Group A seeks to achieve as high a standard of living for B as possible while B seeks to generate as high a profit for A as possible. Each understands, respects, and acts on the interest of the other and appreciates their mutual interests in achieving this outcome.

To illustrate alternative interpretations of the traditional Golden Rule, consider the controversial case of slavery. There are five levels of 'enlightenment' that might be associated with it. Level 1—unenlightened conduct—do unto them what promotes them being good slaves to you. Level 2—constrained self-regarding enlightenment—do unto them what you would have done unto you in slavery. Level 3—constrained other-regarding enlightenment—do unto them what they would have done unto them in slavery. Level 4—unconstrained self-regarding enlightenment—do unto them what you would have done unto you in freedom. Level 5—the reformulated Golden Rule and emancipated enlightenment—do unto them what they would have done unto them in freedom.

To take a less contentious example, consider cutting a cake. Level 1—do unto them what you would have done unto you—you persuade them to let you have the cake. Level 2—do unto them what you would them do unto you—you persuade them to let you cut the cake 'fairly' and take the first slice. Level 3—you cut the cake 'fairly' and let them take the first slice. Level 4—you let them cut the cake 'fairly' and take the first slice. Level 5—do unto them what they would have done unto them—you let them have the cake.

The reformulated Golden Rule is self-sustaining in the sense that I can encourage others to abide by it by offering it in exchange and withdrawing it where it is violated. If you do unto me what I would have done unto me then I will do the same. As a Moral Law, it is even more powerful and enduring than the tit-for-tat of repeated games such as the Trust Game because it is not just me who will withhold reciprocation in the event of you violating it but everyone who is affected by you.

It is an example of Immanuel Kant's categorical imperative: 'Act only according to that maxim whereby you can, at the same time, will that it should become a universal law.'[12] By imprinting my image of your and others' desires and interests on my mind I extend it to encompass the world as others wish it to be. Whether or not you subscribe to the concept of the 'divided brain'[13] with the right and left hemispheres performing different functions, the reformulated Golden Rule promotes the 'collective brain'[14] in a way in which the traditional version does not. I want you to project how I wish you to treat me, not how you want me to treat you, onto your brain.

The formulation of the Golden Rule bears directly on the more material form of trust described above. In its traditional form it encourages a get rich quick mentality—I want you to make me as rich as possible as quickly and safely as possible by investing as little for as short a period as possible in you. In the reformulated version, I want to make the investment that is best suited to you in the knowledge that, as a universal rule, you will do the same for me. In other words, the traditional Golden Rule is transactional, the reformulated is relational.

The current moral foundation of business is individualistic, self-interested, and transactional. The reformulated is collective, mutual, and relational. The importance of the moral law is in bridging the divide which currently exists between property and society. Profiting from producing solutions not profiting from producing problems aligns the private incentives of property with the collective interests of society. The moral foundations of trust derive from an intrinsic commonality of interest in solving our problems in ways that are embracing and inclusive of society as well as enriching and respecting of property.

Unjust Enrichment

The reformulation of the Golden Rule has fundamental implications for our understanding of profit. 'Do unto others as they would have done unto them' implies that we should profit from producing solutions not problems for others and that profit should derive from solving not causing others' problems. It suggests that one should not profit from imposing detriments on others.

The difficulty that arises in implementing this is that there may be no contractual relationship which would allow the losing party to seek compensation for breach of contract. There may be no violation of law or regulation that would allow public law to be invoked. There may be no practical or cheap form in which a tort can provide a remedy, particularly where the aggrieved party comprises an uncoordinated group of disparate individuals.

A more relevant principle is that of 'unjust enrichment', which derives from the Roman Law principle of '*nemo locupletari potest aliena iactura*' (no one can be enriched by another's loss). Unjust enrichment is associated with restitution of property to its rightful owner. It primarily relates to circumstances in which one party has erroneously received something from another party, for example for double payment of an invoice or payment to an incorrect recipient.

Restitution or restoration of the property to its rightful owner is then the correct course of action. This is distinct from compensation for a tort or loss incurred for default on a contractual obligation. Unjust enrichment relates to the gain of the recipient rather than the loss of the claimant. 'The law of restitution is the law of gain-based recovery, just as the law of compensation is the law of loss-based recovery. Thus, a right to restitution is a right to a gain received by the defendant, while a right to compensation is a right that the defendant makes good a loss suffered by the claimant.'[15]

Even so, the onus is on the claimant to demonstrate that there has been unjust enrichment. In contrast, in the equitable principle of 'account of profit', which concerns circumstances in which a trustee has profited from a breach of trust or fiduciary duty, the trustee is required to return the profit they have made to the party that has suffered the loss, for example the trust. Here the onus is on the trustee to establish that the profit was not in breach of the trust or their fiduciary duty.

The distinction comes from the greater responsibility that falls on a trustee to uphold the interests of their beneficiaries. In the case of a tort there is a duty of care but not loyalty since the defendant has not been engaged to act on behalf of the claimant.

What about a business? At present as will be discussed in the next chapter, the director has a fiduciary responsibility to the company and its shareholders, but they do not have a responsibility to other parties except in so far as the interests of those parties contribute to the success of the company for the benefit of its shareholders. In other words, their duties to other parties are derivative of or subordinate to their duties to their shareholders.

That is where the issue of the moral law comes in. The assertion that there is no direct duty to any other party presumes that the company is a freely floating entity whose responsibilities to other parties derive from those to its shareholders. But if the company is perceived as part of a system, then, in discharging their duties to the company and its shareholders, directors have duties to other parties in their own regard. The interests of the company and its shareholders derive from a duty of directors to other parties in the system as well as the converse.

The moral law implies that companies are not just liable to individuals, communities, NGOs, and private organizations through private laws of contracts and torts, and to public institutions and regulators through public laws and regulations. It also requires that directors and controlling owners have duties of loyalty and care under company and corporate law to avoid profiting at the expense of others and to be potentially liable for failures to fulfil this.

Furthermore, alignment of private and public interests of business is achieved not only through the threat of imposition of penalties but also through the inducement of governments and public institutions partnering with companies that abide by the moral law. In the case of regulated utilities, it is reflected in regulators assisting companies whose purposes correspond with their social licences to operate to earn sufficient long-term returns on their investment expenditures through the charges they are allowed to levy on their customers.

Not profiting to the detriment of others (unjust enrichment) and restoration and restitution (account for profit) therefore apply in all circumstances in which the company has profited at the expense of others. Companies have responsibility for the negative effects of their actions on all parties on whom they impact. This extends the legal boundary of the firm beyond its contracts with others and in the process internalizes its negative externalities. It restricts the boundary of the firm to where it is capable of profiting from delivering positive externalities of solutions without problems.

The relevant boundaries may relate to a nation but are often narrower or broader than that. For a small firm they may be constrained to the locality within which the firm is situated; for a multinational organization they can extend beyond national borders. While national regulations are therefore relevant to defining the limitations on the determinants of the profits of an organization, they are not sufficient. In both a local and an international context, the firm should identify the parties with which it is interacting and ensure that it is not profiting at their expense.

Summary

In sum, the reformulated Golden Rule and Moral Law have led us to a recognition that a profit of a business should be regarded as deriving from solving not causing problems for others and that in particular it creates responsibilities to other parties on whom it impacts. The fiduciary responsibility of directors to their shareholders remains as at present but their duties extend to ensuring that the profits their companies earn do not derive from inflicting problems on others.

The next chapter examines how the Moral Law relates to legal systems and the rule of law but before doing that it is important to recognize one important aspect of the Moral Law. While the notion of profit is most naturally applied to business because its fundamental objective is to be profitable and generate a return for its shareholders, it is not in any sense restricted to it. The rule of not profiting at the expense of others applies equally to all organizations and institutions—public or private; for profit or not-for-profit; local, national, or international.

Governments exist not only to promote the interests of their citizens but also to ensure that they are not promoting the interests of some segment of their societies at the expense of others or the interests of their citizens at the expense of those of other nations. Philanthropic organizations exist to promote the interests of the beneficiaries of their charitable purposes and in the process ensure that they do not benefit to the detriment of others. And all organizations must ensure that their human beneficiaries are not benefiting at the expense of non-human members of the natural world.

'Profit' in this context is the benefit of the parties whose interests the organization is there to serve, and it should deliver it without imposing detriments on others. There are similar fiduciary responsibilities on directors, elected officials and trustees to ensure that in solving the problems of some they are not creating problems for others. It is the role of law and legal systems to ensure that the moral law applies to all organizations, institutions, individuals, and natural world within their jurisdictions. And it is to the laws that support this that we now turn.

4

The Role of Law

The law is reason unaffected by desire.

Aristotle, *Politics*, iii

Corporate Law

It was 25 June 2020. I was participating in an online debate in the middle of the COVID-19 pandemic with Lucian Bebchuk, an eminent Harvard Law School professor, on 'Capitalism—The Great Debate: Stakeholder versus Shareholder'.[1] The subject under discussion was whether the current focus of capitalism and corporate law on shareholder interests was appropriate or whether they should be broadened to encompass a wider range of stakeholder interests.

Professor Bebchuk's argument was straightforward. If, as many people suggest, looking after stakeholder interests is simply good business and promotes the success of the company then there isn't a problem. In seeking to maximize the financial interests of their shareholders, companies will take their stakeholders' interests into account.

If on the other hand, looking after stakeholder interests is not simply good business and involves benefiting stakeholders at the expense of shareholders then it is bad business and should not be done. It undermines the performance of firms by presenting those running them with multiple, often conflicting objectives.

Thus, companies will take stakeholder interests into account to the extent that it is desirable to do so from the point of shareholders. As far as Professor Bebchuk was concerned, those running companies are incentivized and rewarded to promote their shareholder interests, and that is how it is.

In contrast to Professor Bebchuk's legal positivist view of what is, I argued from a normative position of whether existing law could be deemed to be 'unjust' and should reflect what ought to be, not just what is. It is only if profits derive from solving problems for others not causing them that the pursuit of shareholder interests is unequivocally good. In the presence of the moral law then Professor Bebchuk's claim is valid but not otherwise.

It is problematic if corporate law does not incorporate the moral law because, even if it were universally recognized as a moral obligation, then the law would not require it and would not prevent those who violated it from undermining, outcompeting, or acquiring more scrupulous companies. Legal systems and moral obligations would not be consistent and there would be no sanction for violation of the moral law.

Corporate law needs to place the purpose of business as being to produce profitable solutions for the problems of people and planet, not profiting from producing problems at the heart of it. It should be the fiduciary duty of directors of companies to determine their company purposes, define the problems they are seeking to solve, ensure that they have the resources and means to deliver on their purposes, measure their performance against delivery on their purposes, consult with relevant and affected parties in evaluating their performance against their purposes, and incur the costs of avoiding inflicting detriments on others.

The appeal of this is that it aligns company law, directors' duties, the purpose and reason for creation and existence of a company, its constitution and governance, and the way in which it accounts for its activities and reports its profits with the delivery of solutions to individual, local, national, and global problems without inflicting detriments. It creates a coherent notion of why business exists and its reason for being that is unequivocally beneficial. It promotes markets, competition, and delivery of benefits, and it encourages runs to the top of solving problems not to the bottom of extracting financial returns at the expense of others.

But is this realistic? Is it feasible to incorporate the moral law in corporate law? Is Lucian Bebchuk right that what is, must be, or can we reasonably expect another world? To answer this, we need to understand how we got to where we are and how we might go from here to where we want to be.

How We Got Here

There are four views of where a company derives its legitimacy.[2] The first and longest standing is that it comes from monarch or parliament. A company is established at the behest of its reigning authority to undertake activities that are dictated by the national interest. It is a concession conferred on a group of individuals to promote the objectives of the state in a form that is set out in a charter or licence.

This concessionary view of the firm reached its apex in the eighteenth century in the period after the scandal of the South Sea Bubble and the passing of the South Sea Bubble Act in Britain in 1720 prevented the formation of joint stock companies without a royal charter. But attitudes changed not least in response to the competition that was emerging elsewhere, especially in France and in the US, from less draconian restrictions on the creation of companies. Prohibition gave way to permission in the nineteenth century and the era of freedom of incorporation to establish joint stock corporations without charter or licence was born.

From a belief that a firm is a concession conferred at the behest of the state on those charged with running it, it rapidly evolved in the opposite direction into a simple aggregation of those individuals, its shareholders, who came together with a desire to form a new enterprise. It was a voluntary club of members established with the intent to create a commercially successful endeavour without requiring the permission of king or country to do so. It was as if the cork had been removed from a pressurized bottle of frustrated entrepreneurs and newly incorporated companies exploded out of it. The right to get rich from business was as much a human entitlement as freedom from oppression and slavery.

But no sooner had the joint stock company been established than its nature became the subject of scrutiny and interrogation. Was it just a body of freely consenting adults who were intent on getting rich or was it not something more than that? Did it not have an existence beyond those who came together as its members to create it?

The twentieth century was a period of intense debate and changing attitudes on what to some might have seemed arcane matters but were of profound importance and ultimately the survival of all of us. Underpinning this was a rapidly emerging professional class of middle and senior management standing between shareholders and employees. For them the firm was neither just a product of the state nor a collection of members but an organization with an existence of its own, distinct from both government and shareholders. Firms were entities with objectives that were determined and implemented by those running them.

Realization of what was happening was a source of mounting concern as rapidly growing corporations of the twenty-first century increasingly became recognized for what they were—fiefdoms and global empires operated for the benefit of their managers. The result was a move back to the conception of the corporation as just being an aggregation of shareholders connected by a 'nexus of contracts' in pursuit of commercially valuable endeavours. In other words, firms were extensions of the property of those who owned them, run for their benefit with management there to serve them as their agents with no discretion to deviate from this objective.

Our current conception of the firm is therefore a rejection of the alternative view that they are entities run for the benefit of the state or in the interests of their management. They are webs of contracts designed to enhance the wealth of their owners. Management has no legitimate basis on which to promote a broader agenda of human, social, or natural world wellbeing.

The real appeal of this notion of the firm is its clarity and simplicity. The objective of the firm is precise and measurable. Everyone—investors, employees, regulators, customers, governments, and managers—can see how well they are doing against the objective of promoting the wealth of their shareholders and be rewarded accordingly. It has a precision that no other formulation of the purpose of the firm comes anywhere near achieving.

The Duty of Directors

Within this context, the duty of directors of a company is clear: the directors must promote the success of the company for the benefit of its members, namely its shareholders. For example, UK company law states that a 'director of a company must act in the way he considers, in good faith, would be most likely to promote the success of the company for the benefit of its members as a whole' (Para. 1 of s.172 of the UK Companies Act (2006)).

The law recognizes the importance of other parties in achieving corporate success when it adds 'and in doing so have regard (amongst other matters) to:

(a) the likely consequences of any decision in the long term,
(b) the interests of the company's employees,
(c) the need to foster the company's business relationships with suppliers, customers and others,
(d) the impact of the company's operations on the community and the environment,
(e) the desirability of the company maintaining a reputation for high standards of business conduct, and
(f) the need to act fairly as between members of the company'.

As conventionally understood, directors' interests in other parties are therefore instrumental and subordinate to those of their shareholders, not intrinsic in their own regard, and directors have fiduciary duties of loyalty and care to their shareholders and no one else. The law binds companies to their shareholders, and wider society is relevant only in so far as it furthers their combined interests.

Any suggestion of business doing anything other than promoting the success of the company for the benefit of its shareholders is not going to get anywhere and rightly so because in creating multiple interests and multiple objectives one creates multiple confusion. There should be one and only one objective of the firm: to create just profit. But just profit should be just that—just—not unjust—undeserved, unmerited, or unwarranted.

The duty of directors to their companies remains sacrosanct and is reflected in profit that shareholders earn, which is deserved, merited, and warranted. It should be the duty of directors to ensure that all profit that shareholders earn is just that. But at present it is not because the duties of directors do not extend to other parties beyond their role in promoting the success of the company.

We are in a self-referential legal bind. The duties of directors are to the success of the company that reflects the interests of others, and the interests of others are defined as those that promote the success of the company as determined by the directors. It is as if I determined what is in your interest by how your interests promote my interest.

And that is precisely the position of self-interest in which directors find themselves as recipients of profit, stock option, and shareholding related incentive schemes. Their judgement of what is acceptable in promoting the success of the company is clouded by self-interest. They are making value judgements of the interest of the company that are tainted by the benefits they themselves are deriving.

Adam Smith appreciated the dilemma when he stated in *The Wealth of Nations*: 'It is the stock that is employed for the sake of profit, which puts into motion the greater part of the useful labour of every society',[3] but he then went on to note that: 'The rate of profit does not, like rent and wages, rise with the prosperity, and fall with the declension, of the society. On the contrary, it is naturally low in rich, and high in poor countries, and it is always highest in the countries which are going fastest to ruin. The interest of capitalists, therefore, has not the same connexion with the general interest of the society as that of landlord and worker.'

Smith therefore recognized both the importance and limitation of profits. They are essential to drive and resource companies, but they do not exclusively or solely derive from the delivery of human and natural world benefits. They also come from the exploitation of both of those parties.

How does one get out of this legal bind without reopening the pandora box of a firm having multiple objectives and beneficiaries? The answer is to retain the sole beneficiary from the success of the company as being the shareholders but to define the success of the company as being conditional on and subject to avoidance of detriments for others. It is in other words a binding condition that success for the benefit of shareholders excludes failing others. It does not require benefiting others, but it must avoid disadvantaging them.

This gives meaning to the assertion that the UK Companies Act is an example of 'Enlightened Shareholder Value'. The current interpretation of the law as making other party interests instrumental and subordinate to those of shareholders is not enlightened in any meaningful sense of the word. Shareholder value that respects the interests of others in their own regard is. It is an illustration of the significance of the reformulated in contrast to the traditional interpretation of the Golden Rule in determining the Moral Law.

A Reconsideration of Director Duties

Arguably, on some interpretations the Moral Law is already incorporated in the UK Companies Act. First, note that the Act states the director of the company must 'promote the success of the company for the benefit of its members as a whole', which means that it must deliver profitable solutions in the sense of solutions that are beneficial for its members. It cannot promote unprofitable solutions.

Second, it states that 'and in doing so have regard (amongst other matters) to … (d) the impact of the company's operations on the community and the environment'. How should that be interpreted? Suppose a proposed course of action has a positive and beneficial impact on the community and the environment. Then there is no problem: in supporting a decision to promote the success of the company for the benefit of its shareholders, it also benefits its communities and environment, and the firm does not profit from producing problems for others.

But suppose the decision has negative, detrimental impacts. It cannot seriously be suggested that what the Act intends is that, in having regard to promoting the success of the company for the benefit of its shareholders, directors must also accept, and indeed seek out, decisions that have detrimental effects on others. That would condemn the firm to treating the community and the environment as dustbins of dirt and disease so long as it is profitable to do so. The 'enlightenment' of the Act would be no more than inflaming the world.

That is not what should have been intended. When having regard to 'these other matters', the Act should have recognized an asymmetry between positive and negative consequences for others in the sense that positive consequences *may* be taken in consideration, but negative ones *must* be avoided. Perfectly appropriately, the Act would then imply that the success of the company for the benefit of its members, namely its profits, derives from producing solutions not problems for others.

Section 172 of the UK Companies Act is currently interpreted as implying that directors should treat the rest of the world as instrumental in promoting the success of the company for the benefit of their shareholders. A more reasonable interpretation is that the duty of directors is to ensure profits are not earned in violation of the interests of: (a) employees, (b) suppliers, customers, and others, (c) the community and the environment, (d) the company's reputation, and (e) the members of the company, now or at any time in the foreseeable future. In other words, the duty of the directors of a company is to uphold the Moral Law for everyone, everywhere, and for all times.

So much for the UK Companies Act, which, on this interpretation, could therefore be seen to be truly enlightened. But what about other countries' company and corporate laws that do not have the supplementary material regarding 'other matters'. How enlightened are they in practice? Let's take one, arguably one of the most important, which was the basis of Lucian Bebchuk's assertions in that Great Debate on Capitalism, namely the US.

US Corporate Law

A majority of publicly listed corporations in the US are incorporated in the State of Delaware. Under General Incorporation Law of the State of Delaware 'the directors of a Delaware corporation entrusted with management responsibility must protect the interests of the corporation and effectively serve as "trustees" for the stockholders (i.e., shareholders) with respect to the interests of the stockholders in the corporation', and 'directors of Delaware corporations … owe a duty of loyalty to the corporation and its stockholders'.[4]

In 2010 the then-Chancellor William B. Chandler III of the Delaware Court of Chancery stated that:

> the corporate form . . . is not an appropriate vehicle for purely philanthropic ends, at least not when there are other stockholders interested in realizing a return on its investment. . . . Having chosen a for-profit corporate form . . . directors are bound by the fiduciary duties and standards that accompany that form. Those standards include acting to promote the value of the corporation for the benefit of the stockholders. The 'Inc'. after the company name has to mean at least that. Thus, I cannot accept as valid . . . a corporate policy that specifically, clearly and admittedly seeks not to maximize the economic value of a for-profit Delaware corporation for the benefit of its stockholders. . . .[5]

In 2015, former Delaware Supreme Court Chief Justice, Leo Strine stated: 'A clear-eyed look at the law of corporations in Delaware reveals that, within the limits of their discretion, directors must make stockholder welfare their sole end, and that other interests may be taken into consideration only as a means of promoting stockholder welfare.'[6]

The American Law Institute has interpreted Delaware Law as:

> the objective of a corporation is to enhance the economic value of the corporation, within the boundaries of the law. In doing so, a corporation *may* consider: (a) the interests of the corporation's employees; (b) the desirability of fostering the corporation's business relationships with suppliers, customers, and others; (c) the impact of the corporation's operations on the community and the environment; and (d) ethical considerations related to the responsible conduct of business. [*italics added*][7]

By limiting the objective of the corporation to economic value without obligations to other parties, the American Law Institute restricts fiduciary duties of directors to financial benefits for shareholders, subordinating other parties' interests to their fulfilment.

Not all states in the US conform to the principles of Delaware Law. There are what are termed 'Constituency Statute' states of the US. The Constituency Statutes were introduced in the 1980s and 1990s to allow, and in some states require, directors to take account of the interests of stakeholders other than shareholders.[8] They were in part a response to the takeover wave of the 1980s and the negative impact that had on other stakeholders.[9]

In practice, there is much scepticism about the degree of protection that constituency statutes afford other parties. Part of the problem is a reluctance of courts to interpret them in terms of anything other than shareholder interest.[10] Another is that other stakeholders have no means of seeking redress if directors fail to take their interests into account.[11] Combined with concerns about the practicality or desirability of businesses adopting stakeholder practices,[12] some observers conclude that 'constituency statutes failed to deliver the benefits to stakeholders that were promised or hoped for in the push for the adoption of these statutes'.[13]

A second legal form that originated in the US to promote stakeholder beyond shareholder interests is the benefit corporation (also known as the public benefit corporation). Benefit corporations are formally established under statutes that require for-profit entities to pursue a dual mission of profits and social purpose.[14] Maryland was the first state to adopt a benefit corporation law in 2010 and 38 states have followed suit.

Critics of this new legislation claim that it is unnecessary as existing legislation permits directors sufficient latitude to adopt the practices of benefit corporations;[15] that benefit corporations are used for promotion or 'purpose washing';[16] and that many are not delivering any social or environmental benefits.[17] One study concluded that benefit corporations are concentrated in consumer-facing sectors where their benefit status is financially lucrative rather than socially transformative.[18]

Attempts to promote stakeholder interests through alternative legal forms have therefore had limited impact on conventional shareholder primacy, and empowering directors to incorporate other parties' interests has not fundamentally altered their behaviour. The effects of Delaware Law remain pervasive even where there are alternatives to it.

Is it realistic to expect anything different, or is Lucian Bebchuk right when he argues from a positivist position that we cannot expect directors of US companies to do anything different from what happens at present, namely pursue the success of their companies for the benefit of their shareholders?[19]

While it may be possible on some interpretations to attribute the Moral Law to the UK and other countries that have adopted a similar form of company law, that is by no means universally the case, particularly in the US. The reason is that neither constituency statutes nor public benefit corporations address the fundamental defect of conventional Delaware corporate law—its failure to prevent profit being earned at the expense of others. Even in the UK, there is ambiguity and controversy about whether company law has really achieved that. To ensure the universal adoption of the Moral Law, we must look elsewhere—to company purpose.

The Law of Purpose and the Purpose of Law

Attempts to introduce purpose into company and corporate law have a chequered history.[20] Early UK Companies Acts[21] in the nineteenth century required companies to adopt object clauses in response to the granting of limited liability and the *ultra vires* doctrine, which established that if companies strayed outside their stated objects, they were acting beyond their designated power.[22]

There were three difficulties with object clauses and their imposition through the *ultra vires* doctrine. The first was the liability directors incurred from acting *ultra vires*. The second was the limitation it imposed on the activities in which companies could engage and the ability of companies to modify their objectives. The third was the inability of parties to enforce contracts that were deemed to be *ultra vires*.

In response, companies specified progressively more general and less meaningful object clauses that served no useful function of clarifying or restricting corporate activities. Attempts by courts to sustain substantive interpretations of the *ultra vires* doctrine became clouded in confusion and obscurity, and progressively the doctrine was weakened until its death knell was sounded in the 2006 UK Companies Act.

How did the early architects of company law get things so wrong and why did the courts persist for the best part of a century in trying to make the impossible possible? The answer is that they were seeking to protect investors and in particular creditors from being lured into companies on false pretences. But they tried to do that by restricting the ability of a company to alter its purpose. This is hopeless for a business that needs to respond to changing circumstances. Furthermore, it failed to recognize that the problem it was trying to solve was not restricted to investors. Past attempts to incorporate corporate purpose in corporate law therefore provide few lessons on what role a suitably specified corporate purpose could play in determining the duties of directors.[23]

In contrast, making it illegitimate for a company to profit at the expense of others while allowing it to profit from anything else recognizes that it should profit from benefitting not harming others. The duty of a director is then not to avoid the creation of problems but to avoid doing so from a position of profit. It is not a 'do no harm' but a 'do not profit from doing harm' condition.

This distinction is important for two reasons. First, one should not incentivize companies to do harm. Second, companies and directors are routinely required to make judgements about conflicting interests of different parties regarding, for example, the employment effects of a decision to relocate from one town or country to another, or to benefit customers with lower prices at the expense of employee wages. For such decisions to be objectively fair and judicious they should not be distorted by the self-interest of profits. That means that firms must incur the costs of rectifying detriments (through, for example, retraining employees) to the point that they are just profitable.

A purpose of 'producing profitable solutions for problems of people and planet not profiting from producing problems' provides an appropriate basis for determining fiduciary relations of directors to both their members (their shareholders) and other parties on whom they impact and depend. First, it clarifies that directors have no right to pursue purposes that do anything other than promote the interests of their shareholders. They can only produce solutions that are profitable. There must therefore be no conflict between the interests of directors and their shareholders.

Second, it determines a profit as deriving from solving not creating problems. In relation to the UK Companies Act, it implies that directors have a duty to ensure that profits are not earned in violation of the interests of (a) employees, (b) suppliers, customers, and others, (c) the community and the environment, (d) the company's reputation, and (e) the members of the company, now or at any time in the foreseeable future. It therefore incorporates the Moral Law by being permissive in conferring positive benefits and proscriptive in preventing negative detriments.

Third, it does not require a company to specify a positive corporate purpose or one that is any more than making money for its shareholders. But it does allow companies to do so if they so wish. Why should companies want to tie their hands rather than have the discretion to do whatever appears appropriate at a particular point in time? The answer is that by fettering their discretion companies may be able to exceed what they can achieve without restraint. By tying themselves to the mast of purpose they can commit to a course of action from which they would otherwise be deflected by the sirens of opportunity.

A purpose that does not have the force of law behind it may be a description of what a firm intends but it can be jettisoned if something better subsequently appears, and it cannot be used to bind successor boards of directors or owners of a company. It cannot therefore act as a device for committing to other parties because the firm cannot give assurance that directors and shareholders will not change their minds in the future.

Firms may in general not wish to bind themselves in this way but there may be occasion on which they would benefit from the reciprocal commitment that other parties—employees, suppliers, customers, communities, and governments—provide in return in the form of investment expenditures, partnerships, and joint ventures. There is one occasion when this is particularly significant.

A hostile bid or hedge fund activist campaign involves a purchaser of a company's shares seeking the support of other shareholders in replacing the existing board of directors with one that will create greater shareholder value. In the process, there may be changes in strategy that involve making employees redundant, replacing existing supply and distribution arrangements, and abandoning environmental protection and community support programmes.

The mere threat of such events occurring at some stage in the future may be sufficient to require potential targets to adopt these policies themselves. Where markets for corporate control prevail in the form of hostile takeovers and hedge-fund activism, it is difficult for firms to commit to policies that do anything other than maximize shareholder value irrespective of the source of profit.

In contrast, where company law is interpreted in conformity with the Moral Law then, even if the hostile bidder or hedge-fund activist is successful, the new owners and directors will be obliged to continue to protect existing employee, supplier, distributor, environment, and community interests as specified in s. 172 when restructuring the target company.

In the presence of a specific positive purpose those interests relate not just to the minimal conditions of not doing harm but also to the legitimate expectations that positive purposes establish in the minds and investments of employees, suppliers, and other parties. That does not mean that acquiring companies and shareholders cannot restructure targets but that the profits they earn cannot simply come from transferring wealth or wellbeing from their stakeholders to their shareholders.

The Limitations and Unlimited Potentials of the Law

A purpose of producing profits from solving not creating problems has an important role to play in aligning the duties of directors to the Moral Law as well as their shareholders and allowing directors to commit their companies to objectives that would otherwise be unattainable in the absence of such binding commitments. It establishes the Moral Law as a condition of incorporation embedded in the firm's constitution and permits but not requires the determination of positive benefits.

As many have noted, corporate law in the UK and US and many other jurisdictions around the world is permissive in allowing companies to adopt any purpose that promotes the success of the company.[24] It already permits companies to commit to a positive purpose, conditional on it being aligned with the duty of directors to promote the success of the firm for the benefit of its shareholders. However, it does not do so in a form in which the Moral Law is a binding condition.[25] That is what incorporation of a purpose of producing profits from solving not creating problems contributes to existing law.

It is neither realistic nor desirable to expect the law to go further in requiring companies to make meaningful statements of why they are created or exist beyond the interests of their shareholders without governments or regulators forcing them to do so. This would take one down the dangerous path of politically determined corporate purposes. Far from inspiring a plurality of corporate purposes which reflect a multiplicity of interests beyond those of the members of a corporation, the imposition of purpose statements by government or regulator risks the incursion of politically inspired and bureaucratically managed motives in corporate objectives.[26]

The law can address negative externalities arising from market failures but not a failure to internalize positive externalities—it can proscribe profiting at the expense of others; it cannot prescribe profiting for the benefit of others. Furthermore, individual national laws cannot address the disparities that might exist at an international level.

To illustrate this, consider what happens if there are two countries in the world—one that respects the Moral Law in the interpretation of its corporate law, call it 'Us', and one that does not, call it 'Notus'. Can Us exist in the presence of Notus if people in both countries are equally self-interested in their own wealth without any altruistic concerns for others, and there are unrestricted flows of products and capital between the two countries?

The answer is no because companies in Us will be unable to compete against the lower costs of companies in Notus and capital will flow from Us to Notus. The burden of the mobile products and capital will be borne by the immobile people of Us who will be forced to accept worse conditions of employment than those in Notus.

The principle of not profiting at the expense of others must be adopted by both countries to avoid the good citizens of Us requiring capital market and trade barriers to protect them from the immoral of Notus. That is why the Moral Law must be universally incorporated into company and corporate law.

While the law cannot force organizations to adopt purposes that they do not wish to pursue or extend their reach beyond their legislative boundaries, it can incorporate organizations that are not profit-making businesses. For example, s. 172 of the UK Companies

Act has a second paragraph that permits companies to adopt a purpose that does not entail promoting the success of the company for the benefit of its members.

The notes to the Act explain what is intended by this paragraph: it 'addresses the question of altruistic, or partly altruistic, companies. Examples of such companies include charitable companies and community interest companies, but any company can have "unselfish" objectives which prevail over the "selfish" interests of members. Where the purpose of the company is something other than the benefit of its members, the directors must act in the way they consider, in good faith, would be most likely to achieve that purpose.'[27]

The company can therefore have a philanthropic, social, or public purpose and it does not have to deliver a benefit for 'the "selfish" interests of members'. What this does is extend the benefits of incorporation to any type of activity with the same condition that 'in doing so have regard (amongst other matters) to—(a) the likely consequences of any decision in the long term, etc.'. In other words, the duties of directors can be to any purposes that do not inflict detriment on others.

The Moral Law then applies to all corporations. In place of a purpose of producing profitable solutions without profiting from problems is a purpose of 'producing solutions not problems for people and planet'. A philanthropic company must support its beneficiaries, a public company its public, a social company its relevant societies and communities, in each case ensuring they avoid inflicting detriments on other parties. The company must ensure a harmonious existence of those both within its system—its sphere of operations—and outside but within its sphere of impact and influence.

It means that when we discuss the nature and organization of the corporation in subsequent chapters, while we will be doing so predominantly in a business context, it applies equally to virtually every form of economic, public, and social activity—a capitalist system of organizations—private, public, and not-for-profit—all operating according to the Moral Law.

The purpose of corporations is the criterion against which their success will be judged. It will be the basis of court judgements of whether directors are discharging their fiduciary duties of loyalty and care to their members. Corporations can, but are under no obligation to, specify, on a non-exclusionary basis, particular problems they seek to solve, and these may then form part of the criteria against which their success and the fiduciary duties of directors will be judged.

The concept of problem-solving organizations provides a framework within which corporate legal responsibilities can be determined.[28] It puts the onus on companies to demonstrate that they do not profit from producing problems for others and have in place the systems and processes required to prevent them from doing that. Those systems and processes relate to four areas—their ownership, governance, measurement, and financial arrangements.[29]

By focusing on whether companies have the right ownership, governance, measurement, and financial structures, the law will have a profound effect on the management and conduct of business, the way in which it is owned and governed, how it measures its activities and impacts, how it finances them, as well as how it evaluates its performance and rewards its employees and investors. In other words, the law has the potential to reverse the detrimental effects that corporations have had on the environment and social cohesion and align their interests with the world around them.

Profit and Prosperity

A corporate purpose of 'producing profitable solutions for the problems of people and planet, not profiting from producing problems for either' is not just a statement of the object of the firm but also of what is deemed to be a legitimate source of profits, namely profiting from solving not creating problems for people or the natural world. The reason why this is critical is that it resolves the conflict that arises between the pursuit of objectives that are in the corporate interest of its members in financial terms and those of society or the natural world more generally in social and environmental wellbeing.

Where the company has effects on others that are not reflected in market prices, there will be externalities that are not internalized in its financial performance. Since they are not priced, they are not included in a company's revenues or costs and therefore not relevant to the management of its profitability. What the reformulation of the company's purpose does is to require a firm to take account of the negative effects of its activities on others, irrespective of whether they are priced.

It expects a company to identify where its activities as a producer, employer, purchaser, neighbour, or consumer of public goods and ecosystem services are having a detrimental effect on the interests and wellbeing of others. It must then determine how it can best mitigate, remedy, rectify, or compensate for the detriments it is causing. If the costs of so doing are too great for it to profit from those activities, then it should desist from undertaking them because, as the first part of the purpose statement says, a company should not undertake activities from which it does not profit.[30]

What this does is align social and environmental interests with those of a company's members. Companies only profit where they create positive societal and environmental benefit, not where they have a negative impact on either.[31] It is no longer an empirical matter of whether there is a positive relationship between profits and problem solving but definitionally true in at least the anticipated sense of the profits that a firm expects to earn.

The purpose of a business clarifies what together the board of a company and its shareholders regard as the legitimate source of its profits and therefore the return on shareholders' capital. It establishes where they understand the company as contributing to enhancing the wellbeing of its customers, employees, suppliers, societies, and environment, and where investors are therefore appropriately rewarded for their investments. What this does is to avoid the current situation by which any profit that is earned without violating regulatory rules or the law is regarded as legitimate. It diminishes but does not eliminate the need for regulation to stop companies from damaging society and the environment.

Corporate purposes of profitably solving not causing problems, together with profits earned from producing solutions not problems, align the interests of shareholders with those of everyone else. Shareholders earn profits and only earn profits where they benefit others without imposing detriments on them. Conflict between shareholders and others becomes cooperation and, instead of seeking to benefit from exploiting others, shareholders recognize their mutual dependence on and responsibility to others.

Far from weakening the link between directors and shareholders, problem-solving business strengthens it. The interest of shareholders in their wellbeing as well as their wealth is reflected in profit being earned from enhancing social and environmental wellbeing. Any conflict that at present exists between shareholders' concerns about earning financial gains at the expense of environmental and social prosperity is extinguished. Shareholders can sleep easy in the knowledge that their financial prosperity is not derived from environmental and social impoverishment.

Not only does this strengthen the link between directors' and shareholders' interests it also connects both with the world beyond. It means that the financial performance of a firm is consistent with its shareholders' own sense of wellbeing, and with the wellbeing of everyone and everything else. It comes from solving the problems of others without causing problems for others. It derives from an intrinsic not just an extrinsic interest in others.

What we have done is link the firm with society and nature at large without eliminating the accountability and fiduciary duties of directors to their shareholders. We have made the interests of shareholders and directors in profit a product of the benefit that they confer on others. In so doing we have connected not only the two together in a stronger bind than existed previously through recognizing the interests of shareholders in their wellbeing as well as their wealth, but we have also connected both with the interests of everyone and everything else.

In essence, we have succeeded in finding a way of linking the interests of the wealthiest investors in the world sitting in their apartments at the top of skyscrapers in New York with the interests of the poorest slumdwellers in Nairobi and with the most endangered species in the Amazon rainforests, provided the means can be found to do this profitably. We have achieved this by recognizing what just profit is and how a purpose of producing profitable solutions without profiting from producing problems delivers just profit.

The investment chain and the multinational corporation are then not just a means of linking the wealthiest with more wealth production but wealth with poverty alleviation and nature conservation. They are linked where profits derive from alleviating not causing poverty and conserving not destroying nature. And by linking them through profits one is also ensuring that the interests of investors in profits correspond with the purpose of business of profitably solving problems. The corporation is the transformer of the system, converting individual self-interest into a collective endeavour by injecting financial investment into a problem-solving purpose.

We therefore almost magically unite the world around the promotion of commercial success. But even more strikingly than creating an intrinsic interest of the most privileged in the most deprived and vulnerable in distant parts of the world, we also establish a natural symbiosis between the present and the future. It is not only current generations of the most deprived and vulnerable that the wealthiest have an interest in but also the most distant future generations.

How so? How can even the most sophisticated corporate structures link the present to the future? The answer is from the perpetual nature of the corporation. Humans are mortal but corporations are not. In principle, they possess the immortality of perpetual existence. Hence in establishing a purpose of producing profitable solutions without problems, they create an obligation of protecting and promoting the interests of not only the most physically and emotionally remote but also the most temporally distant. The corporation must stare not just into the murky horizon of foreign lands but also into unknown futures.

Business is the most powerful instrument created for uniting the world in its entirety and for its eternity and the law has a primary function to ensure that it achieves its full potential to do that. To date, it has done exactly the opposite. It has linked the purpose of the firm with the self-interested concern of shareholders in their financial wealth. It has encouraged exploitation not just protection or furthering of the interests of the most disadvantaged and vulnerable. It has therefore sometimes done precisely the opposite of what the firm is capable of and should be doing.

In the process, it has brought us on occasion to our knees of self-interested impoverishment instead of carrying us to new heights of universal wellbeing. It has imposed an intolerable strain on government and our democratic systems to bridge the divide between those who advocate for the unrestrained operation of markets and businesses, and those who seek to tie them down with the heavy hand of regulation and enforcement.[32]

Summary

The corporation is a product of the law, and the law can fashion it in its preferred form. That is what it did when the corporation was constrained to be publicly chartered and then released to be freely incorporated.

Appropriately interpreted the law can and does ensure the alignment of the corporation's incentives with individual, societal, and planetary interests, and it promotes the resolution of their problems by enabling the most powerful institutional entity that we have created to date alongside governments, namely corporations, to commit credibly to their resolution without causing detriment. Its failings on both counts have been the source of our intensifying crises. We need to acknowledge this and recognize our power to provide a remedy for the cause of crises—namely the laws that create the corporation.

The approach of viewing the law from a systems perspective has not involved centralized governance. On the contrary, it encourages decentralized authority at the level of individual firms by imposing the onus on them to align their interests with those of society and the environment as well as their shareholders.

It encourages market processes and competition by incorporating non-market impacts in the objectives of the firm. It inverts the argument of treating negative externalities as beyond the boundary of the firm by embracing them within its boundaries. That diminishes reliance on external regulation to impose corrections for market failures and allows competition to proceed unimpeded by regulatory requirements.

Furthermore, a purpose of profitably solving without creating problems does not dilute or weaken the fiduciary responsibility and accountability of directors to their shareholders. On the contrary, it strengthens them by aligning the interests of companies with the welfare as well as the wealth of their shareholders. The fact that profits derive from solving not creating problems for others means that shareholders have both an emotional and financial interest in ensuring that their companies deliver on their promised solutions.

There are four key aspects of the nature of the company which influence its ability to fulfil its objectives—its ownership, governance, measurement, and finance. When adjudicating disputes with affected parties, the law has an important role to perform in evaluating the appropriateness of the systems and procedures that companies have in place. In the process, it will then have a profound influence on how companies structure their ownership, governance, measurement, and financial systems and ensure that they are consistent with businesses delivering the global benefits of which they are capable.

This will have the effect of engaging the wealthiest investors in the most prosperous developed parts of the world in alleviating the hardships of the poorest in the lowest income countries, not just today but across generations into the future. It will bring about a transformation of a self-centred, selfish institution into an enlightened and other-regarding one. Far from increasing the complexity of business, it clarifies and simplifies how to deliver what is expected of it.

Critical though the inclusion of the Moral Law in corporate law is to avoidance of the negative, its real significance is in the attainment of the positive. It creates a mutual realization on the part of all of us that our individual gains come exclusively from assisting each other. It thereby establishes a unity of direction and purpose without relying on a central coordinator or governor to do this.

It provides the foundations of a commonality of interest and understanding of how we individually and collectively resolve our challenges and problems as owners, leaders, employees, customers, suppliers, investors, and communities. It is the means of realizing our full potential to flourish and prosper and, above all, restore our sense of humility and humanity.

But how? How can this be done without making business impossible? The answer is simple: let business focus on what it is there to do—own and solve problems that earn just profit.

PART III

THE METHOD

Ownership of business is conventionally considered a property right. It confers considerable authority on the providers of finance. However, it has become less appropriate as firms' dependency on other resources has increased.

The alternative stakeholder approach of conferring rights on other parties is widely advocated but has been a source of confusion and proven complex to implement. Instead of diluting accountability to shareholders, the responsibilities as well as rights of shareholders should be recognized.

Those responsibilities derive from the firm being part of a system. Owners of firms are owners of a part of the broader system in which the firm resides. They therefore have responsibilities to contribute to the resolution of the system's problems, as well as rights to financial claims over private property.

A plurality of forms of ownership is required to solve the multiplicity of problems that exist in the system. Consistent with this is the large variety of forms of ownership observed around the world. These extend from the Anglo-American widely dispersed stock market listed companies to the more commonly observed parallel forms of stable, concentrated, and dispersed ownership. Family and state ownership are prevalent forms of concentrated shareholdings around the world, together with employee and foundation ownership in some countries.

The parallel system combines stable, long-term shareholdings exposed to firm-specific risks with universally diversified, liquid shareholdings that are subject to global systemic rather than specific risks. They therefore perform different functions in the financing and governance of firms.

Ownership of problems is not restricted to dominant shareholders. It is reflected in how companies are led, governed, and run, and it is the role of the board of directors to ensure the determination and effective implementation of problem-solving purposes. Everyone in an organization should take ownership of their part of its purpose.

Corporate governance is not just about aligning the interests of leaders with shareholders. It is the process by which profitable problem-solving purposes are implemented. Leaders should specify, clarify, and exemplify their corporate purpose. They should connect it with the core strategy of the business; they should demonstrate an authentic commitment to its fulfilment; they should ensure that the business's values and culture are aligned with it; they should delegate authority and empower those in the organization to deliver it; and they should resource and reward employees accordingly.

Trust must be placed in those lower down in the organization to deliver the purpose. Those at the top of an organization cannot have a sufficient appreciation or understanding of the problems that confront their customers, communities, societies, suppliers, and distributors in the specific local contexts, environments, and ecosystems in which those problems arise, or the most appropriate solutions, people, or technologies to address them. It is employees in the organization with the contextual and specific knowledge who should be empowered and trusted to build relations with these parties and combine that understanding with codified, generic information from the top in delivering profitable solutions not problems.

5
Owning the Problem

Property is that sole and despotic dominion which one man claims and exercises over the external things of the world, in total exclusion of the right of any other individual in the universe.

William Blackstone (1765), *Commentaries on the Laws of England*, Oxford: Clarendon Press, Book 2, Chapter 1

William Blackstone's statement is the basis of modern theory of property and concepts of ownership. It underpins the two dominant concepts of the firm, namely shareholder primacy and agency theory, and has established modern management education, business practice, and public policy as reaching the triumphal peak of that sole and despotic dominion of the shareholder over the rest of the world.

According to a Blackstonian view of property, capitalism is an economic system of private ownership of the means of production and their operation for profit, and ownership is a bundle of rights over assets that confer strong forms of authority on its possessors. Tony Honoré (1987) describes those rights in 11 constituent components: (1) the right to possess; (2) the right to use; (3) the right to manage; (4) the right to income; (5) the right to capital; (6) the right to security; (7) the incident of transmissibility; (8) the incident of absence of term; (9) the prohibition of harmful use; (10) the liability to execution; and (11) residuary character.[1]

By these criteria, the conventional notions of ownership are arguably neither theoretically justifiable nor practically relevant to business. The Blackstone concept of property is particularly inappropriate and detrimental in the context of commercial activities that have the potential for advancing human wellbeing. Its erroneous application has been a source of economic, social, and political instability and growing crises in distribution of income and wealth, environmental degradation, and disaffection amongst large swathes of developed and developing country populations. The despotic has become the sclerotic and its correction requires a fundamental reconceptualization of the nature of ownership, business, and our capitalist system.

Concepts of Ownership

There are two aspects to the ownership of a firm.[2] The first is a claim over the earnings of a firm and the second is control rights over the governance of a firm that extend beyond those of other parties to the firm. The two are intimately intertwined. The control rights are required to protect shareholders from the risks to which they are exposed of expropriation of their earnings by other parties to the firm, including those employed to manage their assets on their behalf. They have rights of appointment, removal, and remuneration of directors and influence over key decisions taken by the board of directors.

The association of shareholding with property is by analogy. Shareholders invest in companies in a similar way to how they purchase cars, houses, and washing machines. They therefore have similar claims over both the benefits and employment of the assets of a firm. Their influence is mediated by the boards of directors who are appointed as their agents, but ultimate authority resides with shareholders as providers of capital. Impediments to the exercise of those rights are an intrusion on liberty equivalent to that on any other form of property.

There are three reasons why the analogy is vacuous, and even if it were ever of any substance, it is increasingly not so. The first is that shareholders do not manage the assets of the firm. For the most part you can run your car, home, and washing machines essentially on your own. That is clearly not the case for General Motors and not even for anything other than the smallest firms. On the contrary, firms are highly complex methods of coordinating the activities of a vast array of individuals and organizations, which no one individual or group of individuals finances or controls.

Second, while the responsible usage of a car, home, and washing machine has limited effects on others, that is blatantly not true of General Motors or even modestly sized companies—the effects of General Motors are felt globally and the corner shop locally.

Quite reasonably then the property rights of shareholders over firms are much more restricted than individuals over their possessions, but third, even if the property right analogy was ever applicable to firms, it is of rapidly diminishing significance. It emerged in the context of the Industrial Revolution and the rise of manufacturing industry when companies employed physical capital that required large amounts of financing from investors. In contrast, today, it is not plant and machinery on which firms are predominantly dependent but individuals, information, knowledge, computer algorithms, networks, brands, and reputations—what are collectively termed 'intangible assets' to contrast them with their traditional tangible forms.

There are several implications regarding this. The first is that the amount of financing that companies require has diminished appreciably. Typically, a high-tech firm will initially raise relatively modest amounts of finance in stages and then seek to fund its expansion through the revenues it generates.

Second, in marked contrast to traditional manufacturing, firms increasingly do not own the assets on which they depend. They do not own their employees, societies, and environments and they do not own many of the organizations with which they interact in their supply and distribution chains. Instead, they coordinate and invest in a wide array of parties and organizations that lie beyond the property right boundaries of the firm.

The twenty-first-century firm therefore comprises a set of intangible assets of a human, intellectual, and social form that they do not possess but on which they are dependent and have an increasingly significant effect. For example, the impact of Facebook and Google is global, not only in terms of their multinational operations but also in the nature of their products. This has profound implications for the way in which we should conceive of their ownership and governance. It turns the traditional property-right view of the firm on its head.

Firms are no longer bundles of assets owned by those who have financed them, and they do not have owners whose rights derive from the property they have financed. On the contrary, they are dependent and have effects on assets that they have not purchased and do not possess. They are therefore bundles of assets outside of a legal boundary of the firm that require coordination but not through control rights that are associated with their financing.

In other words, the traditional association of control with financing needs to be disentangled. As an economic system of private ownership of the means of production that confers strong forms of authority on their possessors, capitalism presumes the allocation of control rights to providers of capital, particularly those who bear residual risks of profits and losses, namely the shareholders.[3] If that ever was appropriate, and for the reasons mentioned above it is questionable whether it was, it no longer is. The dependence and impact on other parties—employees, suppliers, communities, and nature— makes these groups as, if not more, relevant to the success of a firm and exposed to its risks of failure as the shareholders.

The Stakeholder Fallacy

The inadequacies of the shareholder view of the firm have provoked a counter-reaction that it is not just shareholders but a much broader group of 'stakeholders' that have an interest in the firm. These include its employees, suppliers, customers, communities, creditors, as well as shareholders. According to stakeholder theories of the firm, the board of directors should be seeking to promote the interests of this wider group, not just the shareholders.

The most common debate around notions of capitalism relates to shareholder versus stakeholder theories. Proponents of shareholder capitalism argue that shareholders alone are the owners of a company. They invest risk capital and bear the risks of the business. Proponents of stakeholder capitalism argue that stakeholders collectively invest in the company and bear its risks of failure and success. From an investment and risk-bearing perspective, stakeholders— not just shareholders—have an ownership stake in the business and directors owe duties of care and loyalty to all of them.

Stakeholder advocates seek to broaden the accountability of directors beyond the narrow confines of shareholders to the wider group of all stakeholders with an interest in the firm. They believe that this improves the performance of companies because it recognizes the contribution that all stakeholders—not just shareholders—make to their success. Failure to account for their interests results in a lack of engagement and investment by these parties whose inputs are critical to corporate performance.

But shareholder supporters believe that making directors accountable to everyone makes them accountable to no one and that firms become unmanageable. Performance is no longer simply reflected in financial returns and profits but the returns that all stakeholders earn and the risks as well as rewards they bear. That requires the construction of a broad set of measures of performance which involve subjective assessments of the benefits that different parties derive and cannot be assessed with anything like the precision of profits and financial returns.

Far from improving performance, stakeholder concepts are a source of confusion and judgements of the conflicting interests of different parties that directors and managers of firms are not equipped to make. Furthermore, it is claimed they do not have the legitimate basis on which to make such judgements. It is governments not businesses that are subject to an electoral process which gives them the authority to make such decisions. Boards of companies are appointed by shareholders to deliver success as measured by financial benefits, rather than being appointed by citizens to make political judgements.

This is an age-old debate, and the pendulum has swung repeatedly between one theory and the other without any satisfactory resolution. During the first half of the twentieth century, stakeholder notions gained the upper hand only to fall foul of claims that they allowed managers to exercise wide discretion in how they ran their firms with little accountability to anyone. Consequently, in the second half of the twentieth century, the pendulum progressively swung back to a predominant focus on shareholder interests. Measures of financial performance have been developed that have sharply focused management's attention on shareholder interests, largely to the exclusion of everyone else's.

Over the last two decades, the human, social, and environmental consequences of that have become all too evident and stakeholder notions are in the ascendancy with a belief that, more complex though they might be, without them, all of us—shareholders as well as employees, communities, and the natural world—suffer. The world is therefore very divided between parts of it, such as the US, that remain resolute supporters of shareholder capitalism, and others, such as Continental Europe, that are inclined to stakeholder interests more generally, and a third group, such as the UK, that sit on the fence and advocate elements of both.

It is sometimes suggested that the conflict between shareholder and stakeholder interests is resolved in what is termed 'enlightened shareholder interests', namely enlightened in recognizing the contribution that the wellbeing of others can make to shareholders. It is sometimes put in terms of the 'genius of the *and*'[4]—creating benefits for society *and* greater returns for shareholders—or the phrase 'doing well by doing good'—well for shareholders and good for society.

The problem that this sweeps under the carpet is what happens if there is an inevitable 'or' in choosing between societal and shareholder benefits, and companies do well by doing bad not good, as arguably the 'sin stocks' of alcohol, tobacco, gambling, arms manufacturing, and fossil fuels do all the time. Put differently, businesses should, and directors have a duty to, avoid paying taxes, pollute the environment, minimize their labour costs, source from the cheapest global suppliers to the extent that these do not fall foul of the law, or impose reputational costs that outweigh the savings they make by so doing—what might be regarded as enlightenment in the eye of shareholders but no one else.

It is also suggested that shareholder and stakeholder ideas converge over the long term and that the problem is predominantly one of time, namely 'short-termism'. In the long run, all is revealed, reputations are at stake, regulation is a threat, and business must support its stakeholders to reward its shareholders. So long as companies are focused on creating long-term as against short-term value then all's well that ends well—or preferably doesn't end because the other term that is used in this regard is 'sustainability'—building sustainable businesses for the future.

But rather than reveal and heal, time can conceal and misdeal. Those responsible may no longer be around, accountable, or solvent to bear the consequences of their inactions as well as actions, and those who bear the consequences may not be able to benefit from their remedies. We have witnessed all too clearly the consequences of inaction on climate, inequality, and social exclusion, as well as destruction by business of nature, heritage sites, local communities, and human health. The problem is not just a horizon one but what and whose horizon.

The long term looks bleak for the impoverished if they thereby remain impoverished or for inequality if everyone just progresses in tandem. Slave labour would have continued had it not been abolished. Nature would be well advised not to rely on everything turning out well for it in the end. And sustainability of businesses that is achieved through insurance does nothing to address environmental and climatic problems; it just externalizes and potentially exacerbates them. The problem is not simply as Keynes claimed that 'in the long run we are all dead' but that we will all be dead in the short run.

A third suggested solution is to recognize that at the end of the chain of shareholders are ultimately people who have an interest not only in their wealth but also their health, survival, descendants, and security—namely their prosperity and wellbeing. They are concerned not only about financial returns but also how those returns are generated.[5] This has been reflected in the growth of 'impact investing' in which investors seek positive human, social, and environmental impact from their investments as well as, and potentially at the expense of, financial returns. Shareholders are not all the same. Some are only interested in financial returns; others are not. They have different preferences and time horizons in regard not only to financial performance but societal ones as well.

There are two problems with this resolution. The first is that, while growing, the size of the impact investing market remains modest in relation to the conventional value maximizing one. Institutions therefore still regard their primary function as being to identify and promote the greatest financial returns on their investments. The second problem is that the quality, comparability, and reliability of non-financial measures of corporate performance that are available for investors are poor in relation to their financial equivalents. Institutional investors therefore feel better able to allocate resources to financial than non-financial considerations.

The reason why these discussions about the length and breadth of interests of investors are unsatisfactory is that they do not address the central question, which is not whether investor horizons are sufficiently long or broad but whether they have real intrinsic interests in the wellbeing of others not just in the extrinsic benefit that they derive from others. That is blatantly not the case in an enlightened shareholder value view of the firm, it is not true in the long term as against the short term and it is not true of simply substituting shareholder wellbeing for shareholder wealth.

If, on the other hand, one sees the world through a lens of shareholder versus stakeholder capitalism then, in most cases, one ends up just being confused and uncertain of which camp to support. And with considerable justification because neither is appropriate. We simply have the wrong view of what a firm is.

Neither Product nor Property a Firm Be

A firm is not the property of anyone—shareholder, creditor, employee, customer, supplier, community, or the state. None of them own it. They all have an interest in it—some to a considerable extent, others to a lesser extent. But that interest is not a right of ownership in the sense of Blackstone's sole and despotic dominion. In fact, it is exactly the opposite—it is an obligation not a right. An obligation to do something. Not an obligation to produce something. It might involve producing something but that is not its primary obligation. It is an obligation to identify a problem and provide a solution to that problem.

Why? Why is problem solving the fundamental purpose of a business, namely its reason why? The answer is that if it has a problem to solve, which it and no other individual or organization can solve, then it has a very good reason for existing. If it doesn't, then one might legitimately ask: what is its point? Why does it and why should it exist?

'Don't be so pious and self-righteous', some will say. 'A business might exist to make people happy, not simply to stop them being miserable.' Of course, by problem-solving I do not mean just extinguishing the bad but also creating joy and happiness. 'Yes', others will respond, 'but what about just making the shareholders and investors rich and happy? Is that not a sufficient reason for a business's existence?' Yes, if it does not derive from making others poor and miserable in the process but from making at least some others rich and happy as well. That is exactly what solving problems profitably involves.

The reason for focusing on problem-solving and not products is that products often, if not usually, create detriments as well benefits. Simply looking at a firm as a product producing entity does not adequately establish the nature of its responsibility. The reason for focusing on problem-solving rather than profit is that profit is the product of problem solving without problem producing, not the purpose itself. And the reason for focusing on problem solving rather than wellbeing is that wellbeing is the outcome not the objective. Making people happy, content, or fulfilled is not an operational objective of a firm. It too is a product of a purpose of solving problems, not a purpose as such. But there is another way of looking at this.

Owning the System

A business is a system for producing outcomes. It brings together a variety of different parties in the achievement of those outcomes. The parties are not just the investors and the employees of the firm but also all the suppliers, distributors, customers, and organizations with which the business cooperates and partners. One example is universities that are a source of ideas an innovation and the creators themselves of businesses that are spun out of universities by academics and students. Another is charities, civil society organizations, and non-governmental organizations that are the source of information and knowledge about the needs and objectives of different communities, individuals, and the natural world.

But it is not just that a business is a system that together contributes to the activities of the firm, it is that the business is itself part of a system. The business sits in local, national, and international communities and affects them as well as being affected by them. It contributes to the various systems of which it is a part in both positive and negative ways and those systems are in turn part of larger systems culminating in the planetary system, and especially in years to come, interplanetary systems. Business is part of the system however one might define that.

The traditional view of the firm sees it as an entity in its own regard. In a Blackstonian context the right is that of its possessors, its owners. Within a shareholder primacy context those owners are its shareholders. Within a stakeholder context, they are a broader set of individuals with an interest in the firm. No matter, both notions see the firm as an entity in its own regard.

The notion of the firm that is being advocated here is very different—it is one of a firm that is a complex system that is an integral part of an even more complex larger system. It is incorrect to consider the objective of the firm as being to promote its own success, be it for its shareholders or stakeholders. Its objective is to contribute to and promote the success of the systems of which it is an integral part. Its reason for being is to advance its local, national, and global systems, now and for the indefinite future. In the process it produces benefits for its constituent parts—its investors, employees, suppliers, and so on—but that is a product of its purpose, not its purpose as such.

Why? How do I know that the objective of a firm is not just its own success but its contribution to the broader system of which it is a part? The answer is that this is what we each individually and collectively seek from the firm. It is what we seek in terms of individual liberty, freedom, self-determination, free will, as well as economic prosperity, wellbeing, human and planetary flourishing, and emotional and psychological fulfilment and contentment.

Where does the liberty, freedom, self-determination, and free will come from? The answer is that, far from imposing a limitation on our liberties, a systems perspective unshackles us from existing constraints. Those constraints derive from a disconnect between our individual and collective interests and a need to impose limitations on our self-determination to avoid its adverse consequences for others. That is why we live in societies with ever more complex and intrusive forms of legal and regulatory constraints. We entangle ourselves in webs of rules to avoid our selfish desires and pursuits getting in the way of others.

If, on the other hand, we establish that our individual self-interests derive from resolving not contributing to the problems of others then far from there being a misalignment between individual and collective interests, there is a direct correspondence. Our reason for being becomes the interests of others as well as ourselves and our own wellbeing is conditional on that of others. This is the sense in which a systems approach is liberating not constraining—our recognition and response to the world around us is the basis of the justified trust of others in ourselves.

It means that the evolution and performance of the system is not conducted and directed by a single controlling authority, committee, or heavenly body but by each of us acting independently and collectively according to our own goals and objectives. The system is what it is by virtue of what we individually and collectively wish it to be. Obviously, the degree to which this is true is dependent on our capacity to influence the world in which we live. The extent to which that has been the case has varied hugely over time. But this is the reason why business is such an important component of it because of its capacity to coordinate huge amounts of resources and exploit technological advances.

The central point is though that there is no centre. There does not have to be a central coordinating device to run the system and, as will become increasingly evident, the nature of the world that we inhabit makes it highly desirable that there isn't, because the performance of a central controller or planner would almost certainly lead to worse outcomes. That comes on to the second set of reasons why a systems view of the firm is appropriate, and that is in terms of its contribution to economic prosperity, wellbeing, and human and planetary flourishing. There is no right answer to the question of what we individually or collectively should be doing or indeed what contributes to the best systems outcome.

The notion of nirvana is ill-conceived, not only because of the difficulty of attaining it, but because it presumes the existence of Leibniz's 'best of all possible worlds'.[6] That is a highly oppressive concept not only because it implies that we should all be working for a greater good as defined by someone or something but also because even if it existed, it would suggest that we know how to get there. It is my contention that it almost certainly doesn't exist and even if it did, we even more certainly don't know how to get there and if we thought we did today then we certainly will not tomorrow.

Instead, we should recognize the merits of diversity, experimentation, innovation, plurality, and many blooming flowers. Let everyone pursue their own ambitions and dreams subject to one caveat and that is that they should not prosper or benefit at the expense of others but instead from promoting the prosperity and benefit of others. That way we know that we are all individually and collectively contributing to the wellbeing of others, some in very small ways, others in very significant ones, and, in the process, we are advancing the system locally, nationally, and globally, now and in the future.

Finally, I turn to the psychological benefits of this. Our sense of wellbeing derives not just from our material possessions or from the recognition and esteem with which we are held by others but from our self-evaluation of who and what we are. We come into this world, we are here, and we are gone. What becomes of that? It is not a pot of money or a plot of property. It is not a pile of books or clever ideas. It is not even just a family and a future generation.

It is that we have not abused that privilege. We have done what we can according to the simplest of criteria—have we enjoyed the fruits of our existing by helping others and the world that we inhabited? If yes, rest assured, and if not then remain unsure. Our greatest source of happiness is to know who we are and why we exist.

How Does One Own the Problem?

Owning the problem puts a completely different perspective on ownership. It moves it away not just from the Blackstonian property concept but also from the idea of a claim on a cash flow or a right of control. It shifts it from a right to an obligation—an obligation to identify, determine, and resolve a problem and from that to derive a right to a stream of earnings. It puts the nature of the causation the right way round, away from control that derives from a financial claim over an organization to a financial claim that stems from the application of control by an organization to resolve problems of others.

Perhaps the most significant implication is the way in which it shifts ownership from an exclusive privilege to something that everyone associated with an organization has a part of. Everybody in an organization should feel a sense of ownership of its problem-solving purpose. This is not just semantic rhetoric but substantial reality. Organizations are aggregations of sub-components, each of which has its particular purpose and objective within the framework and umbrella of the corporate purpose. And within that sub-component—business unit, division, branch, or subsidiary—there are individuals and collection of individuals with their purposes.

This places the notion of a business as being part of a system in context because a business itself is a system with sub-systems within it. One of the major inadequacies of the way in which we have conceived of the firm to date is to look at it as a top-down entity owned by someone on high and ultimately answerable to them above all others. That is fundamentally wrong. A business is a unit within a system, the ownership of which derives from those within as well as outside it. The business is in turn part of a larger system and owns components of the problem of the system of which it is a part.

Instead, therefore, of looking at the firm as a Russian doll whose inner elements are just smaller replicas of the larger outer one, we should see the firm as jigsaw of pieces, each contributing its own critical perspective to a larger jigsaw of which the firm itself is an important piece. That lends significance to the sub-components that the mechanical reproduction of the Russian doll cannot demonstrate.

The resulting mosaic and tapestry that the firm can create are therefore infinitely more subtle than the dull uniformity that the traditional notion of the ownership of a firm would suggest. Instead of being a unidimensional organization that extends from the investor at the top to the employees on the shop floor, its breadth of engagement with multiple parties horizontally gives the firm a three-dimensional perspective, which extends into a fourth one once account is taken of the potential its perpetual existence gives to addressing intergenerational as well as current problems.

The firm therefore moves beyond an instrument that simply exists to promote the interests of its investors to one that harnesses their resources to provide resolutions to the problems of others. It is a system for converting the financial resources of investors into the successful resolution of problems of the system of which it is a part.

It does this by recognizing that it has two types of owners it is there to serve: owners of its financial resources and owners of the problems it is there to solve. Both are critical to its success, and it must uphold the intrinsic interests of both if it is to fulfil its objective. The traditional view of corporate ownership recognizes the former but not the latter and in so doing it reduces the rich mosaic of the firm to a dull doll. That is, I regret to say, what current descriptions of the ownership of firm are—dull. They focus on finance and presume that is all there is to ownership. They lack the life and vibrancy of what ownership is all about—owning and solving the greatest challenges of the world.

Owning and solving the problem means having oversight and responsibility for the specification and delivery of the problem that the firm exists to solve. It involves putting in place the internal structures and processes needed to deliver the purpose; promoting the right cultures and values; creating internal measurement and accounting systems; and establishing appropriate incentive and reward systems.

It involves ensuring that the company and its investors do not benefit from causing problems; that the resources exist to deliver the purpose; and that there are adequate provisions to remedy problems and unanticipated shocks and uncertainties. In other words, it is responsible for the credibility of its purpose and the trust that others place in it to live by it.

Being responsible for the problems of others is a liability of the firm from which it profits from solving them in ways that produce assets of greater value than its liabilities. That is a just profit in the sense of delivering a benefit to the firm as well as those affected by the firm. That is not how ownership is currently regarded. It is seen as a right to earn a profit in whatever form the firm can best do that, providing that in the process it does not break the law. It is not regarded as an obligation to do anything except make money out of whatever it chooses to do. It gives rise to a very particular and restricted description of the ownership of firms.

Who Are the Owners?

There is a striking feature of the ownership of firms. It differs markedly across countries. I say striking because if ownership had just one purpose of making money, then we would expect it to be very uniform. Indeed, there is a commonly held view that the form it should take is what is often described as the Anglo-American system of ownership—companies listed on stock markets with many dispersed shareholders each holding a very small share of any one company. Some regard it as the model and the form to which all stock markets will or should converge once they remedy their failures to regulate their activities appropriately.

In fact, while it might be thought desirable, it is not common. Indeed, outside of the UK and US it is rare. In nearly all countries in the world the ownership of even the largest firms listed on stock markets is dominated by holders of large blocks of shares. The most common holders of those large blocks of shares are families and the state. Furthermore, there is no evidence of the predicted convergence on Anglo-American markets occurring.

On the contrary, both countries have witnessed rapid declines in the numbers of companies listed on their stock markets—they halved between the 1990s and 2020s in both the UK and US. That accelerated still further in the UK, with the London Stock Exchange losing its position as being a pre-eminent stock market in Europe.[7]

Furthermore, although the UK and US are generally lumped together when categorizing different financial markets around the world, in fact they are very different. There are more holdings of large blocks of shares in the US and much more use made of dual-class shares in which some shareholders have more voting control over their shares than others.

So, in fact, concentrated control by dominant holders of blocks of shares is the norm not the exception and in the one case where it is not observed, namely the UK, it has been associated with the demise of its stock market. What does this tell us?

The answer is that in companies listed on stock markets, there are generally two classes of shareholders. There are holders of blocks of shares that have dominant voting control over their companies and retain their blocks for extended periods of time, and there are small shareholders who individually have little voting power and take advantage of the liquidity of their stock markets to trade their shares.

The reason for this is that they are performing different functions. The latter group invest their money in the shares of companies but individually have negligible influence over the behaviour of firms in which they invest and instead welcome the ability to trade shares that their liquidity provides.

In contrast, the former group of holders of blocks of shares do not find it so easy to trade their shares but instead exercise significant influence over the firm through their voting rights over the appointment and removal of directors and major policy decisions. That puts them in a position to influence the problems that the company seeks to address and the way it sets about doing it, while the latter group are predominantly interested in the financial return that the problem-solving generates.

The Universal Owners

Over the last few years, there has been a pronounced change in the nature of the investments by the dispersed shareholders. Wide scale dispersion of shareholdings began to emerge at the beginning of the twentieth century with the growth of local stock markets. They were situated in towns across countries and allowed investors to diversify their portfolios across the shares of companies in their localities. During the twentieth century, those local stock markets began to consolidate in a small number of towns, particularly capital cities. In the process shareholders were able to diversify their shares nationally as well as locally.

At the same time, new types of financial institutions emerged that facilitated diversification of shareholdings—pension funds, life insurance companies, and mutual funds. They invested across a broad range of companies nationally and increasingly internationally, reducing the costs of shareholders diversifying their portfolios themselves. Mutual funds began to rise in significance first in the USA and then in Europe and elsewhere allowing investors not only to diversify their shareholdings but also to choose between different types of portfolios depending on the companies in which the funds were invested.

However, the performance of the mutual funds was not always good when measured in relation to the returns that shareholders could earn when they diversified their portfolios themselves. The reason for that was, firstly, the high fees that the funds charged their investors for the services they provided their investors and, secondly, the tendency of the funds to churn their holdings, supposedly stock picking for the benefit of their investors, but frequently reducing the returns on their investments and in the process imposing significant costs of transactions on investors.

In response, investors sought funds which achieved the diversification benefits but without giving fund managers discretion on how to invest their monies. What emerged were funds that tracked readily observable and measurable indices of portfolios of shares in different stock markets around the world—the index funds or trackers that track the indices of the main markets and regions.

What these index funds have allowed shareholders to do is to diversify their investments globally across countries, sectors, types, and sizes of firms. In essence shareholders can now replicate a global portfolio of shares thereby achieving the benefits of international as well as domestic diversification at almost no cost. Furthermore, their holdings in index funds are highly liquid and can be traded instantaneously very cheaply.

The result is that many if not most shareholders are almost oblivious to the risks of individual companies and stocks and only concerned about the collective performance of all companies globally. They are interested in globally systemic risks, such as political, military, regulatory, environmental, social, and pandemic risks, but not the individual risks of specific companies.

Ironically, these 'universal owners', as they are sometimes described, do not 'own' the problem solving of individual companies but exactly the opposite—the global systemic problems of the world. They 'internalize', in the sense of price, the big global risks in the world and seek compensating higher returns for those risks but not the ones of individual companies. I say ironically because when freedom of incorporation first emerged in the twentieth century, the nature of shareholding was exactly the opposite—highly concentrated in the company in which the shareholder was invested.

Family Ownership

The parallel structure of ownership of most listed companies reflects the dual function they must perform of solving problems and generating financial returns from doing that. What the dispersed ownership of fast disappearing UK listed firms lack are the large anchor shareholders who are engaged with the problem-solving nature of the firm's activity as well as its financial performance. This is the reason why so many listed companies in the UK are using private equity firms to take them private, away from the intolerable pressure that the financially dominated stock markets impose on them.

In essence, what the block holding does is preserve the features of the founders of companies. The founder of a company defines its purpose and oversees its implementation by appointing its board and raising its capital. Founders then pass on and sell ownership to others, to their partners, descendants, families, employees, other companies, and institutional and individual investors.

If the shareholdings are passed on to their descendants, then the firm remains within the family orbit. At some stage, the family may sell some of their shares on the stock market to realize part of their capital value and raise external finance but, if they retain a substantial shareholding, then they continue to exercise dominant control over the firm.

Family ownership can bring a long-term intergenerational perspective to the problem solving of companies as families seek to retain ownership and control within the family unit. Succession is a critical issue for family-owned firms and encouraging children to take up the reins is not by any means always straightforward.

In essence, the problem with family ownership is that it is past not present ownership. It is ownership that derives from a vision, energy, and determination of a founder that dims and diminishes as the firm passes through the generations. Subsequent generations are more interested in the firm as a solution to their own family financial problems than the economic, environmental, and social problems of the world outside. They become inward-looking and profit-preserving rather than creatively envisioning and problem-solving.

For the past five years, I have been involved in the Ownership Project at the Said Business School in Oxford, funded by the Ford Foundation—the legacy of one famous and fanatical founder, Henry Ford. We have worked closely with many of the largest family-owned firms in the world with annual revenues or assets under management greater than a billion dollars. This has provided real insights into the workings of family businesses and in particular the interaction between families and their firms.

The interaction is complex, extensive, varied, and varying. It reflects the complexities of the management of large wealthy families, their needs, ambitions, and problems. It extends in many directions across multiple generations and through many forms of participation in the firms they own. It varies across countries, sectors, and individuals and it is varying over time as new generations succeed their predecessors with different interests, goals, and concerns. But above all it is in some respects disappointing.

The great benefit that family ownership brings is the involvement of a shareholder with real skin in the game and a commitment to retaining their shareholding. It is therefore the antithesis of the fancy-free universal owner. Through inheritance, shareholdings are retained within families, bringing long-term, stable, engaged ownership to companies that are otherwise exposed to short-term, liquid, passive stock markets.

An illustration of this is the Swiss pharmaceutical company Roche, which is listed and actively traded on the Swiss stock market but has a controlling family holding in the hands of the Hoffmann and Oeri families. In 2009, Roche bought out a minority shareholding in the biotech company Genentech in which it had a majority shareholding. Although financial conditions at the time, just after the financial crisis, might have suggested issuing equity to fund the purchase of the remaining shares in Genentech, this was rejected by Roche on the grounds that it would have involved diluting the family holdings to a point that they no longer had majority control.

The resulting loss of long-term focus and stability was regarded as an unacceptable price to pay for the equity funding. Many UK family owners have lost control of their firms for precisely this reason, issuing shares to fund acquisitions only to find that family control has been sacrificed in the process.

One might have expected that with their long-term, stable perspective, family firms would bring a strong interest in environmental, social, and governance (ESG) performance. In fact, the evidence is exactly the opposite. Comparing family-owned firms with similar non-family-owned firms in a large data set of companies from across the world in different sectors of the economy reveals that family-owned firms are ESG laggards rather leaders.[8] And it is not entirely surprising. Second-, third-, or higher-generation ownership benefits from neither the fervour of fanatical founders nor the global perspective of the universal shareholder and instead becomes preoccupied with squabbling siblings.

That might be one reason why, unlike in other European countries, family ownership has not persisted in large, listed companies in the UK. The liquid stock markets of the UK in the first half of the twentieth century provided British families with an easy and lucrative exit from the internecine conflict from which their firms would otherwise suffer. The vision and purpose of founders of British family firms were therefore progressively diluted until they were extinguished altogether.

One of the most striking forms of ownership of blocks of shares is found in Denmark where holdings are frequently in the hands of foundations and trusts. This is also widely observed in Germany. The reason this is striking is that while companies often put money into foundations as part of their charitable activities, having a foundation as an owner would not generally be regarded as a desirable form of ownership. But it is found in some of the largest and most successful listed companies in Europe.

As was described earlier in the case of Novo Nordisk, foundation ownership is associated with particularly purposeful companies whose problem-solving is linked to the charitable purposes of the foundations. It may be particularly relevant to such sectors as media that create substantial public benefits (e.g., news and information) whose revenues are hard to capture and public detriments (e.g., abuses of data privacy and security) that are costly to avoid.

Private equity, active institutional investors and sovereign funds are other potential owners of problem-solving purposes. They often have the financial resources and expertise required to provide the funding, advice, and support that companies require. To date, many of them have held equity positions in companies for too short periods to be able to promote anything other than immediate financial returns. But if some of the avenues of exploiting financial benefit are closed in the future by limitations on their ability to profit at the expense of others then they may find themselves forced to take longer-term positions that require greater engagement in problem-solving value creation.

Recognition of the dual function of firms in solving problems as well as generating financial returns for their investors therefore provides a natural explanation for the dominance of the parallel form of ownership that is observed in most stock markets around the world. It also explains the longevity of this form of ownership when traditional views of stock markets would suggest that they should have disappeared in favour of what has turned out to be, as I will explain in Chapter 10, the failed form of dispersed ownership in the UK.

Owning the problem as well as the financial return on the investment needed to solve the problem is a critical aspect of ownership of companies that has not to date been recognized. It is how a company connects its system of solving problems to the larger ones of which it is a part. In the absence of this, then a company is a rudderless vessel floating in a sea of shifting financial tides unable to steer a course to the solution of the problems it is seeking to address.

The wide variety of forms of block ownership is precisely what would be expected of problem-solving ownership. Unlike just financial returns, the pursuit of problem-solving appeals to the emotional, relational, local, communal, scientific, environmental, and planetary interests and concerns of investors. A multiplicity of types of owners with different knowledge, ability, skills, and interests is exactly what is required to tackle the multitude of problems that need to be addressed.

The trillion-dollar US companies discussed in Chapter 2 are good illustrations of stock market listed firms that have flourished on the back of founders and owners with a strong sense of a problem-solving purpose. In many cases, they have used such tools as dual class shares to preserve the focus on problem-solving and avoid becoming dominated by financial considerations. They have in nearly all cases implemented these tools in the face of deep-rooted opposition from financial institutions concerned about the governance consequences of entrenching founders.

Not only have the financial returns proven those doomsayers and critics often wrong but they have also shown why investors are not always the best judge of what is in their own interests. Other companies, such as Boeing, that have been taken over by their financial controllers at the expense of their engineering expertise and excellence, have not only sometimes demonstrated a callous disregard for the interests and safety of their customers and communities, but they have also destroyed an immense amount of financial value for their investors.[9]

The combination of problem-solving and a parallel form of financially focused dispersed ownership provides an appropriate balance between financial and non-financial considerations. We have erred too far in particular in the UK and to a lesser extent in the US in the direction of emphasizing financial over other considerations and lost the balance with problem-solving objectives. We need to re-establish an appropriate balance not only to achieve better outcomes for all of us but also to promote the truly impressive commercial and financial outcomes that problem-solving firms in the world have realized.

The Purpose of Wealth

We understand that many religions are the keepers of the gates to heaven through which, with appropriate credentials, we may pass for eternity. But we are now coming to appreciate that they also offer a possible answer to the question, what is the purpose of wealth?

It was between the fourth and sixth centuries AD in the final years of the Roman Empire that the newly emerging religion of Christianity provided a possible response.[10] The declining empire was faced with the problem of how to support the poor and destitute. A potential solution was for local communities to support them through charitable donations, but they often lacked the means even if they had the motives. Instead, there were others that had the capacity but lacked the conviction to provide a resolution—the wealthy.

Great fortunes in the Empire were founded on a combination of commerce and land. By the fourth century AD, the Roman historian Ammianus Marcellinus chronicled that 'the magnificence of Rome is defaced by the inconsiderate levity of a few, who never recollect where they are born, but fall away into error and licentiousness as if a perfect immunity were granted to vice'.[11] It was the emergence of Christianity that provided the Roman wealthy with their missing purpose in life—to purchase eternity in heaven on death. All that was required was an intermediary to link the two together and that is precisely what the newly aspiring institution of the Church provided.

Through the good offices of the bishops and the clergy there was a recognition of how the wealthy could be absolved of their anxieties and guilt at the same time as the impoverished were relieved of their hunger and misery. By providing a ticket to heaven the Church could both discharge its duties to the poor and satisfy the souls of the rich. Furthermore, like all good intermediaries, the Church could in the process accumulate its own small, and often not so small, fortunes. It was a marriage literally made in heaven.

There were only two problems with this divine revelation. The first was that the bishops and priests needed to distinguish themselves beyond their attire from the masses and establish their credibility as honest brokers. The solution that was found was abstinence from the worldly indulgences of their less-worthy counterparts—abstinence from the greed, pride, and lust that afflicted others. One form of this asceticism was continence and the subsequent adoption of celibacy.

The second problem was scepticism. Not unexpectedly self-denying ordinances were invariably subject to lapses and abuses, and the prize of a ticket to heaven began to lose its allure. So, by the time that we get to the nineteenth century with the newly emerging fortunes from manufacturing, the need to find an alternative purpose for wealth became pressing. The response in the twentieth century was to encourage the wealthy to produce more of it. Wealth begets wealth and forget the rest.

But it is not only the poor who today might well bemoan the demise of the enlightenment of early Christianity in Ancient Rome; so too do the wealthy. Their toil of generating more and more and losing none is both unedifying and unrelenting. For those like me who have studied the world's wealthiest families and people, the most common realization is that many of them are the world's most distraught and unhappy. More wealth begets mental ill-health plagued by persistent doubt as to whether people befriend them or their money. Leo Tolstoy may have been correct in opening his novel *Anna Karenina* with the words 'happy families are all alike', but it is not by virtue of their wealth.

So, what is the twenty-first-century equivalent of heaven? One answer is to give it away through philanthropy but then there is nothing left in life. What is needed is a modern version of eternity and the answer is, of course, perpetuity. In place of life after death comes life after life. Immortalize one's existence by giving rise to another. Create the ever-lasting in the not-yet existing.

Instead of the bishops and the priests linking the rich and the poor through promise of eternity come the trustees and foundations fusing the rich and the poor through a fiduciary duty of deliverance. It is the investment by an enterprise foundation in a company that converts the act of giving away into finding a way of preserving wealth for ever. Through the creation of the modern corporate equivalent of the Catholic Church in the form of the enterprise foundation we have the potential to recreate the magic of early Christianity of opening the doors of heaven to rich and poor by translating accumulated wealth into profitable solutions.

This extends the range of options available to wealth holders to incorporate the perpetual, analogous to how Christianity opened the doors to the eternal. It is achieved without invoking the threat of damnation, merely requiring wealth to be accumulated according to the Moral Law—not at the expense of others. It replaces damnation with restitution.

Frivolous as this analogy between fourth- and twenty-first-century wealth may at first seem, it is in fact very insightful. In essence what parallel ownership of corporations by foundations and financial institutions does is to allow wealth to be allocated to both problem-solving and financial benefit in any combination desired by its possessors.

Asset managers have provided investors with the means to diversify their financial portfolios. Charities could do the same for their problem-solving portfolios if, instead of giving away their money, they diversified their investments across foundation enterprises. In the process they would become the enlightened asset managers of the twenty-first century, with two advantages over their fifth-century Roman equivalents—tax deductibility without continence.

Public Ownership

In 2021, there were 1.8 million people in the world (equivalent to the population of a town slightly larger than Philadelphia in the USA) with wealth of more than $10 million. Together they accounted for $63 trillion of the world's $710 trillion total private and public sector wealth.[12]

In 2021, the market capitalization of all stock markets in the world combined was $124 trillion.[13] If these 1.8 million people had put half their money into listed stock market funds whose purposes were to produce profitable solutions for the problems of people and planet then they would have owned the equivalent of 25% of the stock of every listed company in the world. They would have had what is termed a 'blocking minority', sufficient to veto decisions by companies regarding their changes in control, and ensure that they abided by their purposes.

From a distributional perspective, concentrations of wealth are undesirable. From a control perspective they may also be undesirable since control by so few of so much is highly undemocratic. This is exacerbated by the lack of transparency that frequently surrounds the beneficial ownership of companies.[14] However, if appropriately and transparently invested, concentrations of ownership could act as powerful vehicles to promote adoption of beneficial corporate practices that address global problems in value enhancing forms.

The alternative to the problem of promoting public interest is to transfer wealth to public ownership through a combination of income and wealth taxation. There are four forms of state ownership: direct holdings by national, regional, and local governments; public pension funds; sovereign wealth funds; and holdings by state-owned enterprises. The OECD report that 800 of the world's 10,000 largest listed companies have public sector ownership of more than 50% of equity capital, with direct holdings being the largest source, followed by sovereign wealth funds and public pension funds.[15]

The wave of privatizations that emanated from the UK and US in the 1980s was a manifestation of dissatisfaction with public ownership which became commonplace after the Second World War. While in principle the state should be a promoter of the public and social interest, in practice it is subject to distortions of bureaucracy, corruption, lobbying, and political opportunism. More significantly in a corporate context, it imposes monism and uniformity of ideas and intentions where pluralism and diversity are desired, and it lacks the perpetual existence and capital commitment of which corporate entities are in principle capable.

However, the resulting privatizations are now also subject to growing criticism as their professed benefits fail to materialize and the detriments of the private provision of public goods and services become evident. In particular, the mechanism that was supposed to achieve an alignment of private profit with public interest, namely regulation, has been found to be seriously deficient in avoiding abuses of monopoly and promoting efficiency in the delivery of public services. The response to date, alongside the possibility of renationalization, has been a call for better and more intensive enforcement of regulation.

But there is a limit to what regulation can achieve in a context in which there is such divergence of interest between the regulator in public benefit and corporations in the private pursuit of profit.[16] That limitation comes from the ability of private investors to redeploy their capital from locations of intensive regulation. The response to the financial crisis is an example of that: initial promises of intense regulation were progressively diluted as economic and political realities set in.

We are therefore currently in a limbo between disquiet about public ownership and dissatisfaction with privatization and regulation. And that is the inevitable consequence of a system that seeks to impose extrinsic forms of social benefit on organizations that are intrinsically self-interested. Instead, what is required is a recognition of the inherent obligation on corporations to promote public as well as private benefit, particularly in circumstances in which they deliver important public functions, such as infrastructure and public services, especially in conditions of monopoly, such as utilities. These companies owe a special duty and standard of care to those who they serve. Their commitment to the delivery of their social licences to operate should be intrinsic to their purpose and corporate constitution.

Instead of the ideological divide between private and public ownership of the means of production—the assets—we should be focused on ownership of the problems those assets are there to solve. No one owns most of the assets used in production and no one at present takes ownership of the problems they create. We should start from ownership of problems and then determine the assets needed to fix them. We shouldn't start with the ownership of assets and fix the problems that creates.

Summary

In addressing the question of ownership, it is important to recognize it as a systems design issue. We have developed a coherent and consistent view of capitalism as comprising an economic system of private ownership of the means of production and their operation for profit. In this context, ownership is a bundle of rights over assets that confers strong forms of authority on their possessors. And firms are viewed as nexuses of contracts managed by their boards of directors for the benefit of their owners. In other words, capitalism is private ownership for profit managed by boards that engage others through contracts.

In contrast, the view that is being expressed here is that capitalism is an economic and social system of producing profitable solutions to the problems of people and planet by private and public owners who do not profit from producing problems for people or planet. In this context, ownership is not just a bundle of rights but a set of obligations and responsibilities to uphold the delivery of these purposes. And firms are not just nexuses of contracts but nexuses of relations of trusts based on principles and values enshrined by the boards of directors. This too is a coherent and consistent view of capitalism in which it is about solving problems by owners and boards who engage with others through relations of trust as well as contracts.

Owning a problem involves taking responsibility for solving not causing problems and deriving profits from so doing. The role of ownership of a firm is therefore to determine the problems it seeks to solve and avoid, and ensure that the structure, systems, and processes are in place to deliver the solutions. Ownership of the problems makes them liabilities of the firm that it turns into assets by providing solutions, profiting in the process without creating further problems.

The remarkable variety of forms of ownership around the world reflects the emphasis placed on profiting from problem-solving as against problem creation—prominent in the foundation-owned firms of Denmark and elsewhere, such as Bosch, Carlsberg, Ikea, Maersk, and, the Indian conglomerate, Tata—less so in the dispersed ownership firms of the UK and US.[17] It depends on the types of problems that companies seek to solve—local in small private firms, global in universally owned firms. It reflects the horizons of different owners—short-term in liquid shareholdings and intergenerational in family-owned firms. It is a product of the importance attached to different parties to the firm—employees in employee-owned firms, and the national interest in state-owned firms.

It may be no coincidence that Denmark is, on several criteria, one of the most successful countries in the world. Sceptics attribute this to its small country, coherent political and social system rather than to its business sector and refuse even to entertain the possibility that it might derive from the philanthropic, problem-solving nature of its corporate ownership. However, the influence of the integrity of a corporate sector on a country's social cohesion and shared prosperity should not be dismissed. It is something to which we will return in Chapter 10.

A multiplicity of different forms of ownership encourages a plurality in the types of problems that are solved and competition between them promotes active pursuit of the most effective solutions. Markets for corporate control encourage the identification of natural owners who create the greatest value.

So, Blackstone's notion of ownership as the sole and despotic dominion over the external things of the world is all to the good provided that two important conditions prevail—that the despotic dominion is to the benefit not detriment of the rest of the world and the profits that owners earn are not derived from inflicting problems on others but instead from fulfilling promised commitments to deliver benefits for others.

The question this raises is, how can owners do that? How can they profit from producing solutions without problems for the rest of the world? Even more pertinently, how can a world of profiting from producing solutions rather than problems be made more profitable for business as well as the rest of us? The answer is that not only should the owners of a firm own the problems but so too should everyone in the organization from the board to the shop floor and that is the role of governance and leadership.

6
Leading Solutions

There are no problems we cannot solve together, and very few that we can solve by ourselves.

Lyndon B. Johnson

The Challenge

What's so hard about profiting from producing solutions? Surely that's what business does all the time? Regrettably not, for two reasons. First there is the requirement of profiting from producing solutions without problems and second there is the problem of producing profits from solutions where there may not be an associated revenue stream.

Let's start with the first. It is what most people regard as being the major failing of business. Business profits at the expense of others in numerous ways. The one that is of greatest current concern is obviously the environment and CO_2 emissions. Another is the threat that unrestrained competition between tech companies developing artificial intelligence poses for the future of humanity. A third is tax avoidance through shifting profits to low-tax countries. A fourth is shifting jobs to low-cost countries at the expense of communities in higher-income countries.

But there is a much more pervasive sense in which profit-driven business is always problem-producing as well as problem-solving. The reason is that it is chasing the money. Most people when they start a business think in terms of what look to be profitable market opportunities that haven't been spotted to date and where it is therefore relatively easy to make a financial killing. Chasing the money involves looking where it is, not where it isn't, and pursuing those with it rather than without it.

Few people start by posing the question of where is there a particularly challenging human, social, or environmental problem to be solved and how can it be turned into a profitable business? That is what is normally associated with social entrepreneurship and social enterprise as against regular entrepreneurship or business formation. It is attributed to the do-gooders rather than the do-wellers—the green welly as against the get rich brigade.

In fact, that assertion is precisely wrong, and it is in essence always those who start off with the question, how do I solve an insoluble problem profitably, who end up making the most money. That brings us to the second issue of how one produces profits from solutions without revenue streams.

The reason why this appears particularly challenging is that revenues depend on people's ability to pay, and a large proportion of humanity does not have an income with which to buy anything other than life's most essential needs. Business is therefore in essence disconnected from the problems that most of the world faces and has no interest or capability of solving them. Where they do then it is often to the detriment rather than the benefit of the poorest, for example in replacing water with fizzy, sugary drinks.

Faced with problems of earning revenues from the disadvantaged and impoverished, it is much easier to dump the negative externalities of pollution, low tax revenues, and no or low-wage employment on them and focus on delivering good jobs and the provision of goods and services on the high-income parts of the world. This is a terrible indictment of business and suggests that the inability to solve the second problem is a cause of the first by exacerbating not just income inequalities but also access of the excluded to the global economy.

How does one avoid this? The first requirement is to stop companies profiting from the misfortune of much of the world and require the rich to bear the true costs of what they are consuming. The second is to establish how servicing the poorest and most disadvantaged parts of the world can be a source of the largest potential profitability of business. It is where the most significant problems—not the most serious money—reside, and it is therefore the largest potential source of riches from rags for business. The focus of this chapter is understanding why and how.

Governance

The notion of corporate purpose as being about producing solutions runs quite counter to traditional views as to how business should be governed. Corporate governance is conventionally viewed as being about aligning the interests of management, in particular executive and non-executive directors, with those of shareholders. It is designed to ensure that companies are focused from the top downwards on enhancing the financial performance and profitability of firms. That derives from the view that shareholders are the residual claimants and can therefore reasonably expect that the firm is run in their interests to promote value creation for them.

The question of how returns are earned for shareholders is traditionally regarded as being beyond the remit of corporate governance. That is about management within firms and the responsibility of the board, staffed by directors whose interests are appropriately aligned with those of their shareholders. But that distinction between the what and how of business has been blurred as the how has increasingly impinged on the what.

The way in which profits are earned for shareholders has become of greater concern for shareholders as they have come to appreciate the growing risks associated with how profits are generated. Reputational risks, societal pressures, political interference, and regulatory interventions have posed increasing threats for even the most internationally diversified shareholders.

As a result, over the last few years the role of boards has expanded to include oversight of not only the financial risks of the firm but also the risks arising from environmental, social, and governance (ESG) failures. The risks borne by shareholders in this regard have encouraged them to hold boards of directors to account for the extent to which their companies are exposed to and contribute to ESG problems. Companies are now expected to report regularly on their ESG performance and these risks are priced into their shares.

In essence what this is doing is acknowledging the changing nature of the risks that increasingly internationally diversified shareholders face, away from individual firm risks to the contribution and exposure of companies to globally systemic risks. As will be discussed in Chapter 8, numerous problems have arisen in relation to the measurement of ESG, with multiple providers of information on individual firm ESG performance giving conflicting assessments of their performance without any auditing or verification of the information they provide. Until international standard setters bring some consistency and data assurance to these measures then they will remain the subject of much derision, scepticism, and scandal.

More significantly, these measures do not bear directly on the purpose of business in profiting from problem-solving not producing nature of business. What is required of a governance framework for problem-solving is to recognize that it extends the conventional concept of the firm beyond its inputs and outputs to its outcomes and impacts.

Producing solutions is shorthand for relating the activities of firms (their inputs and outputs) to the changes that come from their activities, namely their outcomes, and the effects that these outcomes have on the wellbeing of others, namely their impacts. Solutions are outcomes that are associated with enhancement of wellbeing and problems with outcomes that are detrimental. Most products produce both in varying degrees.

Take the example of a car. A car company produces vehicles that allow passengers to move at speed and comfort. But they also create noise and environmentally damaging emissions. The inputs are the resources used (materials, labour, capital) in producing the outputs, which are the cars. The outcomes are speed and comfort of travel for the passengers, and noise and pollution for pedestrians and residents. The impacts are positive solutions to problems of mobility and enjoyment for passengers, and negative environmental detriments for pedestrians and residents.

There are therefore two aspects to evaluating the performance of a firm. The first is to determine the changes that occur from what a company does as well as what it produces, in this case not just the transportation benefits and pollution detriments of its cars but also the effect of its production on countries from which it extracts material resources and the communities in which it produces cars.

The second element is to identify the effects of these changes on the wellbeing of affected parties—beneficial for customers, passengers, and employees, detrimental for pedestrians, residents, and local and foreign communities where the cars are produced, and its material resources sourced. The first relates to the internal governance of the firm's productive activities and products, and the second to its external governance and engagement with other parties.

The creation of profits from producing solutions shifts the focus of internal governance away from simply aligning the interests of boards with profits to the process of producing solutions from which profits derive. This requires that profits be derivative of the process of solving problems and that internal governance focuses on the process of identifying the problems that companies are there to solve and how they should solve them.

The avoidance of problems requires external governance that achieves a good understanding of the outcomes of the firm's activities and the impact on those who are affected by its outcomes. What are the detriments associated with the company's activities and what are the potential problems that could emerge at some stage in the future? This involves a careful reflection of what can go wrong not just from the point of view of the firm's customers but also its employees, suppliers, communities, and societies.

The positive aspect of producing solutions relates to the internal governance of the process of formulating and implementing a company's purpose, and those parties on which the firm depends for delivery of its purpose. What problems is it seeking to solve, whose problems and how will it engage with those on whom it depends for solving those problems?

The second aspect of avoiding producing problems relates to the engagement of the firm with those who are impacted by its activities and the determination of the degree to which it is fulfilling its purpose of producing profitable solutions not problems.

How should companies establish the appropriate internal and external governance arrangements to do this? Over the last few years, I have co-led the Enacting Purpose Initiative at Oxford University, which has advised the boards of 60 of some of the largest companies in Europe and North America and 30 financial institutions around the world on how to embed problem-solving purposes in their businesses. It has developed what it terms the *SCORE* framework where the five letters of *SCORE* are an acronym for the core internal and external governance components:[1]

1. Simplifying the corporate purpose to bring clarity to it so that everyone inside and outside the organization really understands and appreciates its significance in addressing a meaningful challenge.
2. Connecting corporate purpose with a company's strategy and capital allocation decisions so that it is core to what the business does daily and is not promotional, marketing, or a form of corporate social responsibility peripheral to its core activities. It is also about the external governance connecting the firm with the other organizations and parties on which it depends for the delivery of its problem-solving purpose and those on whom its activities impact.
3. Owning the problem-solving purpose. This relates in part to the formal ownership by the main shareholders of the business. In addition, it is ownership of the corporate purpose by every employee in the organization so that everyone understands their contribution to delivery of the corporate purpose. There should be a clear sense of ownership from the board, which puts in place appropriate structures, values, culture, and processes, down to the shop floor.
4. Rewarding people in the organization in terms of their remuneration and promotion in relation to measures of their performance in delivering the corporate purpose. This involves

creating measures of the outcomes and impacts of the corporate purpose and relating internal incentives to them.

5. Exemplifying organizational purpose through communication and narratives that bring the purpose to life and demonstrate its authenticity through vivid images of its successes, challenges, and failures from an internal and external perspective.

Let me illustrate in relation to the case of Novo Nordisk, the Danish pharmaceutical producer of insulin discussed in Chapter 2. Recall that the problem Novo Nordisk faced was that 80% of people with diabetes live in low- and middle-income countries. As a result, it was failing to reach a high proportion of those in need of its insulin. Novo Nordisk recognized that it was causing the first class of problems described above—namely profiting from producing problems of inequitable access to treatment—which necessitated addressing the second class—producing profitable solutions that would be affordable by the poorest people in the world.

What did it do? As previously described, it sought lifestyle changes and cheaper treatments that would help people avoid contracting diabetes and coping with it if they did. And how did it do that? First, it *simplified* and clarified its purpose; second it *connected* with doctors, hospitals, universities, governments, and health workers around the world to identify alternative treatments and changes in lifestyle; third, it aligned its purpose with that of its dominant *owner*, the Novo Nordisk Foundation, which, amongst other things, promotes research into treatments for diabetes; fourth, it created measures of its success in achieving its objectives, and linked *remuneration* to them; and, fifth, it vividly communicated and *exemplified* its outcomes and impacts in narratives of success and challenges.[2]

This is analogous to the case of another pharmaceutical company described in this book, namely AstraZeneca, in producing a COVID vaccine that was accessible in low as well as middle- and high-income countries. In this case, it was its (part) UK *ownership* that facilitated its *connection* with Oxford University and the associated research funding. That *simplified* the identification of a vaccine that was both storable and affordable, *rewarding* AstraZeneca at cost without the profit margins charged by its competitors.

Pharmaceuticals might be thought to have specific characteristics relating to enacting purpose, so to understand its application elsewhere, let's look at a very different case—a company operating in one of the most troubled sectors during and after the financial crisis of 2008—banking.

Delegation

Handelsbanken is a Swedish bank that has earned progressively increasing returns for its shareholders from before, during and after the financial crisis.[3] It needed no bailing out during the financial crisis of 2008 or the Swedish banking crisis at the beginning of the 1990s. It is one of the best capitalized banks in Europe, with strong solvency and liquidity ratios and a good credit rating.

Its purpose is to put the interests of its customers and shareholders first, as reflected in the highest levels of customer satisfaction, lowest cost base of any of its rivals and steadily growing return on equity capital. It has been successful on all these scores and has regularly been rated as the bank with highest levels of customer satisfaction, most loyal customers, lowest costs, and growing return on equity capital over several decades.

What marks out the bank are three things. The first is its ownership. Handelsbanken is listed and actively traded on the Swedish stock market. However, it has two dominant holders of substantial blocks of shares: Oktogonen, the bank's own profit-sharing scheme, and Industrivärden, a Swedish holding company, one of whose largest shareholders is Handelsbanken. In other words, it is essentially controlled by a cross-shareholding and the bank owns itself.

This would conventionally be regarded as one of the worst examples of ownership and governance, violating all the standard criteria of good practice. However, it is consistent with the dual ownership structure described in the previous chapter of diversified, liquid shareholdings on a stock market together with controlling blocks of shares. The former facilitates the participation of outside shareholders and the latter the stable ownership required of a problem-solving business.

The second distinguishing feature of the bank is its governance. Most banks are run in a hierarchical fashion from the top. This has intensified since the financial crisis, which led regulators to require banks to have risk committees that monitor and manage risks from the top.

Handelsbanken follows the opposite principle of delegating decision-taking down the bank and making branches, especially branch managers, responsible for most decisions concerning the products they sell to whom, at what prices, and how they are marketed. The degree of delegation is reflected in the mantra of the bank that 'the branch is the bank'.

The significance of this is that it embeds the purpose throughout the organization, and it confers authority on branches to build relations of trust with their customers. They can avoid the type of bureaucracy that afflicts more hierarchical banks and can instead base decisions about, for example, loans on information derived directly from relations with their customers.

In essence, Handelsbanken has recreated traditional local relationship banking in a large multinational organization where its business grows with its corporate customers over the long term in contrast to fee-based income earned from transactions in the short term. There are important lessons to be learnt from this for how multinational organizations in general can promote local and regional relationships in the context of their global operations.

The third distinguishing feature of the bank is the way in which it rewards performance. While we are repeatedly told that banks must pay their staff bonuses if they are to recruit and retain the calibre they require, Handelsbanken pays its employees no bonuses at all, at least until they retire at the age of 60, at which stage they have a share in the bank's profit-sharing scheme, Oktogonen, which, as mentioned above, is one of the two main shareholders of the bank. It is a very long-term incentive arrangement.

The importance of this is that it promotes the trustworthiness of the bank from the perspective of its customers. Incentive arrangements may help to align the interests of employees with their shareholders, but they create a misalignment with customers whose interests are not best served by employees who are motivated to sell them the largest volume of financial products at the highest attainable profit margins.

Instead, what Handelsbanken does is to place emphasis on selecting branch managers, ensure that they are well versed in the principles and values of the bank, and then leave them to run their branches as they see fit. In other words, it places trust in its employees to make decisions that are in line with the principles and values of the bank, which in turn allows the bank to establish relations of trust with its customers. That is not possible in more hierarchical banks that use high-powered financial incentives to align employee interests with those of the bank because of the misalignment it creates with the interests of their customers.

What is important about this is that it extends the notion of ownership of the problem-solving nature of the bank from the formal owners and the board down to the shop floor, the branch of the bank in this case, so that everyone in the organization feels a sense of ownership of their part of the corporate purpose. It does this by delegating decision taking down the organization, emphasizing the values and culture of the organization and placing trust in employees to make decisions.

This allows the bank to establish long-term relations with their customers in a branch system where essentially every employee is a relationship manager. They do not have to refer lending decisions up the bank, wait weeks for a response before telling the borrower that they are terribly sorry, but their application has been declined. They can look people in the eye, gain a real understanding of their and their businesses' nature and prospects, and use that most important of loan criteria, human judgement, to take a decision.

What this brings out is that it is not only authority that needs to flow down an organization; so too does finance and it is the former that allows the latter to happen. It is not only at the top of the organization that there is a duality of ownership: ownership of a problem with ownership of finance. It is true throughout a company.

A company is a system of pairing problem-solving ownership with ownership of finance to resource the solving of problems. The governance of an organization is a way of translating that pairing from capital markets through the board down to the bottom of the organization in a form where everyone in the organization knows their part of the purpose—the problem to be solved—and has the financial resources required to solve the problem profitably.

Investment

There are five types of investment that firms need to make—in people, places, nature, innovations, and ideas. They need to invest in education, skills, and training of individuals; in communities, cities, and regions of nation states; in ecosystems, habitats, and the environment of the natural world; in the innovations of firms, clusters, and technologies; and in the ideas coming out of start-ups, spinouts, and universities.

The way to give the most disadvantaged, excluded, and impoverished the capability to participate in economic activity is through their employment and the knowledge, skills, and education that are required for them to contribute to the workforce. Regeneration of depressed and deprived communities, cities, and regions comes from the creation of vibrant small and medium-sized enterprise sectors and investment in land and infrastructure.

The preservation and restoration of ecosystems, habitats, and the environment require investment in nature-based as well as engineering solutions that recognize the regenerative power of nature. Economic growth derives from corporate innovations, creation of clusters of economic activity, and investment in new technologies. And universities are the source of start-ups, spinouts, and commercialization of new ideas that are the backbone of thriving economies.

What the most successful companies do is to harness the financial resources that come from global capital markets and direct them to investment in individuals and places, utilizing the knowledge and ideas that come from the adoption of new technologies and emerging research to solve their problems. They provide the means of combining global and generic knowledge and resources with very local and specific understanding of personal and communal problems to identify their precise desires and needs and the best ways of satisfying them.

It is this fusion of finance and problem-solving, of generic, codified knowledge and tacit, contextual understanding that is the means of resolving the most challenging and complex problems. It is the combination that lends credibility to the idea that business can internalize some of the most external problems and derive commercial advantage from providing solutions to the problems of the most disadvantaged individuals and communities in the world. To do this, businesses need the right governance, not just at the top but throughout their organizations.

The tacit contextual understanding requires a detailed appreciation of the issues and problems that affected parties face. While investors and boards of directors may possess generic, codified knowledge, they will rarely be able to ascertain the specific requirements of individual customers, suppliers, or communities in distant cities, regions, and countries, especially where the resolution of their problems involves the application of complex techniques and novel research. Instead, the company should delegate authority to employees closest to the relevant individuals, communities, experts, and research departments, and encourage them to use their discretion and judgement in formulating the most appropriate responses.

Obvious though this may seem, large corporations are rarely structured in a way that allows them to do this. Instead, they concentrate control and authority at the top and employ a layer of middle management in head office to adopt bureaucratic rules that control customer- and community-facing frontline employees in distant locations.

The result is that the image the company presents to its customers, communities, and suppliers is of an impersonal, uncaring organization in which it is impossible to engage with people who have an understanding, appreciation, or interest in their needs or problems. All it appears interested in doing is making as much money as possible, only tampered by the possibility of adverse reputational, public relations or social media consequences if it oversteps the mark.

What is missing is a group of people in the organization who have a real interest in customer, community, and supplier wellbeing. That in turn reflects a lack of trust by the company in employees to promote the interest of the firm and a need to subject their conduct to detailed rules and validation by people higher up in the hierarchy. What is required is an inversion of a traditional hierarchical structure and a willingness to delegate authority to those who have direct interaction and knowledge of those whom the company is affecting.

Middle management should be performing this function—not just by transmitting decisions from senior executives to employees but by connecting the company with the communities and societies with which it interacts. They should be actively seeking to understand those on whom the firm depends and impacts. They should have a deep understanding of their problems, their context, and history. They should appreciate what is needed to address the problems and the alternative remedies that are available.

Middle management should provide the legitimacy for those on the shop floor and in the shop stores to establish close relations of trust with their customers, distributors, and suppliers. This promotes the customer loyalty, which is the counterpart of the customer satisfaction in Handelsbanken described above. Individuals and companies are willing to invest and borrow long term, thereby allowing Handelsbanken to engage in relational rather than transactional banking, which has yielded growing, profitable, and stable revenues.

How can this be done without the risk of employees 'going native' and undermining the performance of the firm in the process of assisting others? The answer is through the organizational culture and the values that it places on different parties. The values of the organization should prioritize correcting the problems it has inflicted on others in the past and those it is committed to solve in the future, addressing and solving them, and ensuring that they are adequately resourced. Those values should be reflected in the culture of the entire organization and ensure consistent alignment with delivery of those priorities. Those values in turn create the value that justifies investors' long-term financial commitments.

Profitable Problem-Solving

Mahindra, the Indian multinational company, was founded in 1945.[4] It started in steel manufacturing and expanded to 20 different industries, including automobile manufacturing. Its stated philosophy is to challenge conventional thinking, innovate, and enable positive change for its stakeholders. In 2008, it put this into practice by entering the Indian used car market.

The used car market around that time was equal in size to the new car market but most transactions were informal, with only 15% of transactions in the organized sector. The used car space was disorganized, fragmented, and lacked transparency and trust—a 'social capital deficit'.

Mahindra saw an opportunity as a trustworthy company with capital and access to spare parts to transform the market. It could use its trusted brand name, financial resources, and data to facilitate easier access to sellers and buyers, replacement parts, service repairs, and information on car value and history.

The parent company, Mahindra & Mahindra, delegated authority to a small team in its subsidiary, Mahindra First Choice (MFC), to take this initiative forward. As a separate entity, it could develop a more agile start-up culture that allowed it to take risks and build close relations with partner organizations.

MFC had a general understanding of the bottlenecks in the used car industry, but not a detailed one. It needed to know precisely how used car sales occur and between whom, the associated processes such as repair services and financing, and the specific problems that arose in each of them.

Six key actors were identified: buyers, sellers, car manufacturers, independent used car dealers, independent car service workshops, and banks. MFC set about building detailed customer profiles to identify the specific problems that each party faced and needed to resolve.

Buyers had trouble knowing whether they were paying a fair price for a used car, the history of a car including accidents and number of previous owners, the legitimacy of the paperwork provided by the seller, and obtaining spare parts for repairs. Sellers did not know the value of their car and faced the same issues as buyers when seeking to replace their car. Used car dealers struggled to attract customers and make a profit.

Car servicing workshops had difficulty accessing spare parts and employing and retaining trained staff. Banks lacked information about the history and resale value of repossessed cars and were afraid of being left with repossessed cars without a network in which to sell them.

Armed with a detailed understanding of the problems that afflicted the market, MFC could design solutions. It developed a standardized inspection service and created a multi-brand car dealer franchise to roll out the service. It created a franchise model and provided systems and services in exchange for royalties, including an IT system for inventory and customer relationship management. The data collected on transactions through the IT system enabled MFC to price a warranty model and share the profits with the dealers. They were used to benchmark prices and create the industry's first guide to vehicle valuation in India.

MFC provided an online auction platform so that the banks could sell repossessed cars to brokers, who then sold fleets of these cars to businesses. It developed software to optimize supply and distribution across the country and created small hubs. It made a catalogue available to all garages to provide information about spare part availability and it developed a system to educate repair technicians about diagnostic processes, reducing the high burden of training on employers.

The result was that MFC transformed the second-hand car market in India and built a thriving business on the back of it. This illustrates how a combination of delegated authority, a problem-solving ethos, a detailed understanding of the problems that confront different parties in a market and identification of innovative solutions together can simultaneously create substantial competitive advantage for firms and address significant social problems.

Summary

What emerges is the central role that governance and leadership play in corporations that recognize profit as being derivative of solving, not producing problems. Governance in this context moves well beyond its narrow and damaging focus on just aligning managerial interests with those of shareholders to one that seeks to promote the identification and implementation of the profitable resolution of problems.

The role of the board in this context is not simply to oversee the determination of the corporate purpose, ensure that it is the overarching framework within which strategy is formulated, and establish an internal culture, measurement, and incentive system that aligns corporate values with outcomes and impacts that companies have on others. It is also about ensuring that every part of the organization recognizes its contribution to the problem-solving nature of the business and is given both the latitude and the financial resources with which to realize its objectives. It empowers and enables people within the organization to recognize and realize their role in solving problems in the same way that the combination of problem-solving with financial ownership allows a company to define and implement its purpose within a broader system context.

Governance in this regard is therefore not just about looking up to those above—from boards to financial markets, from middle to senior management, and from the shopfloor to middle management—it is also about transferring authority and empowerment downwards. That in turn allows those with the specific, tacit knowledge that comes from interacting directly with those affected by and affecting the firm to identify the problems that need to be solved and how to fix them. It is therefore the vehicle by which what might appear to be irresolvable problems find resolutions and the financial capital needed to resolve them. It is inspiring and invigorating for everybody in the organization, and enabling and enriching for those outside, especially those least able and least likely to get rich—the non-human members of the natural world.

PART IV
THE PRIZE

Measurement is critical to the allocation of resources in a capitalist system. Nowhere is this more significant than in relation to nature and the environment. There are three approaches that are used: metrics, accounting, and valuation.

Metrics record the extent, state, and condition of natural capital. Accounts report the costs of maintaining and restoring nature. These costs should be incorporated in measures of national and corporate income, profit, and balance sheets to derive estimates net of costs of maintaining and restoring nature. Valuation seeks to attach monetary values to nature and the environment.

Valuation is important in economic analyses of natural capital. It is most relevant in determining how investment in nature can best benefit humans. It provides an anthropocentric view of nature that may not reflect its intrinsic condition. Valuation should therefore be combined with metrics that measure nature's intrinsic scale and condition, and accounts that record the costs of maintaining and restoring it.

This suggests a staged approach of creating an inventory of natural assets; identifying priorities for protection or restoration reflecting their scale and condition; incorporating maintenance and restoration charges in corporate and national accounts; and identifying social costs and benefits of investing in different forms of nature-based solutions.

The above is closely related to concepts of sustainability and sustainable finance. Its relevance extends beyond nature to human and social as well as natural assets.

Measurement is critical to resource allocation within companies and reporting by companies to their investors and other stakeholders. Environmental, social, and governance (ESG) reporting has been the dominant form of reporting to date. It has played an important role in portfolio allocation and investment appraisals by investors and companies. But it has been subject to problems of data quality and assurance, and it does not account for resourcing and performance of a company's purpose.

An organization should measure its performance against its purpose. It should incur the costs involved in rectifying, remedying, and mitigating the detriments it causes. It should provide for future costs of avoiding detriments and undertake investments required to deliver on its purpose. It should account for current and capital costs accordingly.

This is no different from traditional cost accounting applied to companies that incur the true costs of avoiding imposing detriments on others and delivering promised benefits associated with their stated purposes. Projections of true costs, revenues, and just profits are the basis of conventional financial valuations and investment appraisals.

Estimates of non-financial valuations of natural and social assets can also be undertaken to supplement financial valuations of true costs and revenues. These non-financial valuations are most relevant to investment appraisals and resource allocation decisions by companies and investors. Appropriate business models are required to ensure that adequate financial returns are earned on investment expenditures incurred in delivering environmental and social benefits.

7
Valuing the Invaluable

There is only one summit in life—to have taken the measure in feeling of everything human.

Wilhelm von Humboldt

Interpretation of the Golden Rule has special salience in relation to the natural world.[1] The traditional form of 'do unto others as you would have them do unto you' has particular relevance to 'them' when they are blue whales, giant pandas, rhinos, tigers, or the 16,000 other endangered species in the world. What exactly would you have them do unto you, apart from provide you with the meat, horns, skins, and money with which to survive, keep warm, and get rich? Arguably, the Golden Rule is a licence to kill, destroy, and eradicate our natural world. In contrast, its reformulated version of 'do unto others as they would have done unto them' specifies precisely what is required, because, if they did have voice on the matter, probably top of 'their' list would come 'be allowed to survive'.

The question this raises is one of implementation. How does one move from a moral principle to a matter of practice? Fortunately, we have a clear illustration of what is required of business and government to allow the world beyond ourselves to survive and thrive. It demonstrates the importance of measurement and accounting in both private and public spheres.

My country, the UK, in January 2018 became the first in the world to launch a national plan for the enhancement of its natural capital.[2] It sought to do exactly what I have set out in this book as the objectives of a problem-solving organization in the context of government as well as business purpose. It followed a commitment in 2011 by the

UK government to be the first generation to leave natural capital in a better condition than it was inherited.[3] In other words, it sought to avoid imposing detriment and instead confer benefit on nature.

The intentions were noble and the commitment to it no doubt sincere, but delivery is another thing. The 25-year plan conjures up images of an ever more green and pleasant land with clean air and water; thriving pastures, meadows, and woodlands; and abundant species of birds and other animals. It is envisaged as a buttress against the unrelenting pressures that economic and population growth exert on land and nature. It is our protection of the green and pleasant against the brown and concrete.

Or is it? Twenty-five-year plans in general do not have a great record of fulfilment in either sense of the word and there are traps that lie in the way of this one. The approach to the measurement and valuation of natural capital risks having precisely the opposite effect on nature from the one that is expected of it—not just unintended but decidedly unacceptable consequences. Valuation raises issues that go well beyond the comfort zone of economics into moral philosophy and biological evolution.

Uncomfortable though they may be, it is of paramount importance that these issues are aired before we begin the exercise in earnest, because false accounting risks being far more destructive than no accounting. Indeed, so serious is the risk that apparently worthy attempts to protect our natural capital through recognizing its value threaten to have precisely the opposite effect of hastening its eradication.

The Nature of Natural Capital

Some people view natural capital as synonymous with nature. But the addition of the term 'capital' is not as innocent or benign as it might at first sight appear. The term capital denotes something that contributes to the production of wealth and gives rise to claims on that wealth.[4] So human capital is the stock of knowledge, skills, and personal attributes that contribute to economic value, and social capital is the networks and relationships from which individuals and societies benefit.

E.F. Schumacher first used the term 'natural capital' in his book *Small is Beautiful*.[5] It is designed to capture the benefit that we as humans derive from our natural world and natural capital is the stock of natural assets that benefit mankind. The addition of capital to nature therefore focuses attention on the relevance of nature to the wellbeing of humanity and its contribution to the enhancement of human welfare. A 25-year natural capital plan is a plan to promote nature for the benefit of mankind.

There are six stages to the implementation of a plan.[6] The first is to take stock of the natural capital assets that a country, region, municipality, company, or landowner possesses and create an inventory of natural capital assets at a national, local, corporate, and individual level. This is a critical first stage because, while countries, companies, and individuals in general have reasonable records of their material and financial assets, the same is not true of their natural assets.

The second stage is the determination of the condition of those assets. What distinguishes natural from other assets is their capability of regeneration and renewal. They bless mankind with the ability to consume their services and benefits at no cost to the user if they are not over-utilized. However, there comes a point at which this capacity to restore is exhausted and natural assets deteriorate in a state of decline that becomes progressively irreversible. These critical thresholds are points at which renewable assets lose their power to renew of their own accord and threaten in time to become non-renewables or extinct.

There are therefore four classes of natural assets—renewables in an intrinsically healthy state, those close to or at a critical threshold, those in decline and below the threshold, and non-renewables. The preservation of natural assets is in large part an exercise in identifying into which category different assets fall and to concentrate attention on those near or below thresholds.

The third stage involves moving beyond the inventory of the quantity and quality of natural assets to an assessment of the services that they yield. This is the point at which one moves to consider the capital element of natural assets, their contribution to human wellbeing—happiness and health, both physical and mental, prosperity and flourishing, safety and survival. Examples include flood prevention, carbon sequestration, clean air and water, food, and recreation.

Note that thus far no mention has been made of valuation or monetary values. The natural assets and their services and benefits are measured in physical units and indicators. They are a mixture of quantitative and qualitative measures but with no attempt to standardize them in relation to units of account.

It is at the fourth stage, when one moves to assess the relative significance of the benefits derived, that it is necessary to try to standardize the outputs of natural capital. Over the last few years, economists have woken up to the fact that they have failed to account for many of the assets that contribute the most to human wellbeing. To date, the focus has been on material and financial assets. Conventional accounting in both national and company accounts has largely focused on these to the exclusion of other especially intangible assets, such as human and social capital. 'Wealth accounting', as it is termed, is an ambitious project to correct this by looking beyond material and financial capital to other assets from which mankind derives benefits.[7]

Natural capital is one of these assets, one of the newest on the block and one of the most neglected until very recently.[8] The importance of human capital in terms of education and skills has been appreciated for a long time, as have trust and institutions in promoting social capital. But with a few exceptions, natural capital has for the most part been taken for granted and it is only over the last few decades that we have come to appreciate the limitations on the ability of natural assets to absorb the mistreatment to which they have been subject.

With the realization that it is not just land that is a scarce resource but also many of the other components of natural capital has come an appreciation of the need to attach prices and values to them. Of course, many products of natural assets such as timber and food have been traded and priced for millennia, but others have not. It is only recently that we have felt it necessary to price such 'goods' as clean air and carbon sequestration. Alongside the creation of natural capital metrics are therefore natural capital prices and techniques for valuing natural capital.[9]

Having derived valuations of natural capital services then the fifth stage is managing them. As with any good or service there are limited resources with which to do this, and they must be prioritized. The standard way of doing this is to undertake 'cost-benefit' analyses of the goods and services and allocate resources to those for which the net benefits per unit of expenditure are greatest.

Finally, there follow various management requirements, determining property rights and responsibilities in relation to different assets, setting up governance systems, producing strategic plans, measuring performance against targets, and relating incentives to the performance outcomes.

In other words, the management of natural capital is treated like that of any other asset—produce an inventory, assess quality, measure outputs, value them, prioritize them and manage them. The stock of assets produces outputs that yield benefits, and the stock should be managed to yield the greatest net benefits given the limited resources available to do this. We treat nature like a production line—in go natural assets at one end; out come natural capital services at the other; and in between sit managers allocating labour and physical capital to generate the highest value output from the process. Nature is just another factor in the production of human wealth and wellbeing. Only it isn't and if it is then it won't be.

Accounting for Natural Capital

The problem relates back to the age-old debate about the nature of capital, which lies at the heart of this book.[10] As described above capital is an asset that yields benefits for mankind. The valuation of capital is, by definition, the value that man attaches to the services that capital yields. What went into producing it is neither here nor there. It is the output not the input that is of significance and that is what economists seek to measure.

Natural capital is particularly pertinent in that regard because in principle little or nothing manmade went into producing it.[11] It is just there and goes on being there if it is not unduly exploited. It therefore only makes sense to talk about the value of the services that natural capital creates, not about the historic cost of its production or the current cost of its replacement, which are the forms in which accountants typically record assets on the balance sheets of companies and nations.

So, wealth accounting is for the most part undertaken in relation to economic measures of value rather than accounting notions of cost. As will be described in the next chapter, there are formidable problems involved in undertaking such economic valuations because of the frequent absence of precise market prices and reliable approximations to them. However, resort in such circumstances is often made to the quote (precisely wrongly) ascribed to John Maynard Keynes that 'it is better to be approximately right than precisely wrong'. In other words, it is better to attempt to estimate missing values than to ignore them altogether.

However, it is not in fact practical issues of measurement that are the principal cause of concern about economic valuations. Of greater significance are matters of principle. What question are we trying to answer? The observant reader will have noted that the six stages of implementation of a natural capital plan slipped seamlessly from an inventory of the quantity and quality of natural assets to an assessment of the services that they provide. It ended by focusing on the value of outputs because the assets were purely regarded as mechanisms for deriving those outputs.

In contrast to economists, accountants are concerned with assessing the productive capability of a firm or nation and therefore with the presence and condition of the assets required to sustain their capacity to produce. The profit of a firm and the income of a nation are measured net of the cost of maintaining their productive capability. In particular, the entity view of the firm sees the corporate body as distinct from its owners and its profit as being net of the cost of maintaining its capacity to sustain its existing activities. A charge for capital maintenance or depreciation is set against the income of the company and netted off reported profit.[12]

The distinction therefore boils down to a question of what a 25-year plan is seeking to do. Is it seeking to manage natural assets in a way that yields the greatest benefits for mankind or is it trying to manage the assets in such a form as to maintain the productive and reproductive capability of the assets themselves? The former is the economists' proprietary view of natural assets that they are there to serve mankind and should be valued in that regard, and the latter is the accountant's entity view of natural assets as having a productive benefit in their own regard.

The accounting approach in essence suggests a merit in stopping at stage 2 in terms of considering the extent and condition of the stock of natural assets and their capacity to reproduce and sustain themselves, as well as continuing to stage 3 to 6 of evaluating services and the valuations attached to them. In other words, we cannot devise a plan for managing capital assets until we have clarified the purpose behind doing this. And this question of purpose is being lent urgency now not just because of our continuing degradation of natural capital services but also because of our increasing potential to enhance them.

The Purpose of a Plan

Recall that the motivation behind the creation of the natural capital committee and the 25-year plan was to be the first generation to leave natural capital in a better condition than we inherited it. What does that mean? One answer is that at the end of the 25 years, the citizens of the UK will be deriving greater benefits from its natural assets than they were at the beginning. We will have cleaner water, cleaner air, less flooding, better recreational opportunities, and so on. This has a seductive attraction to it, particularly for politicians who are faced with a complex problem of persuading their electorate to sacrifice more housing or employment to accommodate it.

A second answer is that we have more forests, meadows, nature parks, fish stocks, and biodiversity in at least as good or better condition than at present. This views natural capital from an intrinsic perspective of its quantity and quality, and its maintenance and enhancement, as against its extrinsic benefit to the citizens of a nation.[13]

In both cases there are economic judgements that must be made about how scarce resources should be allocated to achieve their purposes. In the first case, economic valuations and cost-benefit analyses are the tools that are used for this purpose. In the second, resources are devoted to those natural assets that are most vulnerable and at risk of decline and to those that would benefit most from restoration or enhancement. In particular, the latter evaluates natural capital in the context of complex interconnections between organisms and environments in ecosystems, as against the partial evaluations of the cost-benefit analyses that evaluate enhancement of specific natural capital services.

The distinction between the two approaches is being lent particular significance by technological advances. While nature might at present be the best way of producing natural capital services, increasingly over time artificial substitutes are becoming available and may in due course surpass natural systems. Astroturf may not be as beautiful as the real thing, but it has advantages as well as drawbacks as a substitute for grass, and carbon sequestration through artificial trees will become an increasingly common alternative to its natural equivalent.

At present, nature can provide a much broader range of services than artificial alternatives and possesses the advantages of self-renewal and adaptability mentioned above, but it would be a mistake to assume that this will always be the case or that combinations of different artificial substitutes might not provide lower-cost solutions than maintenance of nature. Cost-benefit analyses will over time therefore drive cost-conscious policymakers in the direction of synthetic solutions to natural asset requirements.

Far from being the guardian of our natural assets, 25-year plans have the potential to become the creator of their destruction. We could live true to a plan that seeks to enhance the extrinsic benefits of natural capital at the same time as we eradicate our natural assets, as we know them today. A focus on outputs and valuations of natural capital on its own therefore provides no assurance of the maintenance let alone enhancement of nature.

But why should we worry about this any more than we should have worried about the impact of new technologies on replacing outdated forms of production and employment? Surely, we should no more stand in the way of the march of progress in relation to natural capital services than in the production of any other goods or services. To do so would represent as misguided a response as the Luddites to the arrival of the cotton and woollen mills.

There are three reasons why the analogy may not be a good one. The first is an irreversibility argument. We can always choose to reverse the decision to employ new technologies. We can and in some cases have decided to eschew new modes of production and return to traditional forms in, for example, using hand- as against machine-made methods. We do so if there is perceived to be a benefit and a market for such processes.

In the case of natural capital that option is not currently available. Once a particular form of nature has been eradicated then it is lost. That means that there is an option value of natural capital that is extinguished by its destruction. For example, one hundred years ago we valued trees and forests for their aesthetic, recreational, and fuel qualities but not their carbon sequestration properties. We recognized the sun as a source of life, light, and warmth but not of powering production and transportation, and we continue to discover new medicinal properties in plants and soils.[14]

There is therefore a systematic undervaluation of natural capital that comes from our inability to determine the option values that future generations will derive from its preservation and the irreversibility associated with its destruction. The option value does not just come from unanticipated new demands for ecosystem services but also from new forms of services themselves.

This relates to the second issue and that is the living rather than inert nature of renewable assets. They evolve according to processes that we only partially understand and therefore provide benefits in the future that we cannot fully predict.[15] The most insightful way of thinking about this is in relation to artificial intelligence systems of the future.

At present artificial intelligence is predominantly about the application of high-powered processing systems to vast volumes of data to identify new methods of undertaking activities. The algorithms in that respect are not dissimilar to the inert nature of mechanical processes in the past, albeit much more sophisticated. However, as we progress to forms of machine learning in which algorithms evolve of their own accord then they too begin to take on a life of their own.

Will that make the evolutionary processes of the natural world irrelevant? Almost certainly not, since just as we value the diversity of the co-existence of multiple species and their forms of evolution today in terms of their contribution to a rich variety of types of life, so too we will continue to benefit from diversity of natural systems even in the presence of advanced forms of machine learning in the future.

The final argument for acknowledging the intrinsic value of nature beyond its current capital value in a plan for managing natural assets derives from a question of whose assets are they. As noted at the start of the chapter, the underlying assumption of natural capital as against natural assets is that the benefits are those that mankind derives from them. We are schooled in viewing all aspects of life on this planet from the perspective of humans and a production process account of natural capital management presumes that the outputs are for the benefit of mankind just like those of a factory.

There might be some justification for this viewpoint for a factory because humans in large part built it and humans have sacrificed current consumption for the benefits of its future production. But the same cannot be said of natural assets. As previously noted, for the most part we did not make them. We inherited them and we have inherited them because our predecessors chose to preserve them or were incapable of destroying them in their entirety. Our capacity to destroy natural assets and incentives to do so are greater than at any time in the past. We therefore need to be cognizant of our roles and responsibilities as well as our rights and rewards.

This comes back to the question posed by the comparison between the economist's proprietary and the accountant's entity view of assets. To the economist, natural capital like any other asset is the plaything of humans, there to be treated as mankind sees fit. To the accountant, the firm is an entity of which the managers are its stewards. They are there to preserve the firm and to promote its flourishing. So too, we should consider whether it is our right to employ nature in the way in which we see fit or our obligation to act as its steward or trustee.

The economist's is the colonial view of the world. Our supremacy over nature gives us a right as well as an ability to make of it what we will. The trustee view is of a world of which we were not its creator and instead privileged to be its protector. We have inherited the role of the guardian of all living things as we have of our children and their descendants.

It was Schumacher who said: 'To press non-economic values into the framework of the economic calculus … is a procedure by which the higher is reduced to the level of the lower and the priceless is given a price. It can therefore never serve to clarify the situation and lead to an enlightened decision…. The logical absurdity, however, is not the greatest fault of the undertaking: what is worse, and destructive of civilisation, is the pretence that everything has a price or, in other words, that money is the highest of all values.'[16]

A Reconciliation

The above are arguments for suggesting that an economic perspective on natural capital is not without its deficiencies. However, it is equally not a justification for rejecting economic assessments out of hand. We are after all part of the living world that we have duties to protect and so we too have rights to benefit from it. How should we balance these rights and responsibilities?

There is no single answer to this question. Just as social welfare theory has taught us that there are no simple means of balancing the interests of the self with those of others, so there is no straightforward method of reconciling the conflicting interests of human in relation to other species or forms of nature. There might be difficulties in eliciting and aggregating the preferences of individuals, but they pale into insignificance in weighting those of different species.

Thought of in economic terms the problem is almost irresolvable but in relation to the judgemental decisions that trustees routinely must perform on behalf of others they are not exceptional. Faced with such uncertainties, instead of seeking optimizing routines we turn to approximating rules. The one that will be advocated here is precisely that which is conventionally employed by accountants in corporate contexts.

As already mentioned, the accountant's definition of profit differs from that of the economist in considering the income derived net of the cost of maintaining the productive potential of the firm.[17] In other words what the firm has available to distribute to its shareholders is what remains after provision has been made for the maintenance of assets as well as the operational costs of the business.[18]

It is a principle that has direct application to the management of natural assets. Stage 1, create an inventory of natural assets. Stage 2, identify those that are a priority for protection or restoration on account of their significance and condition. Stage 3, incorporate a maintenance charge in the balance sheets and profit and loss statements of nations, municipalities, corporations, and landowners to reflect the liability associated with maintaining or restoring these assets. Stage 4, identify the social benefits of investing in different forms of capital and the costs associated with enhancing them and allocate resources to the highest return investments. Stage 5, manage both the preservation of existing natural assets and investment in the new.

In other words what is being proposed is an accounting entity approach to the protection and restoration of existing critical natural capital assets and ecosystems, and an economist's proprietary approach to evaluating the benefits of new investments in natural capital over and above their maintenance and restoration. This combines a trustee or stewardship role in relation to existing key assets and an economic evaluation process to new investments on the margin.[19] This has not only the advantages of 'no regret' in relation to existing assets but also positive benefits in relation to new ones.

There are clearly numerous matters of detail that need to be resolved in applying this approach. Who should determine which assets are critical and in need of maintenance or restoration? What level of restoration as against maintenance should be employed in stages 2 and 3? How should the complex interactions between different living organisms and environments be modelled and evaluated in the preservation of natural systems? Can one determine the costs of maintenance and restoration with sufficient accuracy?

However, these questions are capable of being answered. For example, regarding the last one, while estimates of maintenance and restoration costs are not without their difficulties, in most circumstances these are modest in relation to those mentioned above of imputing prices to non-traded natural capital assets and services in economic valuations. Problems of measurement are therefore diminished rather than intensified by moving the boundary between accounting and valuation further in the direction of the former and away from the latter.

Regarding the questions of who identifies critical assets and the required degrees of maintenance and restoration, these are public policy issues that should be laid down by national and local governments as obligations on businesses, landowners, and public organizations to protect and promote specified assets. They should be reflected in requirements to account for these assets in corporate accounts and to report measures of profit and loss accordingly.

Mismeasurement is arguably even more of a problem at the macro, national, and international than the micro, business level. It is not only corporate profits that fail to account for the cost of maintenance and restoration of nature; so too does income that is earned by individuals and publicly and not-for-profit owned organizations. More seriously, much activity is merely rectifying, remedying, or reversing

the detriment produced elsewhere in an economy—carbon sequestration to offset CO_2 emissions, water purification to treat harmful
effluents, and flood defences to protect low-lying properties.

Similar double accounting arises in relation to social capital
expended by public health organizations to counteract the detrimental effects of harmful and polluting products produced by the
private sector. For example, purchase of insulin from one enlightened company described in this book, Novo Nordisk, may be
required to offset the diabetes associated with sales of chocolate by
another, Mars. An indeterminate amount of national and international GDP is therefore not a net contribution to aggregate income at
all but merely a reversal of the human, natural, and social detriments
caused by other forms of economic activity.

Sustainability

Replace the word maintain with sustain and one has a natural way
of appreciating the relevance of the above to the extensive discussion
and regulation of sustainability.[20] Sustainability requires the maintenance of natural assets. However, it does so in a more coherent and
comprehensive fashion than is conventionally the case.

First, it emphasizes the distinction, previously described in the
context of corporate law between permissive and proscriptive policy. It is proscriptive in requiring maintenance and restoration of
the intrinsic condition of natural assets, while being permissive
in the promotion of extrinsic human benefits. That draws a line
between what is appropriately addressed through legal and regulatory instruments, and what should be left to commercial and
individual initiative.

Second, it establishes the relevance of sustainability to governments and international organizations at the macro, national, and
international level as well as to businesses, investors and philanthropic institutions at the micro, corporate, and organizational level.

Third, it demonstrates the applicability of the approach not just to
global warming or natural assets in their totality but also to human

and social assets. Without such a comprehensive perspective then ad hoc initiatives to regulate in specific areas risk shifting problems from carbon emissions to biodiversity, from nature to social inequality and exclusion, and from society to infringements of liberty and human rights. We need to recognize the importance of maintaining human, social, and natural world wellbeing in the round to ensure that policy is sound.

Summary

The UK has set a global example through the creation of a 25-year plan for the promotion of natural capital. Its intentions are impressive, and its motivations are sincere. However, its risks are considerable and to date largely unrecognized.

This chapter has sought to argue that the conventional approaches that are being taken to the valuation and management of natural capital have serious deficiencies. Their outcomes could be exactly the opposite of what is intended and expected from the adoption of a 25-year plan. Far from ensuring the preservation of the UK's natural capital, it could be the catalyst for its eradication.

The reason for this is the lens through which natural capital is conventionally viewed and the procedures by which it is measured and managed. It is viewed as part of a production process no different from that of any other good or service. Natural capital is an input into the output of benefits for mankind akin to that of any other form of capital.

What this fails to recognize is that natural capital is very different from other forms of capital and arguably should not be viewed as a capital at all. Its distinctive features are its renewable and restorative properties, its irreversibility, its living and evolving nature, and the fact that it was inherited not created by humans. These properties make it fundamentally different from other forms of capital. They make its option values to future generations particularly large and difficult to evaluate. They make its preservation and promotion of exceptional value, and they impose strong obligations of guardianship and trusteeship upon us.

Unrestrained adoption of economic approaches to managing natural capital is therefore not only unjustified but also inappropriate and potentially catastrophic. On the other hand, a pure intrinsic approach to valuing natural capital risks wrapping it in aspic. The most important argument for advocating the dual approach of using accounting approaches to maintaining and restoring existing assets, and economic valuations to additional investments is that it avoids the stark conflict between the potential destruction of natural assets inherent in the latter and depriving mankind of their potential enhanced benefits in the former. By so doing, countries will not only have set the global standard for aspirations regarding natural capital but also provided the measures and means by which they can be realized. They will have paved the way to enhancing the wellbeing of mankind and ensuring its attainment.

8
Just Profit

They say also that honesty is for the most part less profitable than dishonesty…. For what men say is that, if I am really just and am not also thought just, profit there is none, but the pain and loss on the other hand are unmistakable. But if, though unjust, I acquire the reputation of justice, a heavenly life is promised to me.

Plato (c. 375 bc), *Republic*, Chapter 2, The Individual, The State, and Education

Introduction

Measurement is regarded by many as the holy grail of reforming business. Without it nothing will happen; with it, business can be held to account. But experience of the last few years in the development of 'environmental, social, and governance' (ESG) reporting has demonstrated that this is far from the case.

Measurement is a particularly powerful illustration of the difference between the traditional and reformulated versions of the Golden Rule. It raises questions about the perspective from which companies are assessed—from 'your', the investor—or 'their', affected parties'—viewpoint. In the context of ESG that distinction is sometimes described in terms of 'single materiality'—from the perspective of investors alone—versus 'double materiality'—from the perspective of other parties as well.

Over the past two decades investors have gradually woken to the growing risks they face from environmental and societal considerations, and from poor governance of the companies in which they are invested. In response they have sought means of evaluating the significance of these risks in a similar way to how they assess product market, technology, and other risks. ESG is designed to provide investors with that information and assist them with their portfolio allocations and monitoring.

There has been no shortage of willing providers of such information. As ESG has become fashionable and another lucrative business for consultants and investors, they have jumped on the bandwagon of producing a plethora of ESG ratings. In its extended 'double materiality' form, ESG is also relevant to governments, non-governmental organizations (NGOs), regulators, and those directly affected by a firm's activities.

To date, there has been a problem of measurement arising from inadequate information provided by companies and insufficient standardization and assurance (verification) of the information provided. However, that is changing as some organizations, in particular the European Union and 'international standard setters', most notably the International Sustainability Standards Board (ISSB) of the International Financial Reporting Standards (IFRS) Foundation, determine relevant criteria for the provision of information.

One should nevertheless appreciate the difference between what these initiatives seek to achieve and what they can realize. They first and foremost attempt to improve the information on which financial markets price assets and products and thereby assist investors with their portfolio allocation and engagement decisions. This is an important aspect of the functioning of an economy that affects company behaviour, not least through the cost of the provision of finance for investment.

In its double materiality form, ESG also seeks to inform policymakers and affected parties about the environmental, social, and governance effects of corporate activities. But it doesn't attempt to ensure avoidance of profiting from imposition of detriments or promote profiting from producing solutions to problems. For example, it has not prevented the downgrading of environmental considerations of fossil fuel emissions (the E of ESG) during the current period of energy shortages when social (S) considerations have risen to the fore.

> *When the going gets tough,*
> *Green turns to fluff.*
> *Haven't enough?*
> *Try sleeping rough.*

The issue that lies at the heart of these problems is a misalignment of the interests of companies with solving problems. There are two reasons for that. The first is inadequate account of the detriments that companies impose on others and the second is a failure to incentivize and resource the resolution of problems.

The questions that should be answered are: first, whether a company is correcting and costing the problems it is creating; second, is it appropriately resourcing the problems it claims to be solving; third, is it delivering the solutions it is promising; and fourth, is it profiting from their delivery?

That determines a coherent, comprehensive set of measures that are valuable and important for management and investors. Establishing whether companies profit from producing solutions rather than problems requires measurement of whether solutions or problems are properly resourced, delivered, and profitable.

Understanding the difference between this and the much advocated and maligned ESG is instructive. First, and most significantly, ESG is non-financial reporting. It has no influence on the measured financial performance of the firm and in particular its profits. In contrast, problem-solving purpose establishes the problems that a firm creates, and the costs involved in resolving them. It therefore reports just profit net of the true costs of remedying detriments.

Second, ESG reports the risks of a business arising from its environmental, social, and governance exposures. Problem-solving purpose does this in a more instructive way by determining the problems a company seeks to address and the resources it requires to do that. It therefore provides a financial projection associated with the delivery of a strategy that derives from its purpose, and a basis for determining the value of the company net of the costs of correcting for collateral damage done in the process.

Traditional methods of corporate performance measurement look at the firm as an entity that owns property and contracts with other parties. They record costs, incomes, assets, and liabilities associated with these activities, and make provisions for maintaining physical assets and servicing liabilities. They report the actual costs of the resources that a firm employs and the revenues it earns, distinguishing current from capital expenditures.

What accounts do not currently record are the costs of maintaining assets that a firm does not own but on which it depends, or the liabilities for which it is not contractually or legally obligated but nevertheless responsible because of its impacts on other parties. In other words, accounting is currently aligned with a property but not a responsible owner or problem-solving view of the firm.

As a result, accounts do not at present provide the information required to promote responsible, purposeful business practices. Against that benchmark, profit is overstated where companies cause detriments to other parties and not fully recognized where they invest to the benefit of others.[1] They therefore promote excessive engagement in problem-causing and insufficient investment in problem-solving activities.

This is a serious defect of existing measurement systems and one that needs to be urgently rectified. It is a fundamental reason why, though business has been the source of immense economic progress, it has also been a cause of serious environmental and social problems. We want the former without the latter.

It is a straightforward exercise to create the measurement system that does that, and it does not require a fundamental change in our accounting systems to achieve it. On the contrary, it is merely the application of the most traditional and well-established form of accounting—cost-based accounting—to companies' actual expenditures.

Measuring and Accounting for Outcomes and Impacts

Stop measuring just the inputs that companies use and outputs they sell. Start from the question of what are the changes that the firm's activities are bringing about and the impacts they are having on others. Some of these are positive, some are negative, and in general most companies and products produce a mixture of the two. That is why thinking of companies and measuring their performance from the perspective of the problems they solve and create is much more insightful than looking at them simply as owners of property that produce products.[2]

To take the example of a car from Chapter 6, the outcomes and impacts are the transportation benefits for the passengers, the congestion and collision detriments for other road users, and the environmental detriments for local pedestrians, residents, and global citizens. The outcomes and impacts relate not just to the product and the characteristics of the product but also to the process and production of the car, namely the positive employment benefits, the skills and training which employees receive, the positive impacts on suppliers and distributors, the negative environmental consequences for local communities, and so on.

The first stage then is for a company to determine the changes it brings about (the outcomes). This is an insightful exercise because it provides a company with a comprehensive account of the effects of its activities.[3] It is particularly insightful when it is undertaken in relation to contemplated new activities not just existing ones because it emphasizes the importance of not only considering existing outcomes and impacts but also prospective future ones and the things that might go wrong as well as right.

It therefore encourages an informed assessment of the effects of what the company does and a prospective catalogue of the problems and solutions that might occur in the future. To return to the car example, a manufacturer should contemplate not only the effect that it is currently having on congestion and pollution but also its possible future effects.

The second stage is to determine the actions that need to be taken to correct, rectify, remedy, or compensate for detriments that the company, its products, and activities have and may cause. So, the car causes negative congestion, collisions, and environmental consequences. These will require increased public expenditure on road building and health provision, and private expenditure on car insurance and repairs by other drivers, sound proofing of housing, and so on. There are therefore a variety of expenditures incurred by other parties that are not reflected in the price of the product.

At present the car manufacturer is not bearing the costs of these negative detriments. It is therefore profiting at the expense of others. Internalizing the costs requires the firm to contribute to remedying or rectifying the harms it is producing. Accounting and measurement of profit follow the obligation on firms to avoid profiting from producing problems

The costs are actual expenditures that are incurred by way of settling not only contractual liabilities but also those arising from the need to rectify detriments caused. In essence profits as currently measured are fictitious in not reflecting the true costs of remedying or compensating for harm done. They are profits earned at the expense of others and they are therefore a wealth transfer from others not just wealth creation. The wealth creation of a firm is measured by revenues net of true costs.

Having derived the true cost of the firm then it is possible to establish its true valuation. That is simply the discounted present value of the expected future revenues net of expected true costs. Note that no attempt is made to account for anything other than actual revenues and actual expenditures that will be incurred. There is no imputing of the benefits that the company confers on others over and above the extent to which they are reflected in actual revenues, and no projection of anything other than the true costs it anticipates incurring in remedying detriments. Financial analysis is therefore no different from its current form except that the costs that are projected forward are true costs.

Valuing Benefits

In essence this is one component of a cost-benefit analysis. It takes account of social and environmental detriments by establishing the cost of remedying or rectifying them. It does not value the detriments to the affected party but seeks to internalize them by correcting them. It remains purely focused on the interests of investors and in particular shareholders but recognizes that those interests should not extend to profiting at the expense of others.

Without this, Plato's assertion in the quotation at the beginning of this chapter that injustice is inappropriately rewarded is inevitable. But even if this is corrected, then his first assertion that justice may nevertheless go unrewarded remains true. The reason for this is that benefits conferred on others beyond those reflected in the payments to the company for goods and services provided are not valued. There is no attempt to impute benefits where the firm does not earn a financial return from them.

To do that, those who, in Plato's words, are 'really just' must be 'thought just' by investors who value their activities, governments who can subsidize them where necessary, and customers who should be willing to pay them. Even if profiting from producing detriments is prevented, then going much beyond this to produce profitable solutions requires the support of investors, governments, and customers. This point will be developed in the final part of the book.

While companies can internalize their negative detriments by incurring the expenditures needed to rectify them, they cannot always internalize the benefits they confer through earning greater revenues. That is the business challenge that companies face and need to address through innovative business solutions, committing to value creation over the long term, partnering with others, and receiving financial support from them.

Alternatively, investors might attribute value to the positive non-financial impacts that the company has on other parties. They might attach importance to contributing to addressing human, social, and environmental problems over and above the financial benefit they derive from them. In other words, they might be 'impact investors' who value benefits from non-financial as well as financial returns.[4]

This is sometimes described in terms of the interest that shareholders have in their wellbeing and welfare as well as their wealth.[5] They may care about their health, their environment, the future of the planet or they may have altruistic interests in the wellbeing of others—their children, families, friends, communities, nations as well as the natural world.

For whatever reason investors may be concerned about their welfare rather than their wealth. In responding to the interests of their investors, companies should therefore take account of their positive impacts on others. This would then suggest that companies should value the non-financial as well as the financial benefits that derive from solving problems. They should value the benefits to the planet of reducing their CO_2 emissions, reducing inequality, increasing social inclusion, and improving the health and quality of people's lives.[6]

This implies that companies should not only undertake the cost part of a cost-benefit analysis but the benefit element as well. They should impute values to the non-financial as well as financial benefits they confer on others. One reason for separating this from the derivation of true costs is that it involves an extension to traditional financial analysis.

A second reason is that imputing prices and revenue streams where they do not exist is a highly subjective exercise that does not have the degree of objectivity and verifiability associated with traditional accounting statements and auditing. Such statements might therefore be supplementary rather than integral to financial statements. They are particularly relevant to investors, policymakers, and regulators in appraisals of social and environmental benefits, for example in pricing 'green bonds' that specify and value CO_2, biodiversity, nature-based solutions, and related targets.[7]

The distinction drawn here between positive and negative externalities is not just a matter of measurability but also acceptability. The assertion that a firm should be responsible for remedying the detriments it inflicts on third parties is quite different from suggesting it should be rewarded for uncontracted benefits it inadvertently confers on them. Firms will wish the boundaries of the former to be drawn as narrowly as possible and the latter as widely as possible.

Third parties who are impacted by the firms will wish the opposite and quite reasonably so because they have not created or requested either type of externality. While restricting obligations to their legal boundaries makes measurement more precise, the case for doing so is substantially weakened where negative detriments are inflicted on others. Non-financial valuations that treat positive and negative externalities symmetrically are therefore less relevant than profits that account for unpriced detriments but not benefits.

In summary, the purpose of a company, its strategy, business model, and implementation determine the problems that a company seeks to solve profitably without profiting from creating problems. Its financial accounts, measurement, financial, and non-financial reporting, and valuation derive from its purpose. They assist investors, governments, regulators, customers, communities, suppliers, and society in establishing the degree to which companies are delivering on their problem-solving purposes, profiting from so doing, and avoiding profiting from causing detriments. That distinction between purpose-driven causes, and financial and non-financial reporting of their effects, explains both the role and limitation of non-financial reports, such as ESG.[8]

Measurement is a very natural product of the problem-solving nature of business. Companies should measure the problems they seek to solve and allocate resources to the delivery of those solutions according to their intended timescale. They should make provisions for further costs that might be incurred from failures and unanticipated problems. Furthermore, they should incur the costs of failing to meet intended outcomes and putting the trajectory of the firm back on track.

A company should measure the detriments it imposes on third parties and the costs involved in remedying and rectifying those detriments. That determines a true rather than fictitious cost of the business in terms of delivering benefits and is the basis of a just profit. On that basis, a financial valuation can be estimated of a company which delivers benefits in the form of value creation for all rather than value transfer from some. Finally, the company can also estimate the non-financial value of the benefits it confers on others from imputing prices to the outcomes of activities. This may be particularly relevant to investment appraisals and resource allocation decisions.

Examples

For the past three years, I have been working with a consortium of companies on a project that is based at the Said Business School in Oxford entitled the Rethinking Performance Initiative.[9] The objective of the programme is to assist companies from around the world operating in different sectors of the economy with implementing their corporate purposes of solving problems. We have worked closely with the companies in understanding the nature of their corporate purposes and what they are really seeking to achieve in solving problems. We have then sought to assist them with translating those high-level objectives into practical real policies at the heart of their businesses and in different parts of their organizations.

Key to this is measurement and creating a system of management accounts that can be adopted to assist those working in different units of a business to understand their performance in delivering on their parts of their companies' purposes. The advantage of analysing implementation at this as well as at board level is that it brings to life what it means to seek to solve problems profitably avoiding profiting from creating problems. It is more straightforward to experiment with different forms of management accounts used in a business than with the statutory accounts for external reporting, because the latter are subject to stringent rules and principles that companies must adhere to.

We have partnered with large companies operating globally in four sectors—beverages, construction, energy, and pharmaceutical—headquartered around the world. The problems they are seeking to address range from excessive alcohol consumption, through CO_2 emissions to public health issues. However, an interesting aspect of this is that, while the specific nature of the problems varies, there is one common, underappreciated problem that concerns all of them—access to their products and services, and their affordability.

For example, the problem of a beverage company selling alcohol would appear to about the alcohol content of their products. However, the problem is more insightfully formulated as providing access to no or low alcohol beverages that taste as good, and are as socially acceptable, cheap, and profitable as alcoholic ones. The problem of a fossil fuel company is that it is now an energy company that exists to solve global energy problems of producing environmentally friendly and sustainable sources of energy that are affordable and accessible in all parts of the world, including low- and middle- income countries and regions.

A construction company needs to find ways of delivering the housing and accommodation requirements of individuals and organizations in a form that is zero or less CO_2 intensive than at present, and low cost and affordable. The problem of a pharmaceutical company is in creating solutions for medical problems that are affordable and accessible in low- and middle-income as well as high-income countries around the world.

In other words, the fundamental problem of most companies is not just solving a global need—reduced alcohol consumption, CO_2 emissions or health problems. There is in general a solution, but it is often expensive, not profitable, or unaffordable for large segments of the world's population. It is not just an environmental or a health problem but also a social one of access and affordability. Many companies are therefore not fully identifying the nature of the problems they are seeking to solve, let alone providing solutions.

Having defined the problem precisely, the next task is to determine alternative ways of addressing them. This involves creation of low or no alcohol alternatives to existing alcoholic drinks; alternative forms of packaging to reduce plastic waste; alternative designs, construction methods, and materials to reduce CO_2 emissions in buildings; investment in renewables, electrification, battery technology, off-grid generation to provide affordable low CO_2 emitting energy sources; and alternative forms of treatment, as for example described previously in relation to Novo Nordisk and diabetes, in addition to R&D in new medicines.

But most significantly in this context is measurement of performance in delivering solutions. To what extent is a beverage company able to produce, promote and sell a low/no alcohol beer that appeals to a substantial fraction of the existing alcohol market. Does it substitute for existing alcohol consumption or for other types of beverages? Does it only appeal to a certain segment of the population—old/ young, low/high income, rural/ urban? Does it create problems of its own—sugar content, packaging, sourcing of materials?

Likewise with buildings, energy, and pharmaceuticals. Measures of the success of companies in delivering on their objectives need to be determined that reflect the positive and negative contributions that the firm makes to solving problems and the degree to which it is not only tackling the issues but also doing so in a way that is affordable and accessible. Those measures are the basis on which it must resource the relevant business units and ensure that the necessary current and capital expenditures are made to rectify failures and deliver future objectives.

Most significantly, management accounts should be constructed that record the expenditures associated with meeting targets and capitalizing those that are associated with delivering problem-solving in the future. Based on that, the profitability of solving problems and avoiding profiting from causing problems can be determined. This has significant implications for resource allocation in the business as well as rewarding those involved in delivering outcomes.

Take for example the case of promoting a non-alcoholic as an alternative to an alcoholic beverage. This would on the face of it appear to be an unprofitable activity since the firm has to invest in the new product and, if successful, it will diminish its earnings from existing alcoholic products. However, that is not necessarily the case if the existing activities are properly accounted for. If the problem to be solved is excessive alcohol consumption and it is not addressed through switching consumption to another product, then the firm will have to find another way of avoiding profiting from producing problems.

For example, the firm will have to cut sales of its alcohol products or pay for the public and private health consequences of alcohol disorders. In other words, the just profit of existing products is significantly lower than currently recorded. As a result, introducing an alcohol-free product might well be the most profitable strategy for the company once the profitability of its existing activities is correctly determined.

A similar approach needs to be taken to all investment appraisals. The appraisals are taken against the context of not only existing profitability assessments but also those that account for alternative ways of remedying detriments caused. So, for example, the profitability of fossil fuel production is substantially overstated in failing to account for rectifying and reversing the environmental damage it causes. As a result, affordable renewable energy production may well be an attractive alternative to higher cost ways of compensating or remedying the detriments caused by fossil fuels. This is highly relevant to current debates about switching to renewables during periods of energy shortages when returns on oil and gas are high.

To take another example, pharmaceuticals may have as their objective lives saved, greater longevity and improvements in quality of life. These are measurable statistics of the degree to which a pharmaceutical company contributes to human wellbeing. Setting targets for these influences the expenditures that companies need to make on R&D and the development of new forms of treatment for health problems. Access to medicine in low- and middle-income countries requires innovative business models that may involve partnering with the public as well as the private sector, as Novo Nordisk did in seeking to defeat diabetes.

Some companies attempt to value the social benefit that their medicines confer. They do this by estimating extension to length and improvements in quality of lives achieved. This has economic benefits in terms of enhancing the earnings capabilities of individuals and reducing public health and social care expenditures. For example, Novartis estimates that the social contribution of its medicines is more than $200bn.[10] Its stock market capitalization is also around $200bn so the company creates approximately $1 in social value from its medicines for every $1 in financial value for its shareholders. The ratio of social to financial value of Novartis is approximately one.

One can do the same in relation to environmental costs. Novartis estimates that its environmental costs amount to approximately $8bn, which is predominantly associated with climate, energy and air pollution, land use, water, and waste. Its environmental impacts are therefore miniscule in relation to its social contribution, which is not surprising given the nature of its business. A similar analysis of an energy company would yield very different results.

However, what this analysis does not establish is the financial benefit that Novartis and its shareholders derive from the social benefits it creates. How much feedback is there from social benefit to financial return for investors? This determines the degree to which Novartis can commercialize its social benefits and the degree to which it is therefore incentivized to incur the required investment expenditures.

There are several ways in which a pharmaceutical company might be able to internalize the external benefits it confers on individuals, societies, and the public sector. First, it may partner with governments and local authorities in different countries around the world to improve public health and reduce public expenditures on health care. Second, it might work with other businesses to improve the productivity of their employees. Third, it could become a trusted supplier of information, knowledge, and advice to doctors, hospitals, and health care workers around the world, thereby enjoying increased business and custom from public, private, and professional organizations.

There are therefore many ways in which companies like Novartis can build business models that relate private profit to public benefit, but it is important to realize that impact valuation analyses do not measure profit in the conventional sense of a financial return to a company's investors. A company can internalize its negative external impacts by incurring additional costs in mitigating and offsetting detriments, but it cannot conjure-up profits and financial returns on positive impacts without implementing the business models which do that.

A company will not therefore in general be able to transform all problem-solving benefits into profits and the degree to which it does this will reflect its success in creating a commercial product out of an environmental and societal opportunity. Measuring social impact may therefore be an important consideration in investment appraisal, scenario planning, and resource allocation, but it should not be confused with accounting for the actual costs that companies incur and revenues they earn from implementing problem-solving purposes.

Summary

Drawing together conclusions to date:

> *The Moral Law.* It is moral to profit from producing solutions.
> It is immoral to profit from producing problems for others.
> *The Rule of Law.* What is legal is not always moral.
> The Moral Law should be incorporated in corporate purpose and law.
> *Ownership.* Owners have rights of return from producing solutions.
> They are responsible for avoiding profiting from producing problems.
> *Leadership.* Leaders should direct the production of solutions.
> They should empower managers to produce solutions without problems.
> *Values.* We should maintain and sustain human, social, and natural wellbeing.

Income and profit should be measured net of the cost of so doing.

Profit. We should measure true costs of producing solutions not problems.

Just profit should be measured net of true costs.

The final part of the book turns to the challenge of converting these statements into commercial advantage and social advancement. It describes the vital role that four parties play in achieving this: investors, governments, customers, and educators. We start in Chapter 9 with investors.

PART V

THE COMMITMENT

Finance is central to investment in problem-solving purposes. Risk bearing equity capital is key to this. It encourages investment in bottom of the pyramid entrepreneurship in the poorest countries, in small and medium-sized enterprises (SMEs) in left-behind places, and in problem-solving tech start-ups, university spinouts, and scale-ups.

This requires institutional investors in capital markets to connect with businesses at the bottom of the pyramid, in left-behind places, and in academic institutions with little experience of business. That is the purpose of finance and financial sectors, but it is not one that it is performing at anything like the required scale.

The primary focus of financial institutions is currently on financial risks and returns of their investors. They do not view themselves as being responsible for delivering profitable solutions for other parties. That is the role of business or government not investors. So, finance often involves 'arms-length' transactions between finance and business.

All the examples here illustrate exactly the opposite—financial institutions and multinational companies actively involved in funding and training bottom of the pyramid entrepreneurs; long-term relationship rather than short-term transactional banking funding SMEs in the regions of countries; and business angels, venture capitalists, and professional advisors mentoring, networking, and growing university start-ups, spinouts, and scale-ups.

Institutions should finance and steward implementation of problem-solving purposes in their corporate investments. Global portfolio diversification, inadequate investor expertise, and minority investor regulatory protection have discouraged this. Companies should manage their shareholdings to ensure they have the engaged owners required to fulfil their purposes.

Problem-solving purposes are a driver of human flourishing and shared prosperity. But businesses cannot solve major problems on their own. They must partner with other organizations, particularly government. Profitable problem-solving purposes naturally align private interests of business with public concerns of government.

The UK provides a particularly striking illustration of the failures and potential for this. It has exceptionally poor productivity and high regional inequality caused by dysfunctional finance, regulation, corporate ownership, and centralized government.

Reversing failed countries and regions requires enlightened public policy. This involves devolved, decentralized government to the regions; connecting financial centres with the regions through a presence of local institutions; forging common purpose between public, private, and philanthropic institutions in locality; promoting purposeful local businesses and financial institutions to support this; and rapid experimentation and learning from cases of success and failure.

Forging common purpose is needed in some sectors as well as localities, especially utilities. The purposes of businesses should be aligned with social licences to operate in those sectors and regulators should move beyond just setting and enforcing rules to encouraging the engagement of businesses with their customers and communities on common purposes.

Stronger partnerships should be formed between business and educational institutions. They are required in the design and delivery of leadership and skills training, and in mentoring, networking, and financing new business formations and commercial innovations in universities.

9
Financing Equity

Trust in equity

Introduction

Finance is often regarded as the source of the problem. Business would like to solve problems and engage in meaningful, challenging purposes. But it is held back by financial institutions that are short-term, profit focused, and dividend dominated. They are subject to a herd mentality and irrational waves of optimism and pessimism. They are diversified, disengaged, and passive. They divest of troubled shares and only engage when they expect large capital gains on share trading and takeovers. In other words, financial institutions are leeches sucking the financial blood out of firms and inflicting fatal wounds on those who pursue anything other than short-term financial profits.

In fact, finance is the solution not the problem. It is the lifeblood of firms, and it is what distinguishes business from other organizations that seek to solve problems but lack the financial resources with which to do it. Furthermore, recent innovations in financial markets have massively enhanced their potential to fund the growth of problem-solving business.[1]

Why is the perception of finance so at variance with its significance? The answer is that finance has lost sight of what it is there to do. It exists to finance problem-solving businesses. It is not there to determine the problems to be solved or the way to solve them. It is there to evaluate the problems businesses are seeking to solve, whether they have the capabilities and capacity to solve those problems, how they are going about solving them, and the profitability associated with doing that. On that basis, investors then decide whether to invest and on what terms.

Most investors are not owners. They do not own the problem and they are not there to determine how to solve the problem. That is the role of the owners (as defined in Chapter 5) and those charged with running the firm. The investors provide the financial resources to assist with delivering solutions. As shareholders, they have rights of appointment and removal of directors and proposing resolutions at shareholder meetings. As creditors, they have protective covenants and rights of enforcement in the event of default on the terms of their loans.

In other words, investors can seek to improve and protect the returns on their investments through the appointment of directors, propositions at shareholder meetings, and resolution of contractual failures in the courts. But that is against the background of the problems that the business is there to solve and avoid creating.

If the objective of the firm is to seek to solve problems in as profitable a fashion as possible while not profiting from producing problems, then the role of investors is to assess the potential of the company to succeed in that objective, the likely financial returns from doing so, and ways in which the likelihood of success can be enhanced and risks of profiting from problems can be diminished. Investors' assessments of performance are therefore not just about the size of the profits but their veracity in deriving from problem-solving not problem creation.

In this context, the role of investors is not only as an important source of funding but also as an assurance of the delivery of the firm's objective, the efficiency and profitability with which it is delivered, and the appropriateness of the financial returns that are being earned. They are therefore there to ensure responsibility and sustainability of businesses in avoiding profiting at the expense of others as well as impact in delivering as effective and profitable solutions to problems as possible. Far from operating contrary to the objectives of problem-solving businesses, they are valuable and vital components of firms achieving them.

The problem-solving element of the objective of a company is an anchor around which corporate leaders and investors perform consistent and complementary roles in assisting in the delivery of it. Far from a divergence of interests between investor and firm, there is a strong reinforcing relation between them. Without that anchor then the conflicts which repeatedly surface reflect the pursuit of profits without any clear determination of whether they are being earned on the back of problem-solving or problem creation.

Recognizing the problem-solving not problem-creating aspect of business enhances the ability of finance to provide the means to solve local, national, and international problems, de-risk businesses, and earn greater returns for investors. In assessing existing activities and the financing of new investments, investor engagement is focused on profitable problem-solving without problem creation.

All of finance and the stewardship of existing investments are then devoted to identifying solutions to problems and ensuring that they are delivered as profitably as possible. It means that equity is offered to companies to share the financial risks of existing solutions and to projects to fund profitable new solutions.

That is exactly what finance should be doing. It should be associated with enhancing the wellbeing of those affected by its investments. That makes risk sharing a natural function of financing and the provision of equity a more appropriate form of funding. By aligning the interests of customers, employees, suppliers, and communities with those of investors then equity risk sharing becomes a productive basis of relations between stakeholders and firms.

This chapter will illustrate that in the context of four types of problems—providing employment to some of the poorest people in the world, financing the growth of small and medium-sized enterprises in local communities in some of the most depressed regions of countries, building partnerships in large corporations to address major manufacturing and technological challenges, and aligning the ownership of firms with the delivery of their objectives.

Equity in Poverty

The slums of Nairobi might appear an unlikely setting for an experiment in using equity finance to fund investment in self-employed people at the bottom of the economic pyramid in Kenya. But that is exactly what it has been. For several years, Mars Inc. has been running a programme entitled Maua through its Wrigley subsidiary in Nairobi. This employs an approach that Mars describes as the Economics of Mutuality to promote investment in human, social, and natural capital as well as financial and material capital for the benefit of both the company and its stakeholders.

Maua is what is termed a 'route-to-market' programme that uses micro-distributors, self-employed individuals, to shift Wrigley products from small wholesale outlets, known as stock points, to customers in Kibera. Most micro-distributors travel on foot often carrying heavy bags of products in considerable heat over significant distances. It was clear that the lives and productivity of the micro-distributors could be considerably improved through the provision of bicycles. However, bicycles are expensive to purchase, costing around $100 and therefore need financing.

To the extent that finance is available for the poorest individuals in developing economies, it typically takes the form of loans from microfinance institutions. That indebtedness can impose significant repayment burdens and risk on the borrowers. It is generally used to fund essential consumption rather than more discretionary investments in productive activities which are discouraged by the risks associated with the debt.

Together with several other researchers, I was involved in what is termed a Randomized Controlled Trial (RCT) of the Maua programme—a study in which people are randomly allocated to a group, as in a clinical trial, where in this case the groups were associated with different types of financing.[2] We were interested in establishing whether alternative forms of funding could be provided that shared risk between the providers and users of finance along the lines of what is typically observed in equity rather than debt contracts. What made this possible was the participation of a large international company that could collect reliable data on the sales and profit margins of participating distributors and thereby determine the repayments due on alternative forms of finance provided to fund the bikes.

We looked at a variety of different types of repayment schedules associated with funding the bikes varying between standard debt contracts and performance related equity arrangements with a mixed 'hybrid' form in between. What emerged was striking. First, the risk sharing equity arrangements did not discourage micro-distributors from taking up the bikes and indeed encouraged them to focus on selling more Wrigley as against other products in their baskets, even though they had to share some of the profits on their sales.

Second, the profit earned by distributors on the risk sharing arrangements was greater than on the debt contract because of the larger proportion of Wrigley products sold, the greater effort they exerted in using their bikes, and the bigger risks they were willing to take with the provision of risk-sharing finance. Third, the higher profits earned increased the wellbeing of the micro-distributors in terms of their consumption and health.

This brings out several points: first, the merit of risk-sharing equity as against traditional micro-debt finance in low-income countries; second, the importance of encouraging finance for investment in productive activities as against immediate consumption; and third the role that corporations can play in the provision of reliable information on the performance of those using risk-sharing forms of finance. As technology makes collection of reliable information on the earnings of users of finance more feasible in the future, then the potential to offer risk-sharing finance as against fixed debt obligations will expand considerably.

But this depends on an alignment of interest between the company in making a profit and in seeking to address the low-income problems of the users of finance. If it exploited its access to information to the drawback of the micro-distributors, then there would not be a take-up of finance or a willingness to accept anything other than the fixed debt contracts. That is precisely the problem that afflicts most people in low-income countries—they cannot rely on large powerful organizations to do anything other than seek to exploit their dependency and vulnerability for the company's own advantage. They are therefore restricted to funding arrangements that are ill-suited to their needs and the provision of what is available falls well short of what is required.

But this is not a problem that only afflicts developing economies or only micro-enterprises. It is also found in many of the poorest and most deprived areas of the richest countries in the world and in newly formed start-up companies and small and medium sized enterprises everywhere. Equity finance is not the only source of financing equity; so too is the right type of debt.

Banking on Left-Behind Places

While obviously not equivalent to deprivation in Kibera, developed economies have some very depressed regions.[3] They are generally the result of an economic or political shock or the exodus of big corporations to more prosperous or lower-cost locations. What is surprising about these places is that the traditional economic stabilizers of lower costs of employment, cheaper land, and vacated buildings often do not revive their fortunes. If anything, failure breeds failure—the exodus of the best leaves the rest behind. The most mobile depart, the least employable remain, and new businesses fail to emerge to replace the bankrupt old ones.

Key to this is finance. By far and away the most important source of finance for the emergence and growth of small and medium-sized enterprises (SMEs) is bank finance. The relationship of companies with their banks is critical to their ability to fund their growth and development. I referred earlier to the Swedish bank, Handelsbanken, as an example of a financial institution that, through its devolved organizational structure, has placed a great deal of trust and authority in the hands of its branch managers. These managers in turn have been able to build close relationships of trust with their customers and in particular their corporate borrowers.

As the case of Handelsbanken illustrated, key to successful relationship lending is the trust that banks can place in loan officers and the degree to which decision-taking is devolved to their branches. Companies that suffer interruptions to relationships with their loan officers are less likely to be able to renegotiate loans when they need to, are more likely to experience worse renegotiated terms, and end up seeking alternative sources of finance.[4]

What distinguishes relationship from transactional banking is that, in the former, banks profit from growing their business with their corporate customers, whereas in the latter it comes from margins earned on product sales and transactions. The former aligns the financial interests of banks with their customers and avoids the conflicts that otherwise arise in the latter when fees are earned at the expense of customers.

In banking relationships, banks profit from solving problems of businesses, helping them to thrive over the long term and sharing risks of fluctuations in their performance. Direct interactions between banks and firms allow the banks not only to process data but also to look their borrowers in the eye and form a judgement and opinion on their and their businesses' trustworthiness and reliability.

This, sometimes termed soft or 'tacit' knowledge to contrast it with the hard, 'generic' form that comes from readily available data, includes not only assessments of people but also places and puts the firm and its employees in the context of local conditions in which the firm is operating. The needs and opportunities of firms in the Mid-West of the US are quite different from similar ones on the East and West coasts. Lenders must be in place and have a deep understanding and appreciation of the history, aspirations, and challenges of the communities in the localities in which they are operating.

In the nineteenth century, banking was highly geographically dispersed, and local industrialists, philanthropists, and banks played a key role in the building of modern cities across the UK, mainland Europe, Australasia, and North America.[5] However, throughout the twentieth century, but especially during the last four decades, there has been a widespread movement towards the centralization of banking and a progressive decline in relationship banking.[6]

Many banks adopted a form of financial engineering, commonly known as 'fintech', in which large data sets and powerful computer algorithms were used to make lending decisions. This increased the efficiency of collecting and processing hard, codified information, but it came at the expense of soft, tacit information. The public availability of hard information led to the clustering of banks in well-served locations, for example in London and the South-East of England, while other, often smaller locations, in the rest of the country experienced declines in access to finance as financial institutions exited.[7]

The physical distance between a small firm and a large bank limits the 'soft' information available to a bank in assessing the credit worthiness of a borrower and reduces the likelihood of credit being provided where needed.[8] This is especially damaging for small and medium-sized enterprises (SMEs), particularly those in more distant locations.[9] This in turn exacerbates the decline of left-behind places as bank branch closures lead to persistent falls in local small business lending, particularly during recessions.[10]

Germany is often held up as an example of a relationship banking economy. 'Sparkassen' are savings banks, small to medium in size, which are legally focused on providing services to designated municipalities and counties. As decentralized banks, their focus is on supporting the development of regional economies typically through close relationships with the local businesses to which they lend. Roughly 99% of all German businesses are SMEs which typically do not have access to capital markets.[11] The Sparkassen meet their funding needs by acting as their 'Hausbank' (house bank) for their respective municipalities. They reduce the financial constraints on SMEs and play a critical role in making credit decisions for struggling SMEs where soft information is particularly important.[12]

Financial re-regulation and consolidation in the aftermath of the 2008 crisis increased concentration in both the British and German national banking systems but the outcomes were very different in countries. It led to much greater organizational and spatial concentration in the UK, with only London gaining, whereas Germany did not experience anything equivalent.[13] As a result, bank lending to manufacturing SMEs in the British regions was adversely affected by the increasing distance between the banks and their customers.[14] In contrast, in Germany, 40% of credit extended to SMEs came from the local and regional savings and cooperative banks.[15]

It is not only German banking that is more local and relationship than British, so too is banking in the US, where banks are regulated at the national and the state level. There are approximately 5,000 community banks in the US which specialize in banking for local SMEs and family businesses and these banks account for some 40% of small loans to business.[16] The Federal Deposit Insurance Corporation (FDIC) plays an important role in supporting community and locally based banks in the US by providing insurance, regulatory, and receivership services. As a consequence, community banking has had a positive impact on regional development, in particular employment growth in small businesses in the US and it strengthened regional resilience to declines in employment growth and new business formation during the 2007 to 2009 fiscal crisis and recession.[17]

Entrepreneurship and Equity

Important though bank finance is for SMEs, it is not sufficient. They need equity as well as debt. Much of this initially comes from the founders' own savings or from family and friends. However, higher-risk entrepreneurial businesses also need external equity finance. This is often provided by business angels—current or former businesspeople and founders who have a modest amount of funding that they are seeking to invest in businesses which inspire them.

Business angels play a vital role not only in funding start-ups but also mentoring and connecting them with people who can assist and advise them. It is therefore a very hands-on task, initially in screening and evaluating potential investments and then monitoring and advising on their progress. As in the case of relationship banking, proximity is important and business angels are in general local to the companies in which they invest.

That is where left-behind places are frequently at a disadvantage—the decline leads to an exodus of those who might be able to assist new firms to start-up. The UK illustrates this very clearly. Business angels are heavily concentrated in London and the South-East with between 50 and 60% of the total population being located there. That means that many other parts of the country are largely devoid of business angel communities. The consequence is that many would-be start-ups elsewhere are not only deprived of equity to get going but also do not receive the advice and support that comes from the mentoring and networking required to grow a business.

But the problem does not end there. After the first round of finance, later stages involve the participation of more formal institutions, in particular venture capital and private equity firms in the provision of equity finance. They are the essential link between institutional investors in capital markets, in for example the City of London, and the entrepreneurs developing and growing their businesses in the regions. The provision of equity finance requires engaged, informed investors, intermediating between the large diversified institutional investors in major international financial centres and small growing businesses across the country.

Like business angels, venture capital firms are a vital source of advice and information as well as finance on how businesses should grow. But in Britain they too are heavily concentrated in London and the South-East, with some two-thirds of venture capital firms based there, leaving many parts of the rest of the country without the development capital needed to scale-up their businesses. Furthermore, much private equity in Britain (between 70% and 80%) is focused not on funding new and growing businesses through venture capital but on restructuring existing firms, in particular the buyout of companies listed on stock markets by their management. So, the prospects of raising equity finance for entrepreneurs looking to start and grow their businesses beyond the immediate vicinity of the City of London are bleak.

It is often suggested that the reason why much of Britain, despite having one of the largest and most active international financial markets in the world, has so little in the way of long-term bank finance or start-up or scale-up equity finance is that there isn't the demand for it. It is claimed that there are simply not the companies with viable proposals and business propositions coming forward to justify the provision of finance. In other words, it is argued to be a demand rather than a supply of finance problem and, instead of helping to fund the growth and investment of domestic firms, the City of London turns its back on most of Britain and focuses on financial trading in the rest of the world.

This is implausible as Britain is not only home to one of the world's finest financial markets, but it also has one of the largest numbers of top-ranked universities (per head of population) in the world spread all over the country, many of which are desperate to capitalize on their academic prowess by commercializing their activities and spinning-out new start-up companies. In any event, this a misconceived, age-old debate about whether finance is an independent determinant of the growth and flourishing of firms or just the 'handmaiden' of business responding to needs for it where they exist.[18]

The notion of business as being there to solve problems reveals the fallacy of this distinction. The need to fund businesses across the country arises from the commercial challenges and opportunities that exist all over the UK. Solving those problems requires not just finance and ideas but a knowledge and understanding of how to commercialize those ideas. The expertise and experience that relationship banks, business angels, and venture capital bring are a vital source of information and learning as well as funding for business.

The reason why there do not appear to be sufficient viable opportunities to warrant funding is because there are not enough funders to advise prospective businesses on how to put together compelling business cases that justify the funding. In other words, there are not the people, be they relationship bank managers, business angels, or venture capitalists, between the rich investors sitting at their desks in the City of London and the entrepreneurs and founders hungry to learn how to build their businesses and present credible propositions for getting them funded. From the skyscrapers in London, much of Britain looks like a commercial wasteland, and from the rest of Britain, the City of London might just as well be in New York. And both are right because they are not talking to each other and there are too few people with an interest in connecting them.

One of the finest financial markets in the world is not doing the job that a financial sector should be performing or rather it is only doing half the job. It is doing a fine job of serving half of its relevant constituents, namely its savers—depositors in banks, and investors in asset managers, mutual funds, and life insurance companies. They are well provided for by banks and asset managers that are now regulated up to the rafters with requirements to protect their depositors and investors against risks of failure, and asset management firms that allow their investors to extinguish most of the risk of their equity holdings by diversifying their shares across international portfolios at almost no cost.

The price of this post-financial crisis failure proof financial sector is that it serves almost no useful purpose for much of the UK domestic corporate sector, at least the entrepreneurial and small and medium-sized enterprise (SME) component outside of London and the South-East. It creates riskless bank deposits by investing almost exclusively in working capital that can be withdrawn at will and its equity capital flows largely to the rest of the world in preference to the backwaters of Britain.

What is at fault is a failure of the British financial sector to recognize that it takes three to agree—an investor, an entrepreneur, and an interpreter. The interpreters are the relationship loan officers, the business angels, and the venture capitalists sitting alongside the entrepreneurs translating the local dialect and scientific jargon into financial terms familiar to international investors. Translation is the problem that a domestic financial sector is there to solve profitably and which the British financial sector is lamentably failing to do, certainly by the standards of Silicon Valley and the US venture capital industry.

The result is that from the point of view of investors there are no commercial propositions worth supporting in the regions of Britain, and from the point of view of entrepreneurs there is no funding available to start or scale-up their businesses. Both are right. Both should and could be wrong but regrettably are not because the financial sector has not recognized the problem it is there to solve. But this is a problem that afflicts not just micro-enterprises in developing countries or entrepreneurs and SMEs in developed countries but the largest companies around the world.

Equity Stewards

Stock markets do not on average finance listed companies. This is a feature of stock markets around the world that I first documented in a paper in 1986 called 'New Issues in Corporate Finance'[19] and it has been true ever since. Stock markets take out more from companies through stock repurchases and takeovers than they put in through new equity issues. Nevertheless, they exercise a dominant influence on listed firms.

The reason is that shares confer voting rights that can be exercised at shareholder meetings as well as cash flow rights to dividends and stock repurchases. The voting rights give shareholders a say in the appointment and removal of directors and in some cases on the remuneration of directors. In addition, they can vote on resolutions put up at shareholder meetings and in some countries have rights of approval over large transactions involving, for example, acquisitions of other companies and investment in major projects.

While companies do not in general depend on their shareholders for new equity funding, there are circumstances where they do, when they are purchasing other companies in takeovers and during periods such as the COVID pandemic when companies had serious cash flow problems. But even if they do not look to their shareholders for funding, they depend on them for their support in exercising their approval rights over the appointment of members of the board.

The voice of shareholders therefore counts, but their voice is frequently not heard. There is of course an army of investment analysts who pour over corporate reports, quiz companies about their activities, provide forecasts about their future earnings potential, and make recommendations to buy and sell their shares.

What drives asset managers and analysts is what concerns their investors, namely the financial risks and returns on their investments. As equity is increasingly held in the form of index funds that invest in global portfolios of shares linked to stock market indices, then shareholders become progressively less interested in the performance of individual companies and more concerned about the global risks associated with environmental, social, political, and regulatory factors that affect all shares in their portfolios.

In response, analysts are increasingly focusing their attention on companies' CO_2 emissions and pollution, their exposure to flooding, water, and mineral scarcity, the gender balance of their boards, the ethnic diversity of their workforce, the treatment of their supply chains, income differentials within firms, and all the other topics that risk becoming the next source of social media, political, and regulatory attention around the world. That in turn is encouraging boards of companies to pay growing attention to these topics— environmental, social, and governance (ESG) factors, as described in the last chapter.

At no point is there interest in interrogating companies about why they exist. Statements of purpose by companies are regarded as marketing and promotion tools designed to make companies look good. Institutional investors do not see them as relevant to the underlying activities of firms or the drivers of their financial performance—and with considerable justification, because they are not. In general, they have little or nothing to do with the problems that firms are there to solve and the profitability associated with solving those problems.

As with microfinance institutions in developing countries, transactional banking in developed countries, equity funding of start-ups and SMEs, the focus of financial systems and institutions is on investors, not the companies in which they invest or the lives that they affect. It is not surprising that stock markets do not invest, but instead extract financing from listed companies. They are rent extraction devices.

The financial sector is, with a few exceptions, blind to the interest of the world it affects. It does not see its role as being to help companies get people out of poverty, regenerate left-behind places, address global environmental problems, protect nature, or create a more equal and fairer society, except in so far as these benefit investors. That is for government to sort out and any suggestion that investors should finance or support business to do more than promote their own wellbeing is dangerous and misconceived socialism.

Why should investors be concerned about whether their companies solve problems if this is neither necessary nor sufficient for making money? It is not necessary for making money if money can be made from causing problems, and it is not sufficient if commercial ways cannot be found of solving problems profitably. Problem-solving is then irrelevant to investors. However much one protests or regulates, investors will continue to condone companies that profit at the expense of others.

ESG, non-financial reporting, sustainable finance will all remain side shows so long as the fundamental determinant of profit is not problem-solving rather than problem creation. It is only if profit cannot be made from causing problems but can be made from solving them that investors will take an interest in whether companies are doing the latter and avoiding the former.

And that is exactly what the legal and regulatory system should be expecting of institutional investors. As holders of not just shares in companies but also as companies themselves with voting rights over the appointment of directors of firms in which they invest, it is financial institutions that should have a fiduciary duty to establish whether their corporate investments are profiting from solving problems and avoiding profiting from causing problems. They are the natural stewards of their company purposes in ensuring that companies deliver on solving problems and making a profit from so doing.

Stewardship involves establishing that companies deliver on their purposes of solving problems; creating financial value from so doing; and not profiting from producing problems. Financial institutions ensure that companies have the risk-bearing equity finance they need to deliver their value creating solutions, and the equity provisions to ensure that they can correct problems when they occur.

This is particularly important in high-tech industries where companies sometimes deliver blockbuster benefits for society and investors; generally, generate much more modest gains or losses for both; and occasionally create disasters that can only be corrected at immense expense. Financial institutions should promote the first and avoid the last outcome through encouraging companies to be both ambitious and prudent by providing the risk-bearing equity funding and reserves they need to do that.

But at present they are not. We have built a business and financial system that is entirely deferential. Employees look up to middle management, middle management to the executive, the executive to the board, the board to their asset managers, asset managers to their asset owners, and asset owners to their investors to ensure that the interests of investors are respected. No one looks down and takes an interest in those below—investors in their asset managers, asset managers in the boards of companies, the board in middle management, middle management in employees on the shop floor, or employees in their customers and communities.

We have forgotten that intermediation is a two-way process by which it is the role of the intermediary to look both ways at those below as well as above and promote the interests of those above by prioritizing the interests of those below. It is only when the law establishes that corporate profitability comes solely from the delivery of solutions to, not creation of, problems throughout the investment chain that shareholders will have an interest in ensuring this happens and look to their financial intermediaries to do that.

Managing Ownership

The main consequence of this is that there is a lack of ambition—a lack of ambition on the part of finance to exploit its potential to transform the world in which we live. It is passive, sitting back on the laurels of financial wealth sometimes accumulated to the detriment as well as benefit of others. The problem is seen as arising from 'short-termism' and 'risk aversion'—a failure to provide the long-term, 'patient' capital that business needs to fund its capital expenditure and R&D, and an aversion to the risk of losses in doing so.

But that is the wrong diagnosis. Of course, investors are focused on short-term share price movements and their ability to exit when they have nothing else to go on and can profit at the expense of others. That is why they invest via financial intermediaries. But they should be doing so with a view to achieving something very different, namely ensuring that companies in which they are invested are fulfilling the role they are there to perform, their purpose.

Financial intermediation is not, as it is often characterized, just the transformation of short-term, risk-averse, liquid shareholdings of individual investors into long-term, risky, illiquid investments in companies. It is also about converting ambition into achievement— realizing the aspirations of the impoverished in the slums of Kibera, the precarious family businesses in blighted regions of a country, the inexperienced entrepreneurs in universities, and the most innovative multinational corporations. It is the role of intermediaries to help them to prosper from solving the world's greatest challenges.

While all investors should be involved in stewarding companies to the profitable delivery of solutions without problems, it is those with the greatest degree of exposure and control of companies—the holders of large blocks of shares—who have the greatest incentive to do this. They are the owners, as described in Chapter 5, of the problem-solving company purpose. They should be the shareholders who have an appreciation and understanding of how to deliver it.

Currently companies listed on stock markets in the UK and US for the most part take the structure of their ownership as given to them by purchases and sales of shares on the stock market. Their highly dispersed ownership and absence of owners of substantial blocks of shares subject them to substantial changes in ownership when they are targets of takeover bids by other firms or 'activist campaigns' by other shareholders. The risk of sudden and large changes in ownership makes it difficult for companies to ensure continuity and consistency in their problem-solving purpose.

As described in Chapter 5, the way in which many listed companies outside of the UK and US avoid this is by having owners of blocks of shares—family owners or foundations—at the same time as the remainder of their shares are actively traded on stock markets. This dual or parallel system of shareholding—ownership in the hands of stable holders of blocks of shares and investment by diversified shareholders with liquid frequently traded shares—provides consistency and stability to the problem-solving nature of a business at the same time as it gives it access to pools of financial capital in liquid stock markets around the world.

There is one country in the world which has neither the dispersed shareholdings of the UK and US nor the family control of Continental Europe and much of the Far East. In Japan, the stable shareholdings are in the hands of other companies—intercorporate holdings in which one company holds controlling blocks of shares in another. Those corporate investors purchase blocks of shares in other firms as strategic investments that they manage to the benefit of both firms.

What is particularly interesting about this method of creating stable blocks of shares is that management manages the process itself. They repurchase blocks of shares traded in the market or owned by existing holders of blocks, store them in the company's treasury stock while they look for suitable purchasers, and then sell them as blocks in private transactions. This is an 'internal market for corporate control' in the sense that it is a market in controlling blocks of shares managed by the management of the company in question.

Evidence from Japan reveals that the stock market in general reacts favourably to these transactions when the purchasers of the blocks are other companies seeking to make strategic investments in the firm in question.[20] They are not therefore used by management simply as a way of insulating themselves from external stock market pressures but instead as a means of engaging other companies in the delivery of their corporate objectives and strategy. Both the companies and their outside shareholders benefit from the stable ownership and engagement of the strategic corporate investors.

Japan therefore provides an interesting lesson in how companies do not have to be at the mercy of liquid stock markets and short-term shareholder trading, and how they can create and manage the stable shareholding blocks they require to deliver on their problem-solving purposes. Whether this managerial discretion has been used to best effect for Japan by creating a system of internal intercorporate ownership is questionable. It might have been better deployed in advancing an enlightened form of external block holding, such as the Danish enterprise foundations. Nevertheless, it demonstrates how companies can themselves create stable, supportive problem-solving ownership.

Summary

From the slums of Nairobi to the relationship banks of Germany, from the absence of angel investors and venture capitalists in the depressed regions of Britain to the management of corporate ownership in Japan, we have seen the significance of the financial sector and the provision of equity for promoting problem-solving business.

One policy implication of this is that we should eliminate current tax incentives for companies to employ debt in preference to equity. This incentive comes from the deductibility of interest payments but not costs of servicing equity in computing corporate tax liabilities in virtually every corporate tax system around the world. Taxation should not be distinguishing between different types of finance in this way. It should be neutral or, if anything, encourage the use of risk-bearing equity rather than low risk debt finance.

We have noted the failure of financial institutions to recognize their purposes in solving problems of poverty in Kenya, investing in start-up and growth businesses in depressed regions in Britain, stewarding problem-solving large-listed companies globally and insulating businesses from the vagaries of liquid shareholdings. We have argued that this reflects a serious imbalance between financial intermediaries' interests in their investors and their corporate investments.

What this chapter brings out is how a problem-solving view of business provides fundamental insights into the deficiencies of financial systems and their failure to protect public interests beyond the financial returns of their investors. By predominantly focusing on investors, they ignore the potential for business to promote the wellbeing of citizens at large. Instead, by harnessing finance to address the needs of others as well as investors, capital markets create profitable solutions for the benefit of all.

In the next chapter we go one step further beyond business and finance to establish how problem-solving institutions in the public as well as the private sector can correct the exceptionally poor performance in what until comparatively recently has been one of the most economically powerful and successful nations in the world.

10

Our Common Purpose

Oh, England is a pleasant place for them that's rich and high;
But England is a cruel place for such poor folks as I…
And now I 'm old and going I'm sure I can't tell where;
One comfort is this world's so hard I can't be worse off there.

Charles Kingsley (1858), *The Last Buccaneer*,
first published in *Andromeda and Other Poems*

Powerful though joined up businesses and institutional investors can be, they are not sufficient on their own to solve the world's greatest problems. They cannot do it without government, and governments cannot do it without businesses and institutional investors. What does this much asserted proposition mean in practice?

It was stated previously that the moral law implies that the boundaries of the firm extend beyond its formal ownership and contractual arrangements to include the negative externalities it creates. But its boundaries are constrained to the positive solutions businesses can deliver profitably. The law and regulation can prevent profitable production of problems, but they cannot produce unprofitable solutions. Public policy is required to make unprofitable solutions profitable.

A firm must be supported by the public sector in operating beyond its commercially viable boundaries. The government must deploy its powers of taxation to subsidize unprofitable problem-solving, and of borrowing and monetary creation to co-invest with the private sector in funding it. One of the most valuable investments that the public sector can make is in its business sector.

The force of this is demonstrated by the economic miracles of the Asian tigers, all of which have harnessed the power of cooperation and co-investment between government and business to co-create and co-generate remarkable economic growth.[1] In contrast, the failure of Africa to demonstrate similar economic performance reflects the absence of a thriving indigenous business sector.

The reason why partnerships do not happen as much as they could or should is that they only occur where business and government objectives are aligned. That is not the case if business sees its purpose as being simply to make money, or if government is corrupt or divisive. It is if business recognizes its purpose as being to make money from solving not causing problems, and government to forge common purpose around shared prosperity.

That transforms conflict into cooperation and aligns business and government objectives with society at large. In the process, it corrects the failure of macroeconomic austerity to invest in the human capability and physical capacity required to address inequality in opportunity and income.

The Disunited Kingdom

I am going to illustrate this in relation to the macroeconomic performance of one country—the UK.[2] I use this as an example not only because I am obviously particularly familiar with it but because it is in many respects the most powerful illustration of the policy implications that I want to emphasize. The reason for this is the UK has the feature of being a country with a long history of modern democracy, where the Industrial Revolution started, a country with one of the largest and most successful financial systems in the world, one of the most admired legal systems and forms of investor protection, and one of the best university systems in the world. It was one of the first countries to promote privatization and a carefully structured regulatory system, it has an independent monetary policy committee, and numerous independent organizations evaluating its macro and microeconomic policies.

At the same time the UK has one of the worst economic records of any major economy in the world over the past 15 years. It was one of the main causes and victims of the financial crisis of 2008, it experienced the largest drop in Gross Domestic Product (GDP) during the COVID pandemic since 1709, and was the only G7 country to have failed to recover pre-pandemic levels of GDP three years later by the last quarter of 2022.[3] How so?

The Productivity Puzzle

The UK has experienced an exceptionally bad period of labour productivity since the financial crisis of 2008. Since then, it has endured the largest fall in productivity and productivity growth below their long-run trend since 1760. Its decline in productivity growth been particularly pronounced in comparison with other leading economies such as France, Germany, Japan, and the US.

To the extent that there has been productivity growth in the UK, it has been heavily concentrated in its highest productivity firms. Other companies have lagged appreciably behind, with the bottom 90% of firms in Britain accounting for the absence of productivity growth since the financial crisis. The more productive firms tend to be larger, older, and foreign-owned companies and the least productive are smaller, younger, and domestically owned.

The top and bottom industries by productivity have changed little over time. The most productive are capital-intensive production sectors and the least productive are labour-intensive service industries. That is important to bear in mind when I discuss shortly the performance of the UK in relation to capital expenditure and investment.

What this consistency in performance of different types of companies demonstrates is that productivity gains have failed to diffuse across the economy from leading companies to laggards, i.e., from larger to smaller, from older to younger, from foreign to domestic firms, and from high-productivity to lower-productivity sectors, resulting in a large segment of the UK economy being locked into a syndrome of low productivity and low growth in productivity.

It is as if the knowledge and capability of high productivity firms has failed to permeate elsewhere in the economy. One significant reason for this is another aspect of diffusion that has failed to materialize and that is geographical diffusion. Spatial differences in the UK have been even more pronounced and entrenched.

Regional Inequality

Tables of regional productivity reveal that London has one of the highest levels of productivity of any region in the European Union. But in marked contrast, except for the rest of South-East England, other regions in the UK come near the bottom. As a result, the UK has one of the highest levels of national divergence in labour productivity across the country of any major industrialized nation in the world.[4]

This divergence has occurred over the last 50 years. During the first half of the twentieth century, there was a convergence in productivity across the country resulting in lower levels of disparity between 1950 and 1970 than earlier in the twentieth century. However, thereafter substantial divergences emerged rapidly and by the end of the century they had returned to levels observed near the beginning of the century.

As a result of its higher level of labour productivity, London is one of the regions in Europe with the highest net disposable household income per head. But while earnings per head are lower elsewhere, differences in net disposable income are much less pronounced. So, for example, other parts of the UK, such as the South-West and Scotland, are also better off in terms of disposable income than the average levels of some countries, such as Finland, Italy, and the Netherlands.

The reason for this is that differences in income are also associated with differences in the cost of living between London and the rest of the UK. It is much more expensive to live in London than elsewhere and the primary reason for that is the much greater cost of housing in London. Once account is taken of housing costs, then London moves from being near or at the top of UK regions' household income to being at the median. But the influence of housing costs reveals a second form of even greater inequality in the UK and that is in wealth.

There is a substantial disparity in household wealth between London and the South-East of England, and the rest of Great Britain, with property prices accounting for the much higher level of wealth there than elsewhere. Those variations in property values have significant effects on two major causes of the UK's problems.

The first is the low level of labour mobility in the country, with people living in regions with low property prices being unable to afford to move to the expensive South-East of Britain. The second is that businesses in the rest of the country do not have the property values to offer as collateral when seeking to borrow money from banks. These two features of low mobility and low business borrowing capacity have contributed to the divided kingdom syndrome of the UK.[5]

The question that this productivity record raises is what accounts for the substantial variation in productivity across companies, sectors, and regions and the failure of productivity improvements to diffuse across companies, sectors, and places. The first contributory factor is the UK's dire record on investment—fixed capital formation.

Fixed Capital Formation

Investment has been a consistently lower percentage of Gross Domestic Product (GDP) in the UK than in any other G7 country over the period 2005–17. Even more strikingly, it has been a lower percentage of GDP over the 20-year period 1997–2017 than in any other OECD country and more than 15% below the next lowest OECD country.

While some of this low level of capital expenditure can be attributed to low government expenditure on capital formation in the UK relative to other G7 countries, it is not the lowest in Europe and it is not the main cause of the poor national record. It is non-government expenditure by the private sector, business, on capital formation that has been the main culprit and the lowest of any G7 country.

It is sometimes suggested that an explanation for this is that the UK is a modern, post-industrial country, not as focused on capital intensive manufacturing as it is on the new economy of services, high tech, and research and development (R&D). Plausible though this sounds, it is not convincing. The first indicator that it is not an adequate explanation is the relatively low levels of investment in the 'new' sectors of information and communications technology and intellectual property products in the UK since the financial crisis.

More significantly, R&D intensity relative to GDP in the UK has been only at about the average of the EU in the private sector and well below average in the public sector. Furthermore, approximately half of UK business R&D is performed not by UK-owned businesses but by non-UK owned businesses operating in the UK.

So, the UK does not actually stand out as an R&D intensive economy. The one aspect of R&D where the UK does stand out is in relation to its spatial disparity and geographical concentration in London, the South and East of England, with much lower levels of R&D elsewhere in the country.

In summary, the UK is a country with exceptionally low private-sector capital investment and only average private-sector R&D concentrated in London and the South-East. Low investment lies at the heart of the UK's poor productivity record and its wide regional variation. The question this raises is, what has contributed to such a poor record of the UK in capital expenditure and only a mediocre performance in R&D? Finance is probably one of the culprits but for reasons that it is important for all countries to understand.

Finance

The financial sector is one of the great success stories of the UK. After deregulation of the financial sector in the UK in the 1980s (known as Big Bang), London took off as a global financial centre with an influx of financial institutions from around the world. It boomed as the City of London expanded in all directions, not least upwards. At least it did until 2008 when it ground to a halt with the onset of the financial crisis. The crisis revealed that the boom was built on a financially engineered pack of cards with stark deficiencies and outright scandals emerging from its collapse.

There is a still more serious and deep-rooted deficiency that has prevailed not just since Big Bang but for the best part of a century and which lies at the heart of the failure of the UK financial system, and that is its regional concentration in London and the South-East, described in the previous chapter. It is a problem not simply of the concentration of financial institutions in the City of London, but more significantly of their lack of connectedness with the rest of the country and especially with small and medium-sized enterprises (SMEs) in the regions.

As the previous chapter described, business angels, private equity, venture capital, and equity deals are all concentrated in London and the South-East, with two-thirds of venture capital financing occurring there. But the problem is not just limited to the funding of business. It is also a problem of ownership and governance of UK firms more generally.

Ownership and Governance

As described in Chapter 5, the UK is an outlier in terms of the ownership of its large companies listed on its stock market. The UK's form of ownership is often described as being Anglo-American to contrast it with that in the rest of the world, especially with Continental Europe and the Far East. The Anglo-American system is characterized by large stock markets comprising companies with widely dispersed, predominantly institutional shareholders.

Across the world around 50% of the ownership of companies listed on stock markets is in the hands of families. Family ownership is the most important form of ownership of even the largest listed companies in most countries around the world. But one country that stands out as having an exceptionally low proportion of family-controlled firms is the UK.

The level of dispersion of ownership and control of listed companies in the UK is unusually high and its effects are more pronounced even than in the US. There are several reasons for this, particularly regulatory. The first is that the UK places more emphasis on minority investor protection than other countries, including the US. Until recently, the UK had rules prohibiting the use of dual-class shares by premium-listed companies on the London Stock Exchange, which holders of large blocks of shares in many other countries, including the US, routinely use to retain control.[6]

The UK has mandatory bid rules in takeovers, which do not exist in the US, which limit the ability of shareholders to acquire blocks of shares in companies without bidding for all their shares. Holders of blocks of shares are at risk of being classified as 'insiders' unable to trade their shares if they are party to privileged information, acting in concert if they engage collectively with other shareholders and in violation of related party transactions if they do not fulfil conditions on 'arms-length' transactions in their dealings with companies. Regulation to protect the 'small' vulnerable shareholder is exceptionally strong in the UK.

Secondly, and still more significantly, UK company boards have less protection against threats of takeovers than in the US. For example, the use of poison pills in the US to defend companies against takeovers by hostile bidders is prohibited in the UK by restrictions on what are termed 'frustrating actions' being deployed by target companies. 'Staggered boards', which delay the replacement of members of the boards of target firms by limiting the proportion who can be removed in any one year, have in the past (though no longer today) been widely employed by US corporations. In contrast, there are stronger rights of shareholders to remove directors in the UK than in the US and one-year limitations on terms of office of directors.

Together, these rules represent a significantly greater discouragement for shareholders to acquire controlling blocks of shares in companies in the UK than the US, to engage actively with companies in which they invest, and to support them in the achievement of long-term value creation. UK companies in turn have fewer means of protecting themselves against markets for corporate control in the form of takeovers and short-term activist investors than in virtually any other country in the world. The result is that UK firms are under unusually intense and continuous pressure to maximize their share prices—and the problem is getting worse.

The disappearance of family ownership started in the early part of the twentieth century as stock markets grew rapidly from the beginning of the century. However, initially, the impact of this on UK companies was limited because, while ownership became more dispersed, it remained in the hands of individual locally based shareholders who invested in stock markets that were established in towns all over the UK. For example, stock exchanges opened 'in Oldham (in 1875), Dundee (1879), Cork (1886), Belfast (1897), Cardiff (1892), Halifax (1896), Greenock (1888), Huddersfield (1899), Bradford (1899), Swansea (1903), Nottingham (1909), and Newport (1916)'.[7]

The fact that shareholders were locally based meant that there was a mutual interest of investors in promoting the flourishing of local companies and of directors in protecting local investors, even in the absence of regulatory rules requiring them to do so. However, in the aftermath of World War II, those locally based individual investors were replaced by institutional investors, predominantly life insurance companies and pension funds, headquartered in London, and individual share ownership declined rapidly. Local stock markets merged, closed, and eventually consolidated in one market in London and the local ties between investors and companies were severed.

This mirrored an equivalent profound shift in funding that had occurred in banking in the nineteenth century. The Industrial Revolution was funded in large part on the back of many local banks situated all over the country. Those banks had strong relations with companies in their locality. However, they were therefore heavily exposed to their local economies and when the economies failed, so too did the local banks.

Consequently, there were repeated banking crises, which prompted the Bank of England to promote the merger of banks and the shifting of their headquarters from the regions to London. The result was that, by the beginning of the twentieth century, local banks had disappeared and were replaced by five main banks headquartered in London.

So, in a period of 150 years, the British financial system shifted completely from a locally based relationship banking and then stock market economy to a highly concentrated banking and institutional investment system headquartered in London. The consequences were twofold. First, there was an inversion of relatively unregulated, long-term relationship finance into highly regulated, short-term transactional funding. The second was that British corporate finance and ownership changed from being highly decentralized and dispersed around the country to being in one place—London.

But things were to get even worse, because initially, at least, the new shareholders of companies were relatively long-term domestic institutional investors—pension funds and life insurance companies—which, by the 1980s, together owned half of British equity. However, from the 1990s their shareholdings declined to a point that today their combined holdings amount to just 6% of British equity. In their place have come global shareholders investing through mutual funds and asset management firms. As a result, even the national base of shareholding has been eroded and relatively long-term institutions have been replaced by short-term asset managers.

One of the consequences of the growing dominance of dispersed, anonymous, international ownership of companies and markets in corporate control has been a substantial decline in companies listed on the UK stock market. The number of listed companies halved from 2,000 at the beginning of the millennium to 1,000 now, having halved from around 4,000 in the 1960s.

This reflects a declining number of firms choosing to come to the stock market so that, by 2015, new listings of companies had fallen to approximately the same level as firms de-listing from the stock market. Companies have voted with their feet by exiting through going private and merging rather than entering through initial public offerings.

In effect, the UK has become paralysed by a financial system of absent owners—investors who are not present currently, physically, or emotionally. It does not have the founders, families, or foundations of the US, Continental Europe, or Denmark. It does not have the regional relationship banking system of Germany. It does not have the local business angels and venture capitalists of the US. It has a financial system that does not support the creation, growth, and global expansion of firms with advice or finance outside the South-East of England.

But even more serious than the effect of this on the financial performance of individual firms has been its macroeconomic impact on the aggregate real performance of the UK economy. Let me then turn to the point of this analysis and its impact on productivity and divergences in productivity across firms, sectors, and regions of the UK, with its damaging consequences for inequality and wealth.

Implications for Productivity and Inequality

Discussions of corporate ownership and governance have taken place largely independently of the real economy. They are perceived to be more relevant to the financial performance of firms and returns to investors than to questions about productivity, economic growth, and inequality. This separation between ownership and governance, on the one hand, and the real economy, on the other, reflects a view that has prevailed for the last 60 years that the sole purpose of business is to generate financial returns for their shareholders.

According to this view, it is not the role of business to engage in larger questions around economic or social performance. They do not have the legitimacy or authority to do that, and they should therefore stick to their knitting of making money. However, there is a growing recognition that while the doctrine might bring clarity and simplicity, it does so in relation to the wrong objective.

The purpose of business is not just to promote the interests of shareholders but to do so by delivering benefits for its customers, employees, societies, and the natural world in which it operates. The problem is not just a distributional one of the prioritizing of shareholders over employees or other stakeholders but of the objective of the firm. By placing the success of the company for the benefit of its shareholders at the heart of its purpose, UK company law has promoted a singular rather than collective and communal objective of firms.

Instead of producing solutions to problems that we face as individuals, societies, and the natural world and doing so in a way that is commercially viable, financially sustainable, and profitable, it is focused on delivering profits for its shareholders. Refocusing corporate purpose from profit to profitable solutions connects businesses and shareholders with their customers, communities, societies, and environment. It emphasizes the collective and communal as well as the competitive, and it promotes markets and competition in 'runs to the top' in solving problems rather than profiting from creating them.

As described in the first chapter, the supposed economic efficiency of the profit centric, shareholder supremacy view rests on a series of propositions around competitive markets and regulatory effectiveness that simply do not hold in practice. Consequently, the notion that a strict separation can and should be drawn between business, on the one hand, and the public sector and macroeconomic performance on the other is naïve and damaging for the promotion of both economic success and social well-being more generally.

The UK has gone further than nearly any other country in embracing the notion of 'shareholder primacy' in its regulatory rules. As a result, the UK financial system is characterized by a system of dispersed, anonymous investors who have little interest in the performance of the individual stocks in which they invest and cannot be held responsible for the actions they take.

As described in the previous chapter, what matters more to diversified shareholders are global systemic risks relating to social, political, and regulatory disturbances. They have little interest in individuals, communities, or the natural world, except in so far as they influence their financial performance and have regulatory, political, or reputational repercussions.

This is not true of dominant holders of blocks of shares who are identifiable and substantially invested in individual stocks. They cannot hide behind a veil of anonymity like holders of index funds. The existence of identifiable, long-term committed shareholders who act as owners, as described in Chapter 5, has a significant effect on the policies that companies adopt and the degree to which they account for benefits beyond short-term financial returns. In essence, the system that has emerged in the UK is at an extreme of rent extraction, which prioritizes returns for shareholders over capital investment and training.

This is of fundamental importance not just in relation to the observation of exceptionally low levels of capital expenditure in the UK but also the demise of a domestically owned UK manufacturing industry from a position of dominance in sectors such as electrical engineering, electronics, and chemical engineering to near extinction in 60 years.[8]

It is reflected in a failure of companies to form partnerships with other organizations in the public and private sectors. The sole preoccupation on financial returns has created a fundamental conflict between the interests of public and private sectors, between utilities and regulators, and between commercial and not-for-profit organizations.

It has given rise to a disappointing performance of public–private partnerships and private finance initiatives because of the divergent interests between public organizations in public welfare and private companies in making money.[9] It has resulted in a failure of large parts of the privatized utilities to fulfil their promise, and repeated conflicts between regulators and regulated companies in response to unacceptable performance of privatized firms.[10]

It is not just the ownership and control of companies that has been the cause of a failure of productivity and inequality across firms and regions. So too has finance. The financial crisis was not—as is often suggested—a global phenomenon. It was essentially a crisis in the UK and US with a few other European countries feeling the repercussions of what happened in those two countries. The consequence for the UK has been particularly devastating because of its dependence on its financial sector and the even greater decoupling it has caused of the City of London from the rest of the country.

One of the main victims of the financial crisis was the commercial banking sector, with the result that the dwindling support that SMEs in the regions received from the banking sector was even further undermined. As a result, SMEs around the country became increasingly dependent on equity sources that were also heavily concentrated in London and the South-East.

Concentration of financial institutions in London has contributed to the extreme levels of regional productivity inequality recorded in this chapter. The demise of UK productivity and its devastating regional effects have their origins in UK exceptionalism in the ownership, control, and financing of its corporate sector.

Summary of the UK Experience

The UK has experienced an exceptionally low level of productivity historically and internationally since the financial crisis of 2008. This has been reflected in a marked variation in productivity across firms by size, age, and sector. There are large regional variations in productivity across the UK with substantial disparities between the South and East, and the rest of the country. These in turn are associated with considerable regional income and wealth inequalities. Alongside its poor productivity performance, the UK has recorded an exceptionally low level of business investment (fixed capital formation) and high regional variation in its R&D.

There are two factors that have contributed to this. The first is the financial system and the funding of SMEs. Having once successfully funded the industrial revolution through a local banking system, the UK now has a highly centralized banking sector that provides predominantly short-term working capital. As a result, SMEs are dependent on equity sources to fund their growth and expansion. However, a large proportion of this goes to firms in the south-east of the UK and there has been a failure to connect pools of capital in London with the regions.

The second factor is the ownership and governance of firms. The UK has an exceptionally dispersed form of ownership of listed companies and an absence of owners of significant blocks of shares. Furthermore, having once had locally based individual shareholders, holdings of shares have moved progressively from domestic relatively long-term institutional investors to global short-term asset management firms. The result has been the demise of long-term domestic, local shareholders.

The consequence has been that the UK has extinguished both locally based banks and local shareholders that had close relations with companies they financed and owned. Instead, finance, ownership, and governance have become highly centralized and disconnected from business. It has become a nation of absent owners—investors who are not present currently, physically, or emotionally.

The result is a high level of regional disparities in financing and governance, and the replacement of long-term relationships between investors and firms with short-term, transactional engagements. Those engagements have become increasingly focused on shareholder returns at the expense of the interests of other parties, with adverse consequences for aggregate productivity and the diffusion of productivity gains between firms and across regions.

What is the solution? How can investment in fixed capital, R&D, people, and places by both the private and public sectors be restored?

Regional Prosperity

There have been repeated attempts at promoting regional economic policies in the UK since the 1960s. They have routinely failed. There is another one currently in process around regeneration of left behind cities and regions in the UK. That too is destined to fail unless there is a greater appreciation of the nature of the underlying problems that must be solved.

I have been involved over the last two years in an analysis of the factors that helped turn around seven city-regions in five countries which suffered severe, adverse economic shocks, but have subsequently been able to re-establish more successful development paths. The cities are Dortmund, Duisburg, and Leipzig in Germany; Bilbao in the Basque Country of Spain; Newcastle New South Wales in Australia; Windsor, Ontario Canada; and Pittsburgh Pennsylvania in the US.[11]

What emerges as common features of these cities successful revival are three things. The first is devolved authority from central government to regional and local authorities. Central government does not and cannot know the precise nature of the problems that specific locations of a country face or the way in which those problems should be addressed. It is the people in those places who have the necessary contextual knowledge and understanding of its history, aspirations, needs, and opportunities.[12]

The second key component is connecting finance in national and international financial centres to local financial institutions and the branches of national banks in the location. Investors in financial markets do not have the knowledge or understanding of what is required to build businesses in localities or provide the advice and mentoring those businesses require. This should be done by local financial institutions working in conjunction with local firms.

The third component is the forging of a common purpose between people, public, and private institutions in the locality. People in failed cities and regions are often locked in backward blaming of each other for past failures. To move forward, they need to be given a credible narrative of opportunity and recovery around which they can unify as a combined community.

That takes inspired and inspiring leadership by public leaders, in particular city and regional mayors, and community, business, and local institutional leaders. The need to forge common purpose is why devolved authority in both public and private sectors is so important, not only because of the significance of local knowledge but also the ability to come together physically and emotionally to agree on a common purpose.

Local business and finance play a vital role in realizing that ambition. Recovery requires innovation, investment, experimentation, failure, learning, adjustment to achieve eventually successful outcomes. It is a long, difficult process with many disappointments along the way but one that is all too familiar to entrepreneurs and SMEs who anticipate bankruptcy and failure before success, and to business angels and venture capitalists who expect that out of a portfolio of investments, most will fail, a few will just survive and perhaps one might hit the jackpot required to justify the many other failures.

But even more significantly local business and finance must be motivated by a purpose of profiting from solving not creating problems to contribute credibly to the common purpose. The common purpose involves establishing a partnership between local public authorities and private business and a commitment on the part of both to invest in the revival of the local economy.

Profiting from producing solutions to the problems of the locality avoids the difficulties that frequently arise in such partnerships from a divergence of interests between profit seeking business and publicly motivated local and regional public authorities. It aligns interests where the profit motive of business otherwise creates conflict.

That common purpose then justifies not only investment by the private but also the public sector. State owned development banks (such as the European Investment Bank) play a critical role in financing infrastructure. They also play an important role in financing businesses, particularly on a regional basis within a country. Mention was made in the previous chapter of the German 'Sparkassen', savings banks which are quasi-public enterprises that operate under a public law regime with constraints imposed on their operations by German law. Savings banks are required to limit their branches to the area in which they are authorized to operate and to lend first to commercial, household, and institutional customers in that area.

The UK has a state-owned development bank, the British Business Bank, which offers a variety of forms of funding to the British business sector. It has contributed to, but needs to go significantly further in funding businesses and co-investing with private financial institutions to promote the development of local financial sectors and business angel and venture capital communities in parts of the country which are currently devoid of them. The British Business Bank could be a major conduit for connecting funding from the UK Government and the City of London with businesses in the regions and creating a revival of locally based financial institutions that were so important in funding the Industrial Revolution in Britain in the nineteenth century.

A Scottish Example

There is one part of the UK that is demonstrating how to forge this common purpose between the private and public sector with an ambitious programme of reform. Scotland was the first country in the world to create a Business Purpose Commission and I was in the fortunate position to be its co-chair. What marked out this initiative was a recognition on the part of the Scottish Government not only of the potential of business purpose to enhance Scottish business but more significantly to promote national and local prosperity in Scotland as well. In other words, it recognized that business could be a powerful force for promoting not just financial returns for investors but also national prosperity.

Key to this was an appreciation that the purpose of business is to solve problems profitably, not profiting from producing problems. But equally significantly was a recognition that this must be considered in a broader context of a public policy of promoting prosperity through partnering with purposeful business whose role is to solve problems profitably.

Why is this such a powerful concept? The answer is that it involves forging a common purpose between public and private interests in identifying what is being sought of local and national economies. What has allowed this to happen in Scotland to a degree that has not occurred to date in the rest of the UK is the devolved nature of authority in Scotland. The Scottish Government has powers of administration and revenue raising that are not present in the rest of Britain. That allows Scotland to formulate a common purpose and work with business in implementing it in a way that has not been possible elsewhere.

Why is this devolved authority so important in terms of promoting regional development? The answer is the same as the one that was described in relation to private capital markets and that is centralized control does not allow localities and regions to flourish. Central governments cannot, any more than central capital markets, know the requirements and objectives of different parts of the country. They cannot formulate and implement policy in an informed way in specific localities. One needs to have devolved administrations to do that.

There is a marked reluctance on the part of central government to let the reins of control go and allow localities to have authority over budgets or fiscal revenue sources. There is a fear that local administrations do not have the knowledge, experience, or political alignment to manage substantial public budgets. Across the UK, the powers of local administration therefore remain highly constrained, which makes the case of Scotland particularly interesting.

What the Scottish Business Purpose Commission did was to work closely with businesses in Scotland in identifying the case for the adoption by business of purposes of profitably solving problems without causing them. There was a high level of support for this amongst both Scottish businesses and the Scottish public at large.

Most Scottish businesses regarded it as an appropriate definition of corporate purpose in preference to maximizing profits, and two-thirds of the Scottish public believed that this was what Scottish business should adopt as their purposes. It was regarded as particularly important in decisions by the public about where to purchase goods and services, and where to seek employment. Treatment of customers and employees were therefore regarded by Scottish businesses as particularly significant.

Scottish business emphasized the importance of the provision of equity finance in delivering profitable solutions. In addition to the devolved power of the Scottish government, what marks out Scotland from the rest of the UK is the significance of its financial centre in Edinburgh—the largest in the UK outside the City of London. The key ingredients for the development of a purpose driven economy in terms of devolved public and private administration and finance are therefore in place in Scotland to a greater extent than elsewhere in the UK.

But the main lesson is that any country in the world can establish a business purpose commission to demonstrate the benefits of problem-solving purposeful business and to forge common purpose between the public, private, and not-for-profit sectors in creating shared prosperity. Not only can this happen nationally it can also be organized regionally or at city level to promote common purpose and shared prosperity across every part of a country. And not only is it restricted to place, but it can also be organized by sector, including some of the most important essential service sectors of an economy.

Utilities

At the start of this chapter, I said that law and regulation cannot produce unprofitable solutions and extend the boundaries of the firm to include the internalization of positive externalities. However, the design of regulation can have a significant influence on the ability of firms to do that.

Utilities in the UK—energy, telecoms, transport, and water—were privatized during the 1980s and 1990s. As part of this, a regulatory system was put in place that controlled the charges that the resulting private monopolies were allowed to levy on their customers. The system was designed to encourage efficiency by rewarding companies for reducing the costs of delivering services to their customers.

The utility companies did this initially by reducing their operating expenditures through cutting employment and then sought to do the same with capital expenditures. However, this resulted in declining services and mounting complaints from customers and communities. Disillusionment in privatization was further compounded by the rising dividends and salaries companies paid their shareholders and executives at the same time as they were criticized and fined by their regulators for delivering poor services.

The 30-year experience of privatization in Britain has not been a happy one and has demonstrated the inherent contradictions that exists in a system that relies on private monopolies to deliver essential services constrained by external regulators who cap the charges they can levy on customers. It creates a conflict between private companies with a primary interest in profit and regulators concerned about the public interest of customers and communities.

Regulators set the rules and companies then seek to renegotiate, appeal, and circumvent them. They complain that the system of setting the prices they can charge their customers does not provide the stability they need to deliver their long-term investments, which typically have a lifetime of several generations.

The system inevitably and invariably ends up being confrontational, finishing at appeal bodies such as the Competition Appeal Tribunal in the UK, on which I served for eight years, adjudicating over numerous examples of the complexities of that confrontation. Not only is it not inevitable that the system should operate like this, but it is also vital that it doesn't because it is expensive, inefficient, and damaging. Furthermore, it is relatively straightforward to correct.

What lies at the heart of the problem are two things. The first is a dominant focus of companies on putting profit before problem-solving and the second is a regulatory system that is focused on short-term periodic settlements of the prices utilities can charge. Neither of these features are conducive to a system that is there to promote the long-term wellbeing of customers, communities, and the environment over many generations. The bad record of utilities since privatization is not therefore in the slightest bit surprising.

If instead the objectives of utilities were to provide profitable solutions to the problems of their customers and communities then the conflict between company and regulator would become one of cooperation. What a purposeful agenda does is to encourage careful consideration about the purposes of utility companies and their regulators, and to design both so that they are fit for purpose. It appropriately positions the profits that utilities earn as being derived from the benefits that they confer on their customers, communities, and the environment, not from the detriments they create for any of them.

This comes from a deep understanding by utilities of the problems of their customers, communities, and the environment, and earning profits from solving not exacerbating them. Purposeful regulation is then not just about the rules of the game and their enforcement but also relating the purposes of utilities with what their customers, societies, and environments are expecting of them. This promotes an alignment between corporate purposes and social licences to operate, ensuring that there is a process of consultation and public engagement, through for example citizens assemblies, which identifies a common purpose between utilities and their customers and communities.

The regulatory process should encourage the delivery of those purposes over the long term—not just a few years but intergenerationally. Purposeful regulation does this by reviewing utility companies' activities within the context of strategies that promote intergenerational environmental and societal benefits and, instead of funding investments upfront, rewarding them on delivery of their benefits. Purposeful companies in turn position their strategies with intergenerational purposes to create long-term value from the benefits they confer on their stakeholders and undertake the long-term investments that are required to deliver them.

It is a partnership in formulating common purpose and its delivery. It differs from traditional price cap regulation in an analogous way to how local, long-term relationship banking differs from arms-length transactional banking, as discussed in relation to Handelsbanken in Chapter 8. It is not regulatory capture but an active ongoing engagement that monitors and corrects to ensure that companies remain on track in delivering their purpose. Can this be measured and be accounted for? The answer is yes; it is measurable, and it is increasingly becoming so.

Take for example inclusivity, access, and affordability. Social media and artificial intelligence are together providing methods for obtaining and analysing large volumes of data on the impact that utilities have on their customers and communities. They allow boards of companies to evaluate whether people in their organization and communities believe that they are authentically implementing their purpose. They provide information on the trust people have in the company and its trustworthiness to uphold the interests of its employees, customers, and communities. They inform the company about the wellbeing and welfare of their stakeholders and the degree of distress they are experiencing in relation to the quality and affordability of services. They identify areas of conflict between companies seeking to fund long-term environmental and intergenerational social policies and regulators' concerns about current affordability and charging for services.

How can regulators reconcile these objectives and be sure that companies are not using purpose as a smokescreen behind which to hide excessive costs and profits? The answer is by working with companies in ensuring, first, that companies' purposes are determined through a rigorous process of consultation and dialogue with relevant stakeholders; second, that they have appropriate ownership and governance arrangements for committing to and embedding purpose in their organizations; third, that there is an alignment between the purposes, values, and culture of companies; fourth, that the appropriate way of measuring the resourcing and performance of companies is in place; fifth, that the company is on target to deliver its purpose; and, sixth, that there are error correction mechanisms for putting the company back on track when it isn't. Conversely, regulators ensure companies can levy sufficient charges on their customers to earn adequate rates of return on their investments in the long term.

It is not very different to the process that the legal system must go through in evaluating whether firms are abiding by purposes of problem-solving not creation and the stewardship that institutional investors should undertake in evaluating the societal and environmental as well as financial performance of their investments. Indeed, key to success is to bring all these parties together in terms of how they view their roles and activities, and a powerful way of doing that is to form business purpose commissions at the sectoral level to determine common purposes, shared prosperity, and social licences to operate.

Scotland provides an interesting illustration and contrast to the rest of the UK in this regard. First it did not privatize its water company, Scottish Water, which remained in the possession of the Scottish Government and, secondly, there is a different regulator of water in Scotland from the rest of Britain. This has allowed the regulator in Scotland to take an approach that is not dissimilar to the one described above.

The relation that is being sought of company, owner, and regulator in Scotland is one of a collaborative long-term adoption of purpose. Scottish Water should consult and engage with its stakeholders, its regulator, and its shareholder on its purpose, its strategy in relation to its purpose, its values and culture, its resourcing, the cost of its resourcing, its measures of performance in relation to its purpose, and its performance against the measures. This should build trust between the different parties, establish the trustworthiness of Scottish Water regarding the delivery of its purpose, and allow for long-term value creation from fulfilment of the purpose.

Does the public ownership of Scottish Water, or the fact that there is only one company, make Scotland fundamentally different from England and Wales? Probably not. A company that has as its purpose to solve problems for its customers and communities profitably not profiting from producing problems is aligned with, not in conflict with, a public entity. In fact, it has an advantage. In addition to promoting the public interest, it has a private interest in doing so more efficiently and more innovatively than a public one. And the fact that there are multiple companies in a private industry allows all of them and the regulator to use the information and experience that comes from comparing the experience of each of them.

The same applies to other utilities. Take for example energy. Clearly the main purpose of energy companies is not simply to deliver energy but also to achieve the energy transition of delivering energy that is not environmentally damaging. There is a rush of commitments to net zero over different periods. But still more critical is whether these commitments to embrace not profiting from producing detriments also address the problem of social exclusion—the inaccessibility and unaffordability of energy.

The energy transition will not be achieved if in the process it excludes segments of a country's, or the world's, population or increases their costs of access to a point that it is unaffordable. And the massive investments that will be required in renewables, infrastructure, and reskilling of employees must yield sufficient returns to encourage the private as well as public sector to fund them. In other words, the importance of energy companies recognizing their purposes in profiting from solving energy problems not producing them, and of investors and regulators in both supporting them and ensuring they do this, could never have been greater or more urgent than at present.

Alongside businesses, investors, public authorities, and regulators at local, national, and international levels, there is one other institution that has a vital role to play in forging common purpose and transforming our capitalist system. But it is an institution that is surprisingly not always at the vanguard of such innovations.

Education and Ideas

It was Francesco Petrarca, better known as Petrarch, who originated the humanism movement in fourteenth-century renaissance Italy. He argued that the Aristotelian virtues of prudence, justice, temperance, and courage are not just inherited as a character of human nature but also acquired through educational nurturing. As the Greek philosophers taught us, it is the virtues which mould the character of leadership and inspire great leaders.[13] Education provides a form of 'virtue egalitarianism' by which the attributes of leadership are not restricted to a ruling class but available to all with interest in and access to the source of that knowledge.

Recent experience has reminded us of the ephemeral nature of visionary leadership and how even the most carefully constructed democratic systems cannot assure it. Instead, the emphasis of the book has been on institutions not individuals. In doing this, I have been influenced by the institution in which I have been fortunate to work for most of my life—Oxford University.

Oxford and Cambridge universities are both corporations; in fact, both comprise multiple corporations within them because not only are they themselves corporations established by royal charter, but so too are each of their 39 and 31 colleges respectively. They illustrate particularly well the concept of systems within systems that has been a theme of this book and the fierce competition between the colleges has been a significant source of their educational success.

One indicator of that success is their survival; they are two of the oldest corporations in the world. They have survived plagues, famines, civil wars, world wars, enlightened and oppressive political leadership. Even more remarkably through all that they have consistently retained their position as two of the world's highest ranked research and teaching universities. While survival may not be everything, it certainly is something.

When I returned to Oxford University in 1993 to help set up the University's business school as its first professor, it was against the background of a university that had a deeply ambivalent and, in many quarters, hostile attitude to business. Oxford University was one of the last major universities in the world to establish a business school. Its procrastination reflected a view that business was not a proper subject of study and not worthy of inclusion in as eminent an institution as Oxford. Once it took the hesitant step of creating one it could not quite bring itself to use the word business, so it initially chose to describe it as a 'School of Management Studies' on the grounds that this sounded a bit more intellectually respectable.

The suggestion of Oxford academics being involved in business activities was even more distasteful to much of the scholarly community so the idea of scientists starting companies or the University engaging in the money-grubbing activity of commercializing and spinning them off was regarded with derision.

I mention this not as a criticism of the University at the time but, firstly, to emphasize that the unseemly nature of business is something that pervades many parts of society and, secondly, to demonstrate the potential to change people's attitudes on this, because Oxford University not only now has one of the top business schools but also one of the best records of spinning out and commercializing its activities of any university in Europe. It is a remarkable change in a 25-year period to which the creation of its business school has hopefully made some contribution.

The concerns of those Oxford academics about the sordid elements of business are not without foundation—some parts of it are. But so too are some parts of politics, governments, the law, and virtually every part of societies. The central proposition of this book is that business can and should be a primary institution for promoting societal wellbeing and it will be if there is not a conflict between delivering solutions to societal problems and producing profits. As a derivative of the former, the latter are as honourable as any other activity.

Business schools are a primary influence on the education of current and future generations of business leaders. They communicate what business leaders adopt as conventional wisdom on best practice. They have the power to influence how businesses behave to a degree that few other institutions can achieve. They therefore have a considerable responsibility to be at the vanguard of presenting ideas that challenge as well as communicate prevailing paradigms.[14]

To achieve this, business schools need to position the purposes of businesses as being about profitable problem-solving. They should educate students in being inspiring and motivational founders, leaders, and owners of problem-solving businesses and financial institutions. They should emphasize the common purposes and partnerships that must be forged between public, private, and charitable sectors at local, national, and international levels to deliver this.

To achieve this, they should incorporate the arts with accounting, ethics with economics, the humanities with human resource management, morals with marketing, the sciences with strategy, and values with valuation not just as electives but as courses core to their entire curricula. Furthermore, these courses are relevant not only to business schools but also to public policy, law, and medical schools. In other words, all university disciplines are central to a business school education and concepts of problem-solving are relevant to all university professional schools.

Business education and skills training are not the only ways in which universities contribute to the development of businesses. They play a vital role in stimulating the growth of businesses in their local communities through generating new ideas especially in the physical, life, and medical sciences that are then the basis of start-up and spinout companies. Financial constraints have increasingly pushed universities in this direction to compensate for diminishing public funding. Oxford University's move was not only motivated by a realization of the merits of business but also by rather more mundane monetary considerations.

More significant than a business school is the role that education in all its guises—university, further education, and schools—should play in promoting knowledge and understanding of business. This points to a growing partnership not only between business and the public sector but also with universities, further education colleges, and schools at a local and regional level in developing life-long skills and training.

Business can not only fund research and provide jobs for graduating students but also help mentor and network new start-ups coming out of universities and further education colleges. This creates a symbiotic relationship between business and educational institutions in which the latter are the creators of new ideas that attract funding from private financial institutions to invest in growing firms, and the former are the providers of advice on the design and development of commercial activities spun out of educational institutions.

But the primary impact of education is on neither research nor commerce but students. A purposeful education promotes a yearning for learning as well as earning; meaning, fulfilment, and achievement from the wellbeing of others, as well as oneself; and lifetime community, national, and international service, and contribution as well as remuneration on graduation.

Summary

This chapter has used the UK as an illustration of how conventional views on economics, business, and finance can be profoundly wrong and have disastrous consequences for the performance of economies, nations, and societies as well as firms and their investors. On nearly all criteria the UK was regarded as a model of good macro- and microeconomic practice in the formulation of monetary and fiscal policies, and the ownership and governance of its business and financial sectors. However, by many standards its economic performance has been poor.

Of course, several reasons can and have been suggested for this but the one that lies at the heart of this book is the misconception of the nature of business and finance. The ownership and governance of UK's business and financial sectors have been seriously deficient. They reflect a belief that 'only the bottom-line (i.e., profit) matters', so all below the line at the bottom (i.e., the poor) really don't matter. Far from promoting the investment required to correct that deficiency, the UK's business and financial system has come nearly bottom of the class in failing to do so.

What this points to is a new way of thinking about national and regional public policy, the provision of essential services by utilities, and the role of education and training of business leaders and employees. That approach derives from the central proposition of the book that business and finance are systems within a system and their contribution should be to a common purpose of shared prosperity, profitably solving problems of people and planet.

The End

To What End?
All for Nothing, or Something for All

What Will the Stock Market Be Doing the Day Before the World Ends?

A bizarre question you might say. Collapsing, of course. How could it be doing anything else when there will be nothing worth valuing tomorrow?

But hold on. Nothing is certain, not even that there will be nothing. The world might end tomorrow, but perhaps it will not, or perhaps it will only end next week or in a year's time, or perhaps it will never end at all because we will find a way of avoiding the end altogether. After all, humans are infinitely imaginative, the world has never ended before, technology can come to the rescue, so surely, we will find a way out this time as well.

Build yourself some shelters, hoard food, go to a lonely island which might escape the cataclysm. Businesses will be busy perhaps busier than ever, at least some of them. And of the rest, well they are a great investment because they will be paying out all their reserves as cash to their investors. We might just have a stock market boom the day before the world ends.

I pose this question because to some people this is precisely what is happening now while I am writing this book. We are in a moment of water shortages, floods, fires, wars, energy shortages, food shortages, and pandemics. If I were a religious person, I might describe the coincidence of disasters as of biblical proportions. But as a mere economist I prefer to view them as coincidental random events. Some people are experiencing several of these disasters at the same time. For many, of course the poorest and most deprived in the world, the world may well end tomorrow.

And how is the stock market responding to this? Well, it is booming as I write this in August 2022. At least it was yesterday. Not so much today as yesterday because today the Governor of the Federal Reserve in Washington signalled that he is inclined to retain a tight monetary policy in the USA after the market had anticipated a relaxation of it.[1] And that is all that appears at present to be influencing stock markets and the earnings of shareholders—short-term predictions of the next movements in interest rates.

What of all those crises? Well of course there are many firms doing very nicely thank you out of water, floods, fires, conflicts, energy, food shortages, and pandemics. In fact, across the corporate sector, many parts of the economy probably have something to rejoice about.

I might exaggerate a bit but not much. The world of finance and stock markets seems to most of us to be completely detached from the world that we are experiencing. Perhaps it was ever so, but it seems to be more now than ever. Maybe it is all to the good because at least something is stable in a period of great instability, and it might be positively beneficial for investors and pensioners to be earning healthy returns during periods when there is otherwise great suffering.

But the idea that some are profiting out of suffering is not a comfortable notion. It might be true, it might be explicable, it might just be the way it is but, even so, it does not feel right. And of course, it isn't right. It is thoroughly wrong and that has been the subject of this book—why it is wrong, what is wrong, and how to fix it fast.

Why Is It Wrong?

It is wrong because it is immoral. It is immoral because if there is one basic principle that should guide our economic behaviour it is not to profit at the expense of others. Why? How can I be so self-righteous and assured about that? After all, God did not include it in the Tablets he gave Moses. Or did he?

One of them (number 7 or 8) is 'Thou shalt not steal.' Profiting at the expense of others is stealing—taking something from someone else for one's own benefit. Producing problems is to create hardship for others from which they suffer and incur costs and inconvenience to remedy. Profiting from producing problems is to derive benefit from failing to incur the costs oneself of remedying, rectifying, or compensating the hardship of others.

But that's just business, you might reasonably respond. Businesses deliver benefits and detriments all the time and if, on balance, they do more of the former than the latter then that is all to the good. Provided that they do not break the law, who is to say whether something is a detriment or a problem? And if they do break the law then it is for the legal system to determine the penalty and remedy.

Expecting businesses to identify let alone rectify or remedy all the problems they impose on others is wholly unrealistic, especially in large corporations that interact daily with thousands if not millions of people globally. It is entirely impractical to expect them to do this, they would incur unreasonable costs in doing it, and it would expose them to lobbying, negotiation, obstruction, litigation, and prosecution by every aggrieved and opportunistic party seeking to make a buck out of them.

And after all, what is a business there to do if not profit at the expense of others? That is precisely what competition is—trying to beat another and make a gain at their expense. Am I suggesting that a firm should compensate its competition for the losses it incurs from failing to be as efficient and innovative as it is? Should it have to compensate its employees when it is forced to close an uneconomic plant and transfer its business elsewhere?

The moral law sounds like moralizing from an ivory tower without any appreciation of the nature and complexity of business. It is seeking to transform a straightforward, practical, liberal concept of business as being about promoting the success of the company while staying within the rules of the game and engaging in open and free competition into a gargantuan monster of illiberal, infeasible confusion and impracticality. It should be confined to the dustbin of absurdity from which it should not have been allowed to come.

I could go on and discuss problems of identification, determination, and measurement of problems, the impossibility of fully rectifying or compensating certain damages such as to nature, the environment, or human health, and the fact that businesspeople are neither equipped nor authorized to make such judgements and decisions which are the proper remit of democratically elected governments and political representatives. I could put forward exactly the opposite proposition that businesses of course consider and worry about these issues all the time and it is naïve to suggest that they are not already actively engaged in addressing them.

The book has attempted to demonstrate that these criticisms and concerns are without foundation, but it is perfectly reasonable that they be raised. They are exactly the questions that need to be addressed and considered but at present are not because they are swept under the carpet of 'they are for the law, the government, the regulator, the philosopher, the priest'—everyone except business, to answer. Business should go on its way, oblivious to the complexities of life and indeed to the existence of some forms of life, because that is what it is charged and authorized to do.

By advocating for the moral law, the book firmly rejects that assertion and seeks to move these questions centre stage into business and argues that there should be someone or some people whose primary function is to consider and worry about them. Those people should not be the chief ethics or sustainability officer or general counsel or any other worthy member of the corporation. They should be those much more central to its formation and existence—the owners and directors—because owning and directing a business are about exactly that: owning its problems and leading it towards their resolution.

What Is Wrong?

The system. First, we haven't recognized it and, secondly, we have misconstrued and ill-designed it. Of course, the notion of business as a system is well understood. But what is not so clearly appreciated is the way in which it should be recognized as a system within a system.

The traditional view of business is as a standalone entity pursuing its own path of success with little engagement with broader societal, environmental, and political issues. Business should not address political issues that it does not have a legitimate mandate to consider. It should stick to its knitting of satisfying its customers, employees, and investors.

What is proposed here is very different. The reason why a business exists is to contribute to the broader system of which it is a part, recognizing its position as a system within a system. It is one component of the overall system, delivering certain functions to it. Of course, the interface between firms and economies is a central part of economic models and the billiard ball analogy at the beginning of the book was an illustration of that. But it relies on markets and competition to organize that interface and, where markets and competition fail, it expects regulators and government to constrain firms. It does not grant the billiard ball any independent authority to determine how it interacts with other balls.

It removes self-determination from business in defining its inter-relationship with its society and environment beyond seeking to promote its own success. This book rejects that reductionist approach and argues for a recognition of business as an entity that defines its own place and function within its broader economic, social, and environmental system.

How do I know that the system approach is appropriate? Not simply because markets are incomplete, imperfect, and ill-informed, or that governments and regulators are at least as defective as markets. The real reason is that a systems approach is enriching. It is enriching in the sense that if parties, particularly firms, are cognizant of their position in the broader framework and appropriately motivated to contribute to it then it is to everyone's advantage. It enriches them by enhancing all around them.

But that is not by any means always the case. We suffered decades of attempts by socialist systems to do exactly that. Where they failed was in ignoring the power of markets and competition to organize systems and instead looking to central control structures and planners to perform the impossible task of running them from the top.

Any solution must seek to enhance not diminish the functioning of markets and competition and confer more, not less, liberty and self-determination on their constituent parts. What is needed is a system within a system where every component determines and implements its contribution to the system. Where this book differs from a traditional market approach is in suggesting that is not best done through each component just blindly pursuing its own self-interest but through promoting the interests of others. It argues for an other- rather than a self-regarding view of the firm.

Why? How do I know this is superior to the existing self-regarding system? The answer is simply that if all agents see it as their primary role to assist others, then that is enriching for everyone. The previous chapter described this in the context of the micro and macroeconomic benefits that come from the productive relations that can thereby be created between the private and public sector but at present are undermined by divergent interests. That cooperation promotes public-sector investment in the private sector and private investment in social and environmentally beneficial outcomes at local, regional, and national levels.

But there is one major caveat that was noted at the beginning of the book. This simply will not happen if it is not in everyone's self- as well as other-regarding interest to make it happen. Altruism is not enough. We cannot rely on the goodwill of individuals or organizations to promote the wellbeing of others. The main failing of the stakeholder and much of the responsible capitalism view of the firm is that it relies on exactly that. It expects companies to promote the interests of stakeholders even where that conflicts with those of shareholders.

Proponents of stakeholder theories like to suggest that the two often coincide and that what is good for stakeholders is good for businesses and their investors. But regrettably this is blatantly not always the case and there are obvious examples of businesses that do very well out of dumping their waste and pollution on others, selling addictive products, treating their employees badly, and avoiding paying taxes. It is where there are trade-offs and conflicts that the toughest problems arise.

We must be realistic and recognize that the notion of firms promoting wider interests will not happen if it is not profitable for them to do so. The core part of the book was therefore about how to do that.

How to Fix It?

The purpose of the firm that is advocated here is to produce profitable solutions to problems not profiting from producing problems. This notion of purpose serves two purposes. First it establishes what a profit is—namely it comes from solving not producing problems and, secondly, it determines how self-interest is aligned with the interest of others—through requiring solutions to be profitable. In other words, it invalidates both profits derived from inflicting detriments on others and problem-solving that is not profitable.

It prevents firms benefiting from harming others and helping others without benefiting themselves. It therefore rules out both irresponsible and uncommercial business and requires the commercial to be responsible and the responsible to be commercial. Those on the right of the political spectrum will hate the former and love the latter, and those on the left will do the converse. There will therefore be something for everyone to welcome and criticize, but also the possibility of addressing the concerns of both.

What is proposed here enhances notions of liberty and freedom. By discouraging irresponsibility associated with profiting at the expense of others, it diminishes the need for intrusive regulation. It thereby augments the autonomy and self-determination of firms and promotes the operation of free markets and competition.

It retains the sole accountability of boards to shareholders. It does not require the complexity of multiple forms of oversight and accountability associated with stakeholder theories. The reason is that profit is a necessary and sufficient statistic of problem-solving in the sense that where profits are earned then problems are solved and where problems are solved then profits must be earned. That means that the interests of shareholders and societies are aligned.

This has the implication that the duties of directors under company law can remain solely 'to promote the success of the company for the benefit of their shareholders'. Companies will of course want to engage with and consult their stakeholders in determining the problems they encounter and how best to address them, but formal accountability and rights of appointment and removal of directors can remain solely with shareholders.

That is why the nature of ownership is so important. It is in shareholders' interests to ensure that their companies are solving problems and profiting from doing so, not creating problems. To the extent that they are benefiting at the expense of others, they expose themselves to risks of having to incur costs of remedying, rectifying, and compensating for problems caused. To the extent that firms are not solving problems profitably then they are not earning the returns of which they are capable.

A large proportion of shareholdings are now in the form of global index funds. Those shareholders are exposed to global systemic risks of an environmental, political, regulatory, and social nature but not the risks of individual firms. For shareholders to have an incentive to discharge their duties to oversee and engage with firms in which they invest, there need to be at least some who have sufficient holdings to have a direct interest in the companies in which they are invested.

This explains the parallel nature of ownership of the largest listed companies around the world—widely dispersed shareholdings by predominantly asset management firms combined with concentrated shareholdings by mainly families, foundations, and public-sector institutions. The former are concerned about the exposure and contribution of their companies to global systemic risks while the latter are focused on their success in profitably solving and avoiding causing problems.

The two groups of shareholders require different types of information on their investments. The global investors are looking for the data that environmental, social, and governance (ESG) providers are supposed to supply, while the concentrated owners require information on the specific measures that relate to the success of the company in solving problems. Together these two types of data measure the expenditures companies must incur to solve problems and remedy detriments caused.

They provide the basis on which company accounts can be constructed that reflect true costs of avoiding profiting from causing problems and just profits earned from producing solutions to problems. They align the interests of those working in companies with their shareholders, and the interests of companies and shareholders with the communities, societies, and natural world around them. They ensure that all enterprises, be they the smallest in the poorest parts of the world or the largest international corporations in developed economies, have the financial resources and in particular equity finance they need to implement their stated purposes and problem-solving.

This reconfiguration of business will not only harness the power of the corporation to raise finance but will also bring immense benefits to employees lower down the corporation and those with whom firms will increasingly partner in the future. Solving problems requires a delegation of authority within companies that empowers everyone within the organization to recognize their part and contribution to the company's purpose.

That is how the complexity of handling multiple interactions around the world is made manageable and practical in even the largest international organization. Everybody from the board to shop floor is a custodian of their piece of the company purpose and the recipient of the financial resources they need to deliver on it. In other words, every part of a business is a system of ownership of problem-solving purpose and the provision of equity finance.

It is an inspiring and motivational notion of business which not only makes everyone feel empowered and valued but also resourced to perform the functions they are supposed to undertake. It is the basis on which the corporation engages with other parties and organizations in an economy and forges a common purpose with public, private, and social entities to solve local, regional, national, and international problems. It is a means by which business becomes a natural partner of government and government becomes an investor alongside the private sector in business. It establishes business as a primary contributor not just to the success of its stakeholders and investors but also of economies, nations, and the natural world.

Public and Private in Partnership

The post-Second World War history of macroeconomics has comprised cycles of fiscal and monetary expansion and contraction. The traditional narrative describes the immediate post-war period as one of Keynesian induced government expenditure and expansionary monetary policy ending at the close of the 1970s in growing inflation and unemployment. This was followed by fiscal and monetary austerity from the 1980s until the middle of the 1990s when both were gradually relaxed.

This was interrupted by the financial crisis in 2008, resulting in a move to an unorthodox combination of fiscal austerity and monetary expansion in the 2010s, ending in the COVID crisis of 2020 and a brief return to fiscal as well as monetary expansion. We are now witnessing the imposition of fiscal and monetary austerity as countries seek to address inflation and avoid economic recession, and 'reckless' attempts at pursuing fiscal expansion in such countries as Brazil, Chile, Colombia, and the UK are rapidly abandoned as fiscal 'discipline' is reasserted by international capital markets.

However, there is a more instructive way of viewing the post-war experience as being an oscillation between attempts to use public and private sectors as ways of solving local, national, and international problems. The Keynesian immediate post-war emphasis on the public sector was followed by a Margaret Thatcher and Ronald Reagan induced promotion of the private sector, a more balanced mixture of the two in the early 2000s, a withdrawal of the state and reliance on the private sector in the 2010s, ending in a renewed appreciation of the role of the state in the COVID crisis. As we move into the 2020s, the room for manoeuvre of both private and public sectors appears limited by a combination of inflationary pressures and fiscal constraints.

The failure of private and public sectors reflects a misconceived conception of both as substitutes rather than complements. Instead, the private sector should be recognized as the provider of innovative solutions to problems through experimentation and adaptation that the public sector cannot undertake, and the public sector as the formulator of a framework and funding that the private sector is incapable of delivering. What is required is neither fiscal constraint nor 'reckless' fiscal expansion but a clear framework for forging a common purpose around addressing global problems by the private sector supported by public-sector investment of a duration and scale which the private sector is incapable of achieving alone.

We are currently confusing cause and effect by regarding financial considerations as the solution to problems instead of the solution of problems as the determinant of financial considerations. Define the collective problems to be solved and then the means to fund them by the private and public sector in partnership, not the converse of private and public sectors independently determining their financial objectives as the basis of solving their respective problems. And do this at the local, national, regional, and global level.

If this happens then the crises discussed in this book find a natural resolution. So far, we have not even defined the problems to be solved correctly. COVID-19 was seen to be a problem of determining the nature of the vaccine and its delivery. The energy problem initially concerned the environment and CO_2 emissions and then, with the onset of the Russia–Ukraine conflict, energy shortages, security of supply, and affordability. The perceived problems with alcohol, gambling, fast foods, sugar are their addictive, physical, and mental health effects.

In fact, the problems to be solved are the distribution as well as determination and delivery of vaccines to the poorest as well as the richest parts of the world; the production, delivery, and distribution of renewable sources of energy in accessible and affordable forms everywhere; the delivery of products that bring people pleasure, relaxation, and social interaction cheaply and easily in ways that are not personally, socially, or environmentally damaging. We should identify not just the symptoms but the crux of the problems and who is needed to collaborate as well as compete in solving them.

Two Worlds

There are two worlds: our current world of crisis capitalism—a world of selfish individuals investing in profit maximizing firms earning returns at the expense, as well as to the benefit, of others; and a world of problem-solving capitalism—a world of equally selfish individuals investing in firms that profit from solving not causing problems for others.

The first is based on a legal system that sanctions profit-maximizing firms operating in a regulatory system that establishes and enforces the 'rules of the game'; the second promotes profitable firms that do not profit from producing problems for others, overseen by private and public law that ensures they don't and won't.

The first comprises widely held companies owned by dispersed shareholders investing predominantly in diversified, global portfolios; the second includes companies that have concentrated owners of blocks of shares who have responsibility for ensuring commitment of companies to their problem-solving purposes.

Companies in crisis capitalism are run from the top for the benefit of their shareholders; companies in problem-solving capitalism are decentralized and devolved, empowering those on the shop floor to own and implement their part of the corporate purpose. The former are accountable to their shareholders; the latter are accountable to their shareholders and responsible for those whom they affect and support.

Companies in crisis capitalism measure their outputs and inputs; companies in problem-solving capitalism measure their outcomes and impacts. The former report profits irrespective of whether they are earned at the expense of others; the latter don't—they record their true costs of cleaning up the mess they cause as well as the products they produce.

Companies in crisis capitalism borrow, go bankrupt, and leave others to bear the costs; companies in problem-solving capitalism use predominantly equity finance, provide adequately for the future, and invest equity in others. They make common purpose with those in the public sector internationally, nationally, and locally and receive investment from public institutions that operate at devolved, local, as well as national levels.

Companies in crisis capitalism only internalize negative impacts on others when required by governments or regulators to do so; companies in problem-solving capitalism internalize negative impacts on their own initiative and create positive impacts when incentivized by governments to do so.

Can the second world really exist? Not only can it but, as has been repeatedly demonstrated throughout the book, many aspects of it already do exist. In particular, it exists in a country with one of the highest levels of GDP per capita, lowest levels of inequality, best employee relations, and highest indices of human happiness anywhere in the world. That country has precisely the types of ownership and governance required by problem-solving capitalism, supported by enabling laws and regulation and close partnerships between private and public sectors in delivering the outcomes expected of it. The country is Denmark, and its enterprise foundation law, ownership, and governance are major distinguishing features and contributions to its economic, human, and social success.

Can the two worlds co-exist? Can companies in the second survive in the presence of those in the first? The answer is again not only that it can, but it does. One of the remarkable features of Denmark is that its prosperity has come despite it having to compete as a small open economy in international markets with crisis capitalism countries.

An example of the latter is a country with one of the lowest levels of investment, productivity, and growth, and highest levels of spatial inequality in the developed world over more than two decades and arguably the best part of a century. It is a country with one of the largest financial markets in the world, most dispersed forms of corporate shareholders, strongest protection of minority shareholders and most active markets for corporate control in the world. It has all the ingredients expected of the best performing capitalist systems and yet it precisely exemplifies the failures of crisis capitalism. It is the UK.

So, the benefits of problem-solving capitalism countries shine through as much for them as the rest of us. But nevertheless, we should recognize problem-causing companies for what they are—parasitic, surviving, and thriving on the demise of others. We should not be precious about this. We should impose restraints and penalties on those that profit from foul not fair play and trade at the expense of others. Competition shouldn't and won't be free if it isn't fair. Every country as well as company should recognize their obligation to contribute to promoting the flourishing and success of our global system.

Recommendations Restated

The book has argued that:

> We should reformulate the Golden Rule around doing unto others as they would have done unto them.
> This should be reflected in corporate purposes of producing profitable solutions for the problems of people and planet, not profiting from producing problems for either.
> Corporations should determine their purposes as conditional on not profiting from harming others.
> Directors can then retain a singular duty to their shareholders not to multiple stakeholders.

This requires that:

> Corporate purpose should be placed at the heart of corporate law around the world.
> Appropriate interpretation of existing legislation in some jurisdictions may already provide courts of law with the basis for doing this. Elsewhere, new legislation will need to be enacted.

Dominant shareholders should take ownership of the problems their companies exist to solve and promote their profitable resolution without detriments.

Leaders should bring clarity and commitment to their organization's purposes, values, and culture, and delegate authority and resources to those responsible for their implementation.

Measurement and finance are critical:

Corporate profit and national income should account for costs of sustaining the wellbeing of those outside as well as within their formal legal boundaries, including in the natural world.

Organizations should incur the costs of rectifying and remedying the problems they create and account for them in both their internal management and external reporting.

International standards should set principles of accounting and reporting for corporate purpose; accountants and auditors should assure adherence to them.

Institutional investors should provide adequate risk-bearing, predominantly equity capital for delivery of problem-solving purposes and steward their profitable delivery.

Public and private sectors should work together:

Leaders of public and private sector organizations should forge common purposes to create shared prosperity inclusive of left-behind people, places, and nations.

Central governments, financial institutions, and organizations should delegate authority and finance to those best placed to deliver shared prosperity.

Regulators should align the purposes of dominant corporations and essential service providers with the interests of their customers, communities, societies, and environment.

Universities and other educational institutions should provide leaders and employees with the knowledge and skills required to support their purpose-driven organizations.

In the Beginning

On Tuesday, 13 December 2022, as I came towards the end of writing this book, on a freezing cold day in Britain when many people wondered whether they would be able to afford the energy they needed to heat their houses, an announcement was made heralding a new era in the history of the world. It was the day on which the US Department of Energy confirmed the achievement of 'fusion ignition'—the energy breakeven where more energy is produced from fusion than the laser energy used to create it.[2] The age of abundant energy may have dawned.

Together with the ability of humans to create and manipulate living organisms (*l*) and to generate artificial intelligence (*i*), abundant energy (*e*) has the power to transform the world we inhabit. But it also requires a newfound form of human feeling (*f*) between them to ensure that the combination of these new technologies create a better *life* not a disastrous *lie*—a heaven on earth that avoids passing hell before reaching heaven. A stock market boom like no other may result from the science but, even if the technologies fulfil their promise, the boom must result from rather than cause the science for the science to avoid being the cause of our demise.

If this reconceptualization of capitalism around profit, systems, and problem-solving offers so much, why did we not design it that way in the first place when it was originally granted freedom of incorporation in the nineteenth century? The answer is because of the growing belief at the time in the ideas that were emerging around the power of competitive markets to deliver societal benefits—it was a triumph of ideology and dogma over pragmatism and pluralism.

There is a salutary lesson in this because while it might have been the right framework around which to build businesses at that time when they were small, family-owned, and local, it became increasingly problematic as they grew to be bigger, institutionally owned, and international during the next century.

That brought government into conflict with business in many different areas, for example anti-trust bodies, regulators, and tax authorities. It thrust a major burden on the public sector to constrain the ever-more avaricious, powerful, and wealthy corporations that emerged. It has recently been subject to increasing divisiveness and confrontations and has put an immense strain on our political as well as economic systems.

One objective behind the agenda of aligning corporate, investor, and public interests is to try to mend those divisions and provide the basis on which we can establish common purpose across communities, nations, and societies. This is not about the 'me' of individualism and neoliberalism or the 'we' of communitarianism and socialism but the 'they' of humanism and humanitarianism. It does not rely on either the human character of Aristotelian ethics or the education of humanism but the nature of the company we keep.

It is about the structure and conduct of our institutions, organizations, businesses, and governments, and how a reformulated version of the Golden Rule establishes a Moral Law that determines the Rule of Law that is the basis of their creation and existence, and the income and profits that resource and incentivize them. It is an appeal to appreciate what was intended when the foundations of capitalism were laid and how we can rediscover the humanity and wisdom of their moral sentiments as well as the source and success of their wealth of nations.

However, there is an important warning that emerges as well. What look to be good ideas, models, and approaches for business, economic, and political systems at one point in time may be wholly ill-suited to another. What is described here should provide a way of resolving many of the serious defects that we currently observe in our system. Most significantly, it offers the potential for identifying how the world can avoid self-destructing.

But it too will have limitations and a time-limited life as new problems emerge, and different responses are required. For, as T.S. Eliot observed, 'we shall not cease from exploration, and the end of our exploring will be to arrive where we started and know the place for the first time'.[3]

It was Milton Friedman, the Nobel Prizewinning economist, who said: 'only a crisis—actual or perceived—produces real change. When that crisis occurs, the actions that are taken depend on the ideas that are lying around. That, I believe, is our basic function: to develop alternatives to existing policies, to keep them alive and available until the politically impossible becomes the politically inevitable.'[4] How many more crises will we have to endure before the change to capitalism we deserve and wish to serve becomes a political reality?

The answer is many more until we are no more, unless we recognize that Friedman's other famous quotation that 'there is one and only one social responsibility of business—to use its resources and engage in activities designed to increase its profits so long as it stays within the rules of the game, which is to say, engages in open and free competition without deception or fraud'[5] must include the words 'and not profit from producing problems for others'.

Thank you for coming with me on this exploration of alternatives to existing policies and helping to keep them alive and available. I will trouble you no more.

Further Readings

The following is a list of some recently published books that are closely related to this book.

On Capitalism

Acemoglu, Daron and James Robinson (2012), *Why Nations Fail*, New York, NY: Crown Publishers.

Aghion, Philippe, Celine Antonin, and Simon Bunel (2021), *The Power of Creative Destruction*, Cambridge, MA, Harvard University Press.

Akerlof, George and Robert Shiller (2016), *Phishing for Phools: The Economics of Manipulation and Deception*, Princeton, NJ: Princeton University Press.

Allen, Danielle (2023), *Justice by Means of Democracy*, Chicago, IL: Chicago University Press.

Atkinson, Anthony (2015), *Inequality: What Can Be Done?*, Cambridge, MA: Harvard University Press.

Bowles, Samuel (2016), *The Moral Economy: Why Good Incentives Are No Substitute for Good Citizens*, New Haven, CT: Yale University Press.

Carney, Mark (2021), *Value(s): Building a Better World for All*, London: William Collins.

Case, Anne and Angus Deaton (2020), *Deaths of Despair and the Future of Capitalism*, Princeton, NJ: Princeton University Press.

Christakis, Nicholas (2019), *Blueprint: The Evolutionary Origins of a Good Society*, New York, NY: Hachette.

Collier, Paul (2018), *The Future of Capitalism: Facing the New Anxieties*, New York, NY: Harper.

Collier, Paul and John Kay (2020), *Greed is Dead: Politics after Individualism*, London: Allen Lane.

Coyle, Diane (2021), *Cogs and Monsters: What Economics Is, and What It Should Be*, Princeton, NJ: Princeton University Press.

DeLong, Bradford (2022), *Slouching towards Utopia: An Economic History of the Twentieth Century*, London: Basic Books.

Haskell, Jonathan and Stian Westlake (2017), *Capitalism Without Capital: The Rise of the Intangible Economy*, Princeton, NJ: Princeton University Press.

Henderson, Rebecca (2020), *Reimagining Capitalism in a World on Fire*, New York, NY: Hachette.

Henrich, Joseph (2016), *The Secret of Our Success: How Culture Is Driving Human Evolution, Domesticating Our Species, and Making Us Smarter*, Princeton, NJ: Princeton University Press.

Henrich, Joseph (2020), *The Weirdest People in the World: How the World Became Psychologically Peculiar and Particularly Prosperous*, London: Allen Lane.

Kay, John and Mervyn King (2020), *Radical Uncertainty: Decision-Making for an Unknowable Future*, London: Bridge Street Press.

Mazzucato, Mariana (2021), *Mission Economy: A Moonshot Guide to Changing Capitalism*, New York, NY: Penguin Random House Press.

Piketty, Thomas (2014), *Capital in the Twenty-first Century*, Cambridge, MA: The Belknap Press of Harvard University Press.

Putnam, Robert and Shaylyn Garrett (2020), *The Upswing: How America Came Together a Century Ago and How We Can Do It Again*, New York, NY: Simon & Schuster.

Rajan, Raghuram (2019), *The Third Pillar: How Markets and the State Leave the Community Behind*, New York, NY: Penguin Random House.

Sandel, Michael (2012), *What Money Can't Buy: The Moral Limits of Markets*, New York, NY: Farrar, Straus, and Giroux.

Sandel, Michael (2020), *The Tyranny of Merit: What's Become of the Common Good?*, London: Allen Lane.

Smith, Vernon and Bart Wilson (2019), *Humanomics: Moral Sentiments and the Wealth of Nations for the Twenty-First Century*, Cambridge: Cambridge University Press.

Wolf, Martin (2023), *The Crisis of Democratic Capitalism*, London: Penguin Random House.

Zuboff, Shoshana (2019), *The Age of Surveillance Capitalism*, New York, NY: Hachette.

On Business

Edmans, Alex (2020), *Grow the Pie: How Great Companies Deliver Both Purpose and Profit*, Cambridge: Cambridge University Press.

Gulati, Ranjay (2022), *Deep Purpose: The Heart and Soul of High-Performance Companies*, New York, NY: Harper Collins.

Harris, Ron (2020), *Going the Distance: Eurasian Trade and the Rise of the Business Corporation, 1400–1700*, Princeton, NJ: Princeton.

Keefe, Patrick (2021), *Empire of Pain: The Secret History of the Sackler Dynasty*, London: Picador.

Oreskes, Naomi and Erik Conway (2011), *Merchants of Doubt: How a Handful of Scientists Obscured the Truth on Issues from Tobacco Smoke to Climate Change*, New York, NY: Bloomsbury.

Polman, Paul and Andrew Winston (2021), *Net Positive: How Courageous Companies Thrive by Giving More Than They Take*, Boston, MA: Harvard Business Review Press.

Wylie, Bob (2020), *Bandit Capitalism: Carillion and the Corruption of the British State*, Edinburgh: Birlinn.

On Finance

Admati, Anat and Martin Hellwig (2013), *The Bankers' New Clothes: What's Wrong with Banking and What to Do about It*, Princeton, NJ: Princeton.

Gorton, Gary (2010), *Slapped by the Invisible Hand: The Panic of 2007*, Oxford: Oxford University Press.

Kay, John (2016), *Other People's Money: Masters of the Universe or Servants of the People?* London: Profile Books.

O'Hara, Maureen (2016), *Something for Nothing: Arbitrage and Ethics on Wall Street*, New York, NY: Norton.

Tooze, Adam (2018), *Crashed: How a Decade of Financial Crises Changed the World*, New York, NY: Viking.

On Law

Armour, John et al. (2016), *Principles of Financial Regulation*, Oxford: Oxford University Press.

Dagan, Hanoch (2021), *A Liberal Theory of Property*, Cambridge: Cambridge University Press.

Davies, Paul (2020), *Introduction to Company Law*, Oxford: Oxford University Press.

Eisinger, Jesse (2017), *The Chickenshit Club: Why the Justice Department Fails to Prosecute Executives*, New York, NY: Simon and Schuster.

Garrett, Brandon (2016), *Too Big to Jail, How Prosecutors Compromise with Corporations*, Cambridge, MA: Belknap Press.

Kershaw, David (2018), *The Foundations of Anglo-American Corporate Fiduciary Law*, Cambridge: Cambridge University Press.

Kraakman, Reinier et al. (2017), *The Anatomy of Corporate Law: A Comparative and Functional Approach*, Oxford: Oxford University Press.

Kuran, Timur (2011), *The Long Divergence: How Islamic Law Held Back the Middle East*, Princeton, NJ: Princeton University Press.

Pistor, Katharina (2019), *The Code of Capital: How the Law Creates Wealth and Inequality*, Princeton, NJ: Princeton University Press.

Stout, Lynn (2012), *The Shareholder Value Myth: How Putting Shareholders First Harms Investors, Corporations, and the Public*, San Francisco, CA: Berrett-Koehler.

On Philosophy

Boucher, David and Paul Kelly (2017), *Political Thinkers: From Socrates to the Present*, Oxford: Oxford University Press.

Briggs, Andrew (2021), *Human Flourishing: Scientific Insight and Spiritual Wisdom in Uncertain Times*, Oxford: Oxford University Press.

Brown, Peter (2012), *Through the Eye of a Needle: Wealth, the Fall of Rome, and the Making of Christianity in the West, 350–550 AD*, Princeton NJ: Princeton University Press.

Hankins, James (2019), *Virtue Politics: Soulcraft and Statecraft in Renaissance Italy*, Cambridge, MA: Harvard University Press.

Hanley, Ryan (2019), *Our Great Purpose: Adam Smith and Living a Better Life*, Princeton, NJ: Princeton University Press.

Runciman, David (2022), *Confronting Leviathan: A History of Ideas*, London: Profile Books.

Sachs, Jonathan (2020), *On Morality: Restoring the Common Good in Divided Times*, London: Hodder and Stoughton.

Siedentop, Larry (2014), *Inventing the Individual: The Origins of Western Liberalism*, London: Allen Lane.

Wolff, Jonathan (2023), *An Introduction to Political Philosophy*, Oxford: Oxford University Press.

On Science

Brasier, Martin (2012), *Secret Chambers: The Inside Story of Cells and Complex Life*, Oxford: Oxford University Press.

Ellis, George and Mark Solms (2018), *Beyond Evolutionary Psychology: How and Why Neuropsychological Modules Arise*, Cambridge: Cambridge University Press.

Gigerenzer, Gerd (2022), *How to Stay Smart in a Smart World: Why Human Intelligence Still Beats Algorithms*, Cambridge, MA: MIT Press.

Ginsburg, Simona and Eva Jablonka (2019), *The Evolution of the Sensitive Soul: Learning and the Origins of Consciousness*, Cambridge, MA: MIT Press.

Heyes, Cecilia (2018), *Cognitive Gadgets: The Cultural Evolution of Thinking*, Cambridge, MA: Belknap Press.

McGilchrist, Iain (2009), *The Master and His Emissary: The Divided Brain and the Making of the Western World*, New Haven, CT: Yale University Press.

McGilchrist, Iain (2021), *The Matter with Things: Our Brains, Our Delusions, and the Unmaking of the World*, London: Perspective Press.

Noble, Denis (2016), *Dance to the Tune of Life: Biological Relativity*, Cambridge: Cambridge University Press.

Noble, Raymond and Denis Noble (2023), *Understanding Living Systems*, Cambridge: Cambridge University Press.

Seth, Anil (2021), *Being You: A New Science of Consciousness*, London: Faber and Faber.

Shapiro, James (2022), *Evolution: A View from the 21st Century. Fortified. Why Evolution Works as Well as It Does*, Chicago, IL: Cognition Press.

Tallis, Frank (2021), *The Act of Living: What the Great Psychologists Can Teach Us about Surviving Discontent in an Age of Anxiety*, London: Little Brown.

Walker, Sara, Paul Davies, and George Ellis (2017), *From Matter to Life: Information and Causality*, Cambridge: Cambridge University Press.

Wilson, Edward (2012), *The Social Conquest of Earth*, New York, NY: Liveright Publishing.

Notes

Prelims

1. While *Prosperity* referred to the first half of this statement of corporate purpose, it did not include the second half on 'not profiting from producing problems', which is prominent in this book, and, as a result, it did not make the central connection of this book between purpose and profit, and what this implies for a legitimate profit.
2. Speech to Conservative Party Conference, 8 October 1976.
3. Drawing on Plato's Epistle 9, to Archytas, 'No one of us exists for himself alone, but one share of our existence belongs to our country, another to our parents, a third to the rest of our friends, while a great part is given over to those needs of the hour with which our life is beset' [quoted in R.G. Bury (tr.) (1966), *Plato in Twelve Volumes, Vol. 7*, Cambridge, MA: Harvard University Press], Marcus Tullius Cicero's stated in *De Officiis (On Duties)*: 'non nobis solum nati sumus ortusque nostri partem patria vindicat, partem amici'. ('We are not born for ourselves alone; a part of us is claimed by our nation, a part by our friends.') *De Officiis*, Bk 1, Sec. 22. In Bk 3, Secs 23 and 26 of *De Officiis*, Cicero continued that a man should 'never act so as to seek what is another's, nor to appropriate for himself something that he has taken from someone else.… Therefore, all men should have this one object, that the benefit of each individual and the benefit of all together should be the same.' [Quoted in James Hankins (2019), *Virtue Politics: Soulcraft and Statecraft in Renaissance Italy*, Cambridge, MA: Harvard University Press, p. 111.]
4. Noberto Bobbio (1996), *Left and Right: The Significance of a Political Distinction*, Cambridge: Polity Press; and Geoffrey Hodgson (2018), *Wrong Turning: How the Left Got Lost*, Chicago: University of Chicago Press.

Introduction

1. These are described in what is termed 'the Fundamental Theorems of Welfare Economics'. See, for example, Peter Hammond (1997), 'The Efficiency Theorems and Market Failure', https://web.stanford.edu/~hammond/effMktFail.pdf
2. Friedrich Hayek (1945), 'The Use of Knowledge in Society', *American Economic Review*, 35, 519–530 is a classic description of the functioning of markets

and his 1944 book *The Road to Serfdom*, Chicago: Chicago University Press, a powerful indictment of central planning.

3. For an extensive discussion of the problems with capitalism, see Paul Collier, Diane Coyle, Colin Mayer, and Martin Wolf (2021), 'Capitalism: What Has Gone Wrong, What Needs to Change, and How It Can Be Fixed', *Oxford Review of Economic Policy*, 37, 637–649 and the other articles in the same issue of the *Oxford Review of Economic Policy*.

4. Adam Smith (1776), *An Inquiry into the Nature and Causes of the Wealth of Nations*, London, Strahan and Cadell.

5. See George Stigler (1971), 'The Theory of Economic Regulation', *The Bell Journal of Economics and Management Science*, 2, 3–21 for a classic description of regulatory capture.

6. Another widely cited survey of trust is the Edelman Trust Barometer, https://www.edelman.com/sites/g/files/aatuss191/files/2022-01/2022%20 Edelman%20Trust%20Barometer%20FINAL_Jan25.pdf.
   While Ipsos-Mori is restricted to the UK, the Edelman Trust Barometer is international. It records that trust in business globally is not on average as low as that reported in the UK by Ipsos-Mori. However, it also reports considerable international variation with low levels of trust in business in the UK, US, and several other countries, in line with Ipsos-Mori's results.

7. Mark Twain (1869), 'An Open Letter from the Humorist to the Great Railroad King', *Marysville Daily Appeal*, Volume XIX, Number 72, 27 March 1869.

8. A phrase sometimes but not conclusively attributed to Horace Greeley, *New-York Daily Tribune*, 13 July 1865.

9. Matthew Josephson (1934), *The Robber Barons: The Great American Capitalists, 1861–1901*, New York: Harcourt, Brace and Co. and Burton Folsom (1987), *The Myth of the Robber Barons: A New Look at the Rise of Big Business in America*, Herndon, Virginia: Young America's Foundation,

10. Rudolph Peritz (1996), *Competition Policy in America: History, Rhetoric, Law*, Oxford: Oxford University Press.

11. Jonathan Haskel and Stian Westlake (2017), *Capitalism Without Capital: The Rise of the Intangible Economy*, Princeton: Princeton University Press.

12. Note that this statement relates to the ratio of these companies' stock market to their book values. It is not true of the ratio of the book value of their intangible to tangible assets. For example, Alphabet's book value ratio of its intangible assets to its property, plant, and equipment tangible assets in 2021 was 24.4/ 110.6 = 0.22, whereas BASF's, a German chemical company, was nearly three times larger at 13.5/ 21.6 = 0.63, see https://www.wsj.com/market-data/quotes/GOOG/financials/annual/balance-sheet and https://www.wsj.com/market-data/quotes/BASFY/financials/annual/balance-sheet respectively. I am grateful to Fuat Eccer for drawing my attention to this point.

13. Nick Bostrom (2014), *Superintelligence: Paths, Dangers, Strategies*, Oxford: Oxford University Press; Stuart Russell (2019), *Human Compatible: AI and the Problem of Control*, New York: Viking.

14. Stephanie Assad, Emilio Calvano, Giacomo Calzolari, Robert Clark, Vincenzo Denicolò, Daniel Ershov, Justin Johnson, Sergio Pastorello, Andrew Rhodes, Lei Xu, and Matthijs Wildenbeest (2021), 'Autonomous Algorithmic Collusion: Economic Research and Policy Implications', *Oxford Review of Economic Policy*, 37, 459–478.

15. See Gerd Gigerenzer (2022), *How to Stay Smart in a Smart World: Why Human Intelligence Still Beats Algorithms*, Cambridge, MA: MIT Press.

16. Joseph Henrich (2016), *The Secret of Our Success: How Culture Is Driving Human Evolution, Domesticating Our Species, and Making Us Smarter*, Princeton, NJ: Princeton University Press.

17. See Raymond Noble and Denis Noble (2023), *Understanding Living Systems*, Cambridge: Cambridge University Press.

18. The problem was noted by Francesco Petrarca, better known as Petrarch, one of the first humanists in early Renaissance fourteenth-century Italy, who noted that 'the chief element in human actions is the intention of the agent, and it makes a great difference with what motive you tackle an undertaking. And it is not the undertaking itself but your mind (*mens*) which deserves praise or blame: that is what turns good actions into an evil and what seems evil into a good thing.' As a result, whoever 'has been the readier to drag the resisting and unwilling law to match his whim has fulfilled the service of a legal adviser and earned the reputation of a learned man; but if any rare person, far from these wiles, were to seize the right path of bare truth, apart from having no share in profit and influence, he would suffer the ill repute of being a simple and foolish fellow'. Quoted in James Hankins (2019), *Virtue Politics: Soulcraft and Statecraft in Renaissance Italy*, Cambridge, MA: Harvard University Press, p. 10.

19. 'Neither cities nor States nor individuals will ever attain perfection until the small class of philosophers whom we termed useless but not corrupt are providentially compelled, whether they will or not, to take care of the State, and until a like necessity be laid on the State to obey them; or until kings, or if not kings, the sons of kings or princes, are divinely inspired with a true love of true philosophy. That either or both of these alternatives are impossible, I see no reason to affirm: if they were so, we might indeed be justly ridiculed as dreamers and visionaries.' Book VI in *Plato in Twelve Volumes*, translated by Paul Shorey (1969), Cambridge, MA: Harvard University Press.

20. Adam Smith (1759), *The Theory of Moral Sentiments*, London: Strahan and Cadell, VII.ii.I.20.

21. Adam Smith (1776), *An Inquiry into the Nature and Causes of the Wealth of Nations*, London: Strahan and Cadell, Bk 1, Chapter 2.

22. Ryan Patrick Hanley (2019), *Our Great Purpose: Adam Smith on Living a Better Life*, Princeton: Princeton University Press, provides a wonderful account of the significance of *The Theory of Moral Sentiments*.
23. See Roger Crisp (1997), *Mill on Utilitarianism*, London: Routledge.
24. See, for example, Leonard Hobhouse (1911), *Liberalism*, London: Williams and Norgate.
25. 'Nature has placed mankind under the governance of two sovereign masters, pain and pleasure. It is for them alone to point out what we ought to do, as well as to determine what we shall do.' Jeremy Bentham (1789), *An Introduction to the Principles of Morals and Legislation,* see Herbert Hart (1982), *Essays on Bentham*, Oxford: Clarendon Press. The term *homo economicus* is attributed to John Stuart Mill who described economic man as 'a being who desires to possess wealth, and who is capable of judging the comparative efficacy of means for obtaining that end', John Stuart Mill (1836), 'On the Definition of Political Economy; and on the Method of Investigation Proper to It', *London and Westminster Review*, October.
26. Bernard Mandeville (1705), 'The Grumbling Hive: or, Knaves Turn'd Honest', reprinted in 1714 as 'The Fable of the Bees or Public Vices, Public Benefits', available Phillip Harth (1989), *The Fable of the Bees*, London: Penguin. See also Jonathan Bennett (2017) https://www.earlymoderntexts.com/assets/pdfs/mandeville1732_1.pdf.
27. For several illustrations of this, see George Akerlof and Robert Shiller (2016), *Phishing for Phools: The Economics of Manipulation and Deception*, Princeton, NJ: Princeton University Press.

Chapter 1

1. Thomas Hobbes, *Leviathan*, Part 2.
2. There is a large literature on complex adaptive systems and complexity in economics. See, for example, Brian Arthur (2015), *Complexity and the Economy*, Oxford: Oxford University Press; John Miller and Scott Page (2007), *Complex Adaptive Systems: An Introduction to Computational Models of Social Life*, Princeton, N.J.: Princeton University Press; and Melanie Mitchell (2009), *Complexity: A Guided Tour*, Oxford: Oxford University Press.
3. One of the most influential books on reductionism in science was Ernest Nagel (1961), *The Structure of Science: Problems in the Logic of Scientific Explanation*, San Diego: Harcourt, Brace and World.
4. Matthew Lieberman (2013), *Social: Why Our Brains Are Wired to Connect'*, Oxford: Oxford University Press.
5. Denis Noble (2012), 'A Theory of Biological Relativity: No Privileged Level of Causation', *Interface Focus*, 2, 55–64.

6. https://www.ft.com/content/c4f4745c-5f98-11e5-9846-de406ccb37f2.
7. M. Contag et al., 'How They Did It: An Analysis of Emission Defeat Devices in Modern Automobiles', 2017 IEEE Symposium on Security and Privacy (SP), San Jose, CA, 2017, pp. 231–250, doi: 10.1109/SP.2017.66.
8. https://www.ft.com/content/964a2f72-e898-11e6-967b-c88452263daf.
9. See the British Academy (2018), 'Reforming Business for the 21st Century: A Framework for the Future of the Corporation' the British Academy Future of the Corporation Programme, https://www.thebritishacademy. ac.uk/publications/reforming-business-21st-century-framework-future-corporation/
10. Southwest Airlines is a well-known example of a company successfully exploiting complementarities as a low-cost carrier. Michael Porter (1996), 'What Is Strategy?', *Harvard Business Review*, November–December, 37–55 and Mu-Jueng Yang (2021), 'The Interdependence Imperative: Business Strategy, Complementarities and Economic Policy', *Oxford Review of Economic Policy*, 37, 392–415. However, its performance is not by any means always faultless: https://www.ft.com/content/b16f6a6a-19a7-47da-919f-eb589fa51136.
11. Joseph Schumpeter (1942), *Capitalism, Socialism and Democracy*, New York: Harper & Brothers.
12. Source: Oxford English Dictionary.
13. Source: Oxford English Dictionary.
14. A director 'shall discharge their duties with the care that a person in a like position would reasonably believe appropriate under similar circumstances' (US Business Model Corporation Act (2002)) and 'the general knowledge, skill and experience that may reasonably be expected of a person carrying out the functions carried out by the director in relation to the company' (s.174 of the UK Companies Act 2006).
15. *Marchand v. Barnhill*, 2019 WL 2509617, at *15 (Del. 18 June 2019), citing *Caremark Int'l Inc. Deriv. Litig.*, 698 A.2d 959, 971 (Del. Ch. 1996).
16. Narcis Serra and Joseph Stiglitz (eds) (2008), *The Washington Consensus Reconsidered: Towards a New Global Governance*, Oxford: Oxford University Press.
17. Michael Sandel (2020), *The Tyranny of Merit: What's Become of the Common Good*, New York: Macmillan.
18. Alasdair MacIntyre (1981), *After Virtue: A Study in Moral Theory*, Notre Dame: University of Notre Dame Press.

Chapter 2

1. https://www.theguardian.com/world/2020/dec/18/belgian-minister-accidentally-tweets-eus-covid-vaccine-price-list and https://www.bbc.co.uk/news/business-55170756.

2. https://www.ox.ac.uk/news/2020-11-23-oxford-university-breakthrough-global-covid-19-vaccine-0.

3. https://www.gov.uk/government/news/government-launches-vaccine-taskforce-to-combat-coronavirus.

4. https://www.bbc.co.uk/news/health-52394485.

5. https://www.ft.com/content/ddf8ec8c-dc30-43b3-847e-c412704a0296.

6. https://www.ft.com/content/bc90afe6-fc10-11e5-a31a-7930bacb3f5f.

7. https://www.bbc.co.uk/news/business-55170756.

8. https://www.nature.com/articles/d41586-020-02450-x.

9. Bridget Kustin, Mary Johnstone-Louis, Colin Mayer, Judith Stroehle, and Boya Wang (2020), 'Business in Times of Crisis', *Oxford Review of Economic Policy*, 36, 242–255.

10. Danielle Allen, 'A Better Way to Defeat the Virus and Restore the Economy', *The Washington Post*, 26 March 2020.

11. Roswell Quinn (2013), 'Rethinking Antibiotic Research and Development: World War II and the Penicillin Collaborative', *Am J Public Health*, 103(3): 426–434.

12. George W. Merck, 1 December 1950, Commemoration of Founders Speech at Medical College at Richmond.

13. https://www.ft.com/content/844ed28c-8074-4856-bde0-20f3bf4cd8f0 is the 19 June 2020 article; https://www.ft.com/content/f8251e5f-10a7-4f7a-9047-b438e4d7f83a is the updated 1 January 2021 article.

14. Robert Eccles, Colin Mayer, and Judith Stroehle (2021), 'The Difference between Purpose and Sustainability (aka ESG), Harvard Law School Forum on Corporate Governance', 20 August.

15. https://www.ft.com/content/340501e2-e0cd-4ea5-b388-9af0d9a74ce2.

16. https://www.gfanzero.com/press/amount-of-finance-committed-to-achieving-1-5c-now-at-scale-needed-to-deliver-the-transition/.

17. https://assets.bbhub.io/company/sites/63/2021/11/GFANZ-Progress-Report.pdf

18. 'By 2030 Microsoft will be carbon negative, and by 2050 Microsoft will remove from the environment all the carbon the company has emitted either directly or by electrical consumption since it was founded in 1975.' https://blogs.microsoft.com/blog/2020/01/16/microsoft-will-be-carbon-negative-by-2030/.

19. https://www.ft.com/content/8d0c1064-881e-42b4-9075-18e646f3e1ad.

20. David Flood et al. (2021), 'The State of Diabetes Treatment Coverage in 55 Low-Income and Middle-Income Countries: A Cross-Sectional Study of Nationally Representative, Individual-Level Data in 680102 Adults', *The Lancet Healthy Longevity*, 2, 340–351, p. 340, https://www.thelancet.com/journals/lanhl/article/PIIS2666-7568(21)00089-1/fulltext.

21. Jeffrey Sonnenfeld, Steven Tian, Steven Zaslavsky, Yash Bhansali, and Ryan Vakil, 'It Pays for Companies to Leave Russia' (18 May 2022). Available at SSRN: https://ssrn.com/abstract=4112885 or http://dx.doi.org/10.2139/ssrn.4112885.

Chapter 3

1. See for example, Paul Babiak, Craig Neumann, and Robert Hare (2010), 'Corporate Psychopathy: Talking the Walk', *Behavioral Sciences and the Law*, 28, 174–193; Joel Bakan (2004), *The Corporation: The Pathological Pursuit of Profit and Power*, Simon & Schuster; and Martin Brueckner (2013), 'Corporation as Psychopath', in Samuel Idowu, Nicholas Capaldi, Liangrong Zu, Ananda Gupta (eds), *Encyclopedia of Corporate Social Responsibility*, Berlin: Springer.
2. See, for example, Anat Admati (2021), 'Capitalism, Laws, and the Need for Trustworthy Institutions', *Oxford Review of Economic Policy*, 37, 678–689.
3. Paul Polman and Andrew Winston (2021), *Net Positive: How Courageous Companies Thrive by Giving More than They Take*, Boston, MA: Harvard Business Review Press.
4. For an excellent account of how early Christianity transformed our understanding of the nature of wealth and gave it a 'higher purpose' in alleviating poverty in fourth to sixth century AD Rome see Peter Brown (2012), *Through the Eye of a Needle: Wealth, the Fall of Rome, and the Making of Christianity in the West, 350–550 AD*, Princeton NJ: Princeton University Press.
5. Simon Blackburn (2006), *Plato's Republic: A Biography*, New York: Atlantic Monthly Press.
6. This can be regarded as a form of what Nathalie Gold refers to as 'non-self-regarding motivations'—Nathalie Gold (2014), 'Trustworthiness and Motivations', in Nick Morris and David Vines (eds), *Capital Failure: Rebuilding Trust in Financial Services*, Oxford: Oxford University Press.
7. Joseph Heath (2014), *Morality, Competition, and the Firm: The Market Failures Approach to Business Ethics,* Oxford: Oxford University Press. proposes a Market Failures Approach based on promoting Pareto efficient outcomes. As Richard Endörfer and Louis Larue (2022), 'What's the Point of Efficiency? On Heath's Market Failures Approach', *Business Ethics Quarterly,* 1–25 note, this suffers from being both being over-demanding in seeking to address market inefficiencies arising from, for example, incomplete information, transaction costs and problems of the second-best, and under-demanding in failing to incorporate distributional considerations. Instead, one should start from moral principles that may have distributional and Pareto efficiency benefits, not the converse.
7. Ken Binmore (2011), *Natural Justice*, Oxford: Oxford University Press.

8. George Bernard Shaw said in *Man and Superman* (1903) in 'Maxims for Revolutionists—The Golden Rule': 'Do not do unto others as you would that they should do unto you. Their tastes may not be the same.' For an extensive discussion of the emergence and interpretation of the Golden Rule see Jeffrey Wattles (1996), *The Golden Rule*, Oxford: Oxford University Press.

9. It is sometimes suggested that the criticism of the Golden Rule in failing to incorporate differences in preferences is misconceived because you wish them to incorporate your, not their preferences in what they 'do unto you', so you should do the same in what you do to them. However, this at best demonstrates the lack of clarity of the traditional Golden Rule, which the reformulated version resolves.

10. Furthermore, the reformulated version of the Golden Rule emphasizes the importance of its universal adoption. One should not assist others to violate its application in how they in turn conduct their affairs. In other words, it requires account to be taken of the consequential effects further down a chain of individuals or, for example, the supply and distribution of goods and services.

11. Immanuel Kant (1785), *Groundwork for the Metaphysics of Morals*, edited and translated by Allen Wood (ed.) (2018), New Haven, CT., Yale University Press.

12. Iain McGilchrist (2009), *The Master and His Emissary: The Divided Brain and the Making of the Western World*, New Haven, CT: Yale University Press; and Iain McGilchrist (2021), *The Matter with Things: Our Brains, Our Delusions, and the Unmaking of the World*, London: Perspective Press.

13. Joseph Henrich (2016), *The Secret of Our Success: How Culture Is Driving Human Evolution, Domesticating Our Species, and Making Us Smarter*, Princeton, NJ: Princeton University Press.

14. Peter Birks (2005), *Unjust Enrichment*, Oxford: Oxford University Press, Chapter 1. An important feature of unjust enrichment is that it may not involve any aspect of unconsciousness by any party. It is this which renders restitution of the property rather than compensation for the loss sustained as the appropriate response. Birks gives the following example: 'You go shopping with a friend. As you are leaving a department store an assistant comes running up to tell you that he has accidentally given you change for £50 when you had in fact paid with a £20 note. He gave you £30 more than he owed. You may be tempted to insist that you were entirely innocent. It is no doubt true that you were chatting to your friend and did not even notice how much change you were being given. But you will immediately see that a retort of that kind will not strengthen your case to keep the £30. Your innocence is irrelevant. Nor would it do you any good to make a show of anger at the shop assistant's want of care. He himself will admit to having been careless. The fact remains that, so long as you still have the mistaken money, there is no answer to the shop's demand to have it back.' (Chapter 1.)

Chapter 4

1. https://www.youtube.com/watch?v=cUpyL1zVF50.
2. See David Millon (1990), 'Theories of the Corporation', *Duke Law Journal*, 39, 201–262; and Michael Phillips (1994), 'Reappraising the Real Entity Theory of the Corporation', *Florida State University Law Review*, 21, 1061–1123.
3. Adam Smith (1776), *An Inquiry into the Nature and Causes of the Wealth of Nations*, London, Strahan and Cadell.
4. William Lafferty, Lisa Schmidt, and Donald Wolfe (2012), 'A Brief Introduction to the Fiduciary Duties of Directors Under Delaware Law', 116 *Penn St. L. Rev.*
5. *eBay Domestic Holdings, Inc. v. Newmark*, 16 A.3d 1, 34 (Del. Ch. 2010).
6. Leo Strine (2015), 'The Dangers of Denial: The Need for a Clear-Eyed Understanding of the Power and Accountability Structure Established by the Delaware General Corporation Law', 50 *Wake Forest Law Review* 761,768.
7. American Law Institute (2022), Corporate Governance. https://www.ali.org/projects/show/corporate-governance/; Stephen Bainbridge (2022), 'A Critique of the American Law Institute's Draft Restatement of the Corporate Objective', UCLA School of Law, Law & Economics Research Paper No. 22-07; and Eric Orts (2022), https://clsbluesky.law.columbia.edu/2022/06/06/the-alis-restatement-of-the-corporate-objective-is-seriously-flawed/.
8. Ronn Davids (1995), 'Constituency Statutes: An Appropriate Vehicle for Addressing Transition Costs?', *Columbia Journal of Law and Social Problems*, 28, 145–147.
9. Jonathan Springer (1999) 'Corporate Constituency Statutes: Hollow Hopes and False Fears', *Annual Survey of American Law*, 85.
10. Anthony Bisconti (2009), 'The Double Bottom Line: Can Constituency Statutes Protect Socially Responsible Corporations Stuck in Revlon Land', *Loyola of Los Angeles Law Review*, 42.
11. Jonathan Springer (1999), 'Corporate Constituency Statutes: Hollow Hopes and False Fears', *Annual Survey of American Law* 85 at 108.
12. Lucian Bebchuk and Roberto Tallarita (2020), 'The Illusory Promise of Stakeholder Capitalism', *Cornell Law Review*, 106, 91–177.
13. Lucian Bebchuk, Kobi Kastiel, and Roberto Tallarita (2020), 'For Whom Corporate Leaders Bargain', SSRN Working Draft, 367155.
14. Shannon Vaughan and Shelly Arsneault (2018), 'The Public Benefit of Benefit Corporations', *Political Science & Politics*, 51, 54–60.
15. Joan MacLeod Heminway (2018), 'Let's Not Give Up on Traditional For-Profit Corporations for Sustainable Social Enterprise', *University of Missouri-Kansas City Law Review*, 86, 779.
16. Kennan El Khatib (2015), 'The Harms of the Benefit Corporation', *American University Law Review*, 65, 151.

17. Ellen Berrey (2018), 'Social Enterprise Law in Action: Organizational Characteristics of U.S. Benefit Corporations', *Transactions: The Tennessee Journal of Business Law*, 20, 21–114.

18. Michael Dorff, James Hicks, and Steven Davidoff Solomon (2021), 'The Future or Fancy? An Empirical Study of Public Benefit Corporations', *Harvard Business Law Review*, 11, 114–158.

19. Some believe that it is realistic; see, for example, Martin Lipton (2019), 'Directors Have a Duty to Look Beyond Their Shareholders', *Financial Times*, 17 September 2019. They argue that success of the corporation should be evaluated in the long term and in the long run the interests of the corporation and those affected by it coincide because their success and survival are so closely intertwined. But even if that were true that does not address divergences of interests in the short term or the fact that short-term gains in such firms as the 'sin stocks' of Chapter 2 appear to be remarkably durable.

20. This chapter refers to Colin Mayer (2022), 'What is Wrong with Corporate Law? The Purpose of Law and the Law of Purpose', *Annual Review of Law and Social Science*, 18, 283–296 with permission from the *Annual Review of Law and Social Science*, Volume 18, copyright 2022 Annual Reviews.

21. E.g., Companies Act (1862).

22. Chrispas Nyombi (2014), 'The Gradual Erosion of the Ultra Vires Doctrine in English Company Law', *International Journal of Law and Management*, 56, 347–362.

23. There are two categories of fiduciary responsibility—those reflecting the holding of property where the fiduciary has control over the property and those where the fiduciary is entrusted to act on behalf of the beneficiary, not in his own interest. In the first case, the fiduciary must keep the property separate from his own and must not use it for his own benefit. In the second case, the fiduciary must act on the behalf of others not himself.

    A fiduciary obligation therefore arises where the individual 'has control of another's property or has undertaken to act on another's behalf and for that other's benefit and not the fiduciary's own benefit'. (Sarah Worthington (2021), 'Fiduciaries Then and Now', *Cambridge Law Journal*, 80, 154–178, at p. 163. See also Len Sealy (1962), 'Fiduciary Relationships', *Cambridge Law Journal*, 20, 69–81; Len Sealy (1963), 'Some Principles of Fiduciary Obligation', *Cambridge Law Journal*, 21, 119–140; and Len Sealy (1967), 'The Director as Trustee', *Cambridge Law Journal*, 25, 83–103.) This gives rise to equitable duties and responsibilities. It establishes the moral hazard risks which a fiduciary is required to avoid.

    It is the breach of avoidance of conflict and the profit requirement that mark out a fiduciary duty. 'A fiduciary must act in good faith; he must not make a profit out of his trust; he must not place himself in a position where his duty and his interest may conflict; he may not act for his own benefit or the benefit of a third person without the informed consent of his principal…. Mere incompetence is not enough. A servant who loyally does his incompetent best for his master is not unfaithful and is not guilty of a breach of fiduciary duty.' (*Bristol and West Building Society v. Mothew* [1998] Chapter 1, 16, 18 (C.A.) (Millett L.J.).)

Fiduciary responsibility does not derive from trust and confidence. It is proprietary rather than personal. It is not predominantly based on power or influence. The principal determinant is the avoidance of personal gain. It is proscriptive in defining what should not be done, especially in avoidance of conflicts and taking unauthorized profits, not prescriptive in laying down what should be done.

Contractual undertakings and acting with care and skill are not fiduciary responsibilities and apply to non-fiduciaries as well as fiduciaries. They give rise to contractual and tortious duties. Breaches of influence and confidence are not therefore fiduciary in nature. Likewise, those in a position of power do not have to be in denial of self-interest but merely acting in good faith in the pursuit of the endeavour. For the power holder it is the purpose that matters not the avoidance of self-interest.

Lord Justice Leggatt defines an obligation of good faith as requiring 'a party to subordinate its own commercial interests to those of the other party to the contract. Good faith is not altruism. It does not require one party to put the other party's interests before its own. That is the nature of a fiduciary duty. Good faith is different. Good faith demands loyalty, not to the other party, but to the agreement itself—to the bargain the parties have made through which each has sought to advance its own commercial interests by mutual collaboration.' Georg Leggatt (2016), 'Contractual Duties of Good Faith', Lecture to the Commercial Bar Association on 18 October 2016, available at https://www.judiciary.uk/wp-content/uploads/2016/10/mr-justice-leggatt-lecture-contractual-duties-of-faith.pdf. In other words good faith relates to the purpose of the contract as against the interests of the parties to it.

In contrast, the duty of the fiduciary is to act in the interests of the beneficiary and not in the self-interest of the fiduciary. This does not diminish the significance of contract or tort but is supplementary to them in the obligations imposed on fiduciaries and the remedies that can be sort of them. Nor does it diminish the significance of power relations being exercised in good faith and for proper purposes, which relate to constitutional and governance matters.

Fiduciary responsibilities go beyond these in establishing that the fiduciary has additional responsibilities to avoid self- at the expense of other regarding benefits. They do not impose a duty to act in the interests of others per se because they do not require the fiduciary to act at all but if he does then he must lay aside his own self interests in determining the interests of others. The remedy for a breach of fiduciary duty is therefore appropriately in relation to the restoration, remedying or repair of the property not repairing the harm to the claimant herself. It is the control of the assets and the consequence for the assets that is the focus of the fiduciary responsibility, not the consequence for the individual.

24. Reinier Kraakman, John Armour, Paul Davies, Luca Enriques, Henry Hansmann, Gerard Hertig, Klaus Hopt, Hideki Kanda, Mariana Pargendler, Wolf-Georg Ringe, and Edward Rock (2017), *The Anatomy of Corporate Law*, Oxford: Oxford University Press; and David Kershaw (2018), *The Foundations of Anglo-American Corporate Fiduciary Law*, Cambridge: Cambridge University Press.

25. Asaf Raz dismisses the suggestion that corporate law should be classified as public rather than private law. He notes that 'it is no coincidence that corporate statutes, such as the Delaware General Corporation Law, state that corporations may only engage in "any lawful act or activity." Indeed, "[t]he modern practice of allowing corporations to broadly state their purpose as pursuing 'any lawful activity' still reflects a public-regarding limit on corporate activity." This statement is entirely accurate; yet, it is crucial to remember that "public regarding" is not the same as "public law," and does not mean that the "state" is directly involved in corporate affairs—not any more than contract law's prohibition on unlawful provisions turns contract law to public law, or makes the state party to every contract.' Asaf Raz (2021), 'Why Corporate Law is Private Law', SSRN Working Paper No. 3991950, p. 27.

26. 'Happy are those who live under a discipline which they accept without question, who freely obey the orders of leaders, spiritual or temporal, whose word is fully accepted as unbreakable law; or those who have, by their own methods, arrived at clear and unshakeable convictions about what to do and what to be that brook no possible doubt. I can only say that those who rest on such comfortable beds of dogma are victims of forms of self-induced myopia, blinkers that may make for contentment, but not for understanding of what it is to be human.' Isaiah Berlin (1997), 'The Pursuit of an Ideal', in Henry Hardy and Roger Hausheer (eds), *The Proper Study of Mankind*, Chatto and Windus, p. 14.

27. Explanatory Notes to the UK Companies Act 2006, s.172 note 330.

28. British Academy (2022), 'Implications of the British Academy Future of the Corporation Findings for Corporate Legal Responsibility', Discussion Paper for the Standing International Forum of Commercial Courts (SIFoCC).

29. See the British Academy (2019), 'Principles for Purposeful Business', the British Academy Future of the Corporation Programme, https://www.thebritishacademy.ac.uk/publications/future-of-the-corporation-principles-for-purposeful-business/; and British Academy (2021), 'Policy and Practice for Purposeful Business: The Final Report of the Future of the Corporation Programme', https://www.thebritishacademy.ac.uk/publications/policy-and-practice-for-purposeful-business/

30. Oliver Hart and Luigi Zingales (2017), 'Companies Should Maximize Shareholder Welfare Not Market Value', *Journal of Law, Finance, and Accounting*, 2, 247–274; Eleonora Broccardo, Oliver Hart, and Luigi Zingales (2020), 'Exit vs. Voice', European Corporate Governance Institute, Finance Working Paper No. 694/2020; Oliver Hart and Luigi Zingales (2022), 'The New Corporate Governance', ECGI Working Paper, 640/2022; and Paul Brest, Ron Gilson, and Mark Wolfson (2019), 'How Shareholders Can (and Can't) Create Social Value', *Journal of Corporation Law*, 44, 205.

31. There are reasons beyond profit why they may wish to confer benefits on other parties. See, for example, Roland Bénabou and Jean Tirole (2010), 'Individual and Corporate Social Responsibility', *Economica*, 77, 1–19.; and John Armour, Geeyoung Min, Brandon Garrett, and Jeffrey Gordon (2020), 'Board Compliance', *Minnesota Law Review*, 104, 1191.

32. Martin Wolf (2023), *The Crisis of Democratic Capitalism*, London: Penguin Random House.

Chapter 5

1. Tony Honoré (1987), *Making Law Bind*, Oxford: Clarendon Press 1987, 166–179.

2. This chapter draws on Colin Mayer (2020), 'Ownership, Agency, and Trusteeship: An Assessment', *Oxford Review of Economic Policy*, 36, 223–240 and other papers in the same issue of the *Oxford Review of Economic Policy*.

3. Residual right and agency theories in economics are particularly associated with Ronald Coase (1960), 'The Problem of Social Cost', *Journal of Law and Economics*, 3, 1–44; Harold Demsetz (1967), 'Toward a Theory of Property Rights', *American Economic Review*, 57, 347–359; Sanford Grossman and Oliver Hart (1986), 'The Costs and Benefits of Ownership: A Theory of Lateral and Vertical Integration', *Journal of Political Economy*, 94, 691–719; Oliver Hart (1995), *Firms, Contracts and Financial Structure*, Oxford: Oxford University Press; Michael Jensen and William Meckling (1976), 'Theory of the Firm: Managerial Behavior, Agency Costs and Ownership Structure', *Journal of Financial Economics*, 3, 305–360.

4. Jim Collins (1994), *Built to Last*, London: Random House Press.

5. Oliver Hart and Luigi Zingales (2017), 'Companies Should Maximize Share-holder Welfare Not Market Value', European Corporate Governance Institute, Finance Working Paper Series, no. 521.

6. See Maria Rosa Antognazza (2016), *Liebniz: A Very Short Introduction*, Oxford: Oxford University Press.

7. https://www.thetimes.co.uk/article/paris-overtakes-london-as-europes-biggest-stock-market-k05h785d2.

8. Belen Villalonga, Peter Tufano, and Boya Wang (2022), 'Corporate Owner-ship and ESG Performance', Working Paper, Said Business School, University of Oxford.

9. https://www.justice.gov/opa/pr/boeing-charged-737-max-fraud-conspiracy-and-agrees-pay-over-25-billion.

10. See Peter Brown (2012), *Through the Eye of a Needle: Wealth, the Fall of Rome, and the Making of Christianity in the West, 350–550 AD*, Princeton NJ: Princeton University Press.

11. Ammianus Marcellinus (c.330–395 AD), *History, XIV.16: The Luxury of the Rich in Rome, c. 400 A.D.* William Stearns Davis (ed.) (1912), *Readings in Ancient History: Illustrative Extracts from the Sources*, 2 Vols, Boston: Allyn and Bacon, Vol. II: Rome and the West.

12. Global net private wealth is the sum of all financial and non-financial assets held by the private sector. See Lucas Chancel, Thomas Piketty, Emmanuel Saez, and Gabriel Zucman et al., *World Inequality Report 2022*, World Inequality Lab, https://wir2022.wid.world/www-site/uploads/2022/03/0098-21_WIL_RIM_RAPPORT_A4.pdf.

13. World Federation of Exchanges, *2021 Market Highlights*, https://www.world-exchanges.org/storage/app/media/FY%202021%20Market%20Highlights%20v3.pdf.

14. Financial Action Task Force (2022), https://www.fatf-gafi.org/publications/fatfrecommendations/documents/r24-statement-march-2022.html.

15. Adriana De La Cruz, Alejandra Medina, and Yung Tang (2019), 'Owners of the World's Largest Companies', OECD Capital Market Series, Paris.

16. John Armour (2020), 'Shareholder Rights', *Oxford Review of Economic Policy*, 36, 314–340 notes that lobbying and political contributions to weaken regula-tion appear to yield positive returns to shareholders, particularly in regulated and concentrated industries—John Coates (2012), 'Corporate Politics, Gover-nance, and Value Before and After Citizens United', *Journal of Empirical Legal Studies*, 9, 657–696.

17. Peter Hall and David Soskice (2001), *Varieties of Capitalism: The Institu-tional Foundations of Comparative Advantage*, Oxford: Oxford University Press.

Chapter 6

1. Enacting Purpose Initiative (2020), 'Enacting Purpose within the Modern Corporation: A Framework for Boards of Directors'.
2. https://www.novonordisk.com/about/defeat-diabetes.html.
3. Niels Kroner (2011), *A Blueprint for Better Banking: Svenska Handelsbanken and a Proven Model for More Stable and Profitable Banking*, Petersfield: Harriman House.
4. Ben Jackson and Joy Genevieve (2021), 'Mahindra First Choice: Orchestrating the Used-Cars Ecosystem', in Bruno Roche and Colin Mayer (eds), *Putting Purpose into Practice: The Economics of Mutuality*, Oxford: Oxford University Press.

Chapter 7

1. This chapter is a revised version of Colin Mayer (2019), 'Valuing the Invaluable: How Much is the Planet Worth?', *Oxford Review of Economic Policy*, 35, 109–119.
2. HM Government (2018), *A Green Future: Our 25 Year Plan to Improve the Environment*.
3. HM Government (2011), *The Natural Choice: Securing the Value of Nature*, CM 8082.
4. Natural Capital Coalition (2016). *Natural Capital Protocol*. London: Natural Capital Coalition.
5. Ernst Schumacher (1989), *Small is Beautiful: A Study of Economics as if People Mattered*, Harper Perennial.
6. Natural Capital Committee (2014), *The State of Natural Capital: Restoring Our Natural Assets: Second Report to the Economic Affairs Committee* and Natural Capital Committee (2017), 'How to Do It: A Natural Capital Workbook'.
7. Kenneth Arrow, Partha Dusgupta, Lawrence Goulder, Kevin Mumford, and Kirsten Oleson (2012), 'Sustainability and the Measurement of Wealth', *Environment and Development Economics* 17, 317–353; Kirk Hamilton and Cameron Hepburn, (2017), *National Wealth: What Is Missing, Why It Matters*, Oxford: Oxford University Press; and United Nations (2014), *System of Environmental Economic Accounting 2012—Central Framework*.
8. In fact, concerns about the environment have a long pedigree. As early as 1800, Alexander von Humboldt warned that humankind had 'the power to destroy the environment and the consequences could be catastrophic', Alexander von Humboldt, Diary, 4 March 1800, quoted in Andrea Wulf (2016), *The Invention of Nature: The Adventures of Alexander von Humboldt, The Lost Hero of Science*, London: John Murray.

9. Natural Capital Committee (2017), 'Economic Valuation and Its Applications in Natural Capital Management and the Government's 25-year Environment Plan', Working Paper.

10. Friedrich Hayek (1935), 'The Maintenance of Capital', *Economica*, 2, 241–274; John Hicks (1965), *Capital and Growth*, Oxford: Clarendon Press; John Hicks (1974), 'Capital Controversies: Ancient and Modern', *American Economic Review*, 64, 307–316.

11. Dieter Helm (2015), *Natural Capital*, New Haven, CT: Yale University Press.

12. Jeremy Edwards, John Kay, and Colin Mayer (1987) *The Economic Analysis of Accounting Profitability*, Oxford: Clarendon Press.

13. John Piccolo (2017), 'Intrinsic Values in Nature: Objective Good or Simply Half of an Unhelpful Dichotomy?', *Journal of Nature Conservation*. 37, 8–11.

14. For a recent example in relation to antibiotics, see Bradley Hover et al. (2018), 'Culture-Independent Discovery of the Malacadins as Calcium-Dependent Antibiotics with Activity against Multidrug-Resistant Gram-Positive Pathogens', *Natural Microbiology*, 3, 415–422.

15. For evidence on the speed at which such evolution can occur, see Sangeet Lamichhaney et al. (2017), 'Rapid Hybrid Speciation in Darwin's Finches', *Science*, 23, 224–228.

16. Ernst Schumacher (1989), *Small Is Beautiful: A Study of Economics as if People Mattered,* Harper Perennial.

17. Colin Mayer (2013), 'Unnatural Capital Accounting', Natural Capital Committee Discussion Paper; Colin Mayer (2016), *Introduction to the Natural Capital Committee's Corporate Natural Capital Accounting Project*. London: ICAEW.

18. Natural Capital Committee (2015), *Corporate Natural Capital Accounting*. London: Natural Capital Committee.

19. This mirrors the case that Edward Barbier sets out that 'scientists who advocate the need for planetary boundaries to limit human capital impacts on critical global sinks and resources are aligning with the strong substitutability perspective, which argues that some natural capital may not be substituted and are inviolate'. See Edward Barbier (2019), 'The Concept of Natural Capital', *Oxford Review of Economic Policy*, 35, 14–36. See also David Pearce (1988), 'Economics, Equity and Sustainable Development', *Futures*, 20, 598–605 and Eric Neumayer (2013), *Weak vs Strong Sustainability: Exploring the Limits of Two Opposing Paradigms* (4th edition), Cheltenham: Edward Elgar.

20. See Alex Edmans and Marcin Kacperczyk (2022), 'Sustainable Finance', *Review of Finance*, 26, 1309–1313, and other papers in the same issue of the *Review of Finance*; Dirk Schoenmaker and Willem Schramade (2019), *Principles of Sustainable Finance*, Oxford: Oxford University Press; the European Green Deal, https://commission.europa.eu/strategy-and-policy/priorities-2019-2024/european-green-deal_en;   the   Corporate

Sustainability Reporting Directive, https://finance.ec.europa.eu/capital-markets-union-and-financial-markets/company-reporting-and-auditing/company-reporting/corporate-sustainability-reporting_en; the Sustainable Finance Disclosure Regulation, https://eur-lex.europa.eu/legal-content/EN/TXT/PDF/?uri=CELEX:32019R2088&from=EN; and the EU Taxonomy, https://finance.ec.europa.eu/sustainable-finance/tools-and-standards/eu-taxonomy-sustainable-activities_en.

Chapter 8

1. EU Regulation on sustainability-related disclosures in the financial sector recognizes the need for no-harm performance measurement. (EU) 2019/2088 states in section (17) that 'it is necessary to lay down a harmonized definition of 'sustainable investment' which provides that the investee companies follow good governance practices and the precautionary principle of 'do no significant harm' is ensured, so that neither the environmental nor the social objective is significantly harmed'. See https://eur-lex.europa.eu/legal-content/EN/TXT/?uri=CELEX:32019R2088.
2. For a more extensive discussion of these issues see Clara Barby, Richard Barker, Ronald Cohen, Robert Eccles, Christian Heller, Colin Mayer, Bruno Roche, George Serafeim, Judith Stroehle, Rupert Younger, and Thaddeus Zochowski (2021), 'Measuring Purpose: An Integrated Framework', https://papers.ssrn.com/sol3/papers.cfm?abstract_id=3771892.
3. Robert Kaplan and Karthik Ramanna have proposed a solution to the problem of attributing environmental detriments in supply chains using the concept of *E-liability*, which reflects the incremental environmental impact (for example CO_2 emission) that a company causes in its supply chain. It is analogous to attributing the value added contributed by a company in a supply chain to the value of the final product. See Robert Kaplan and Karthik Ramanna (2021), 'Accounting for Climate Change: The First Rigorous Approach to ESG Reporting', *Harvard Business Review,* November-December https://hbr.org/2021/11/accounting-for-climate-change
4. See: https://thegiin.org/impact-investing/need-to-know/.
5. Oliver Hart and Luigi Zingales (2018), 'Companies Should Maximize Shareholder Welfare Not Market Value', *Journal of Law, Finance and Accounting*, 2, 247–274; and Oliver Hart and Luigi Zingales (2022), 'The New Corporate Governance', European Corporate Governance Institute, Law Working Paper, No. 640/2022.
6. See the Impact-Weighted Accounts Project at Harvard Business School, https://www.hbs.edu/impact-weighted-accounts/Pages/default.aspx, and the Value Balancing Alliance, https://www.value-balancing.com/.

7. See, for example, Malcolm Baker, Daniel Bergstresser, George Serafeim, and Jeffrey Wurgler (2022), 'The Pricing and Ownership of US Green Bonds', *Annual Review of Financial Economics*, 14, 415–437. The Green Bond market is currently estimated to be around $2 trillion globally—https://www.climatebonds.net/2022/11/green-bond-market-hits-usd2tn-milestone-end-q3-2022#:~:text=The%20total%20green%2C%20social%2C%20sustainability,by%20the%20end%20of%20Q3.

8. For an extensive discussion of the relation between corporate purpose, business models, accounting and reporting, see Colin Mayer, Anette Mikes, and Sudhir Rama Murthy (2023), 'Responsible Business Theory and Accounting', mimeo, Said Business School.

9. See: https://www.sbs.ox.ac.uk/research/centres-and-initiatives/oxford-initiative-rethinking-performance.

10. Novartis (2021), 'Measuring and Valuing Our Impact', https://www.reporting.novartis.com/2021/novartis-in-society/our-approach/how-we-create-value/measuring-and-valuing-our-impact.html.

Chapter 9

1. Raghuram Rajan and Luigi Zingales (2003), *Saving Capitalism from the Capitalists: Unleashing the Power of Financial Markets to Create Wealth and Spread Opportunity*, New York: Crown Publishing.

2. Francesco Cordaro, Marcel Fafchamps, Colin Mayer, Muhammad Meki, Simon Quinn, and Kate Roll (2022), 'Microequity and Mutuality: Experimental Evidence on Credit with Performance-Contingent Repayment', National Bureau of Economic Research Working Paper No. 30411.

3. This section draws on Colin Mayer, Philip McCann, and Jacob Schumacher (2021), 'The Structure and Relations of Banking Systems: The UK Experience and the Challenges of "Levelling-Up"', *Oxford Review of Economic Policy*, 37, 152–171.

4. Melina Papoutsi (2021), 'Nothing Compares to Your Loan Officer—Continuity of Relationships and Loan Renegotiation', *European Central Bank, Research Bulletin*.

5. Colin Mayer (2013), *Firm Commitment: Why the Corporation Is Failing Us and How to Restore Trust in It*, Oxford: Oxford University Press; and Colin Mayer (2018), *Prosperity: Better Business Makes the Greater Good*, Oxford University Press.

6. Thorsten Beck, Ross Levine, and Alexey Levkov (2010), 'Big Bad Banks? The Winners and Losers from Bank Deregulation in the United States', *The Journal of Finance*, 65, 1637–67; Sean Becketti and Charles Morris (1992), 'Are Bank Loans Still Special?', *Economic Review—Federal Reserve Bank of Kansas*

City, 77, 71–71; John Boyd and Mark Gertler (1993), 'US Commercial Banking: Trends, Cycles, and Policy', *NBER Macroeconomics Annual*, 8, 319–368; and Jan-Pieter Krahnen and Reinhard Schmidt (2004), *The German Financial System*, Oxford, Oxford University Press.

7. Hoai-Luu Nguyen (2019), 'Are Credit Markets Still Local? Evidence from Bank Branch Closings', *American Economic Journal: Applied Economics*, 11, 1–32.

8. Sumit Agarwal and Robert Hauswald (2010), 'Distance and Private Information in Lending', *Review of Financial Studies*, 23, 2757–2788; and Andrea Bellucci, Alexander Borosiv, and Alberto Zazzaro (2014), 'Do Banks Price Discriminate Spatially? Evidence from Small Business Lending in Local Credit Markets', *Journal of Banking and Finance*, 37, 4183–4197.

9. Allen Berger and Gregory Udell (1995), 'Relationship Lending and Lines of Credit in Small Firm Finance', *The Journal of Business*, 68, 351–382; Rodrigo Canales and Ramana Nanda (2012), 'A Darker Side to Decentralized Banks: Market Power and Credit Rationing in SME Lending', *Journal of Financial Economics*, 105, 353–366; Hans Degryse and Steven Ongena (2005), 'Distance, Lending Relationships, and Competition', *The Journal of Finance*, 60, 231–266; and Gabriel Jiménez, Vicente Salas, and Jesus Saurina (2009), 'Organizational Distance and Use of Collateral for Business Loans', *Journal of Banking & Finance*, 33, 234–243.

10. Hoai-Luu Nguyen (2019), 'Are Credit Markets Still Local? Evidence from Bank Branch Closings', *American Economic Journal: Applied Economics*, 11, 1–32.

11. Christopher Simpson (2013), *The German Sparkassen (Savings Banks)*, London: Civitas.

12. Franz Flögel (2018), 'Distance and Modern Banks' Lending to SMEs: Ethnographic Insights from a Comparison of Regional and Large Banks in Germany', *Journal of Economic Geography*, 18, 35–57.

13. Dariusz Wójcik and Duncan MacDonald-Korth (2015), 'The British and the German Financial Sectors in the Wake of the Crisis: Size, Structure and Spatial Concentration', *Journal of Economic Geography*, 15, 1033–1054; and Britta Klagge, Ron Martin, and Peter Sunley (2018), 'The Spatial Structure of the Financial System and the Funding of Regional Business: A Comparison of Britain and Germany', in Ron Martin and Jane Polland (eds), *Handbook on the Geographies of Money and Finance*, Cheltenham: Edward Elgar.

14. Hans Degryse, Kent Matthews, and Tianshu Zhao (2018), 'SMEs and Access to Bank Credit: Evidence on the Regional Propagation of the Financial Crisis in the UK', *Journal of Financial Stability*, 38, 53–70.

15. Stefan Gartner and Franz Flögel (2013), 'Dezentrale vs. Zentrale Bankensysteme? Geographische Marktorientierung und Ort der Entscheidungsfindung als Dimensionen zur Klassifikation von Bankensystemen', *Zeitschrift für Wirtschaftsgeographie*, 57, 105–121.

16. *The Economist* (2019), 'They Know Their Customers—The State of America's Community Banks: Don't Write off the Admirable Bantamweights of the

Industry', 9 May, see: https://www.economist.com/finance-and-economics/ 2019/05/11/the-state-of-americas-community-banks.
17. Luke Petach, Stephen Weiler, and Tessa Conroy (2021), 'It's a Wonderful Loan: Local Financial Composition, Community Banks, and Economic Resilience', *Journal of Banking and Finance*, 126, 1–20.
18. Robert King and Ross Levine (1993), 'Financial Intermediation and Economic Development', in Colin Mayer and Xavier Vives (eds), *Capital Markets and Financial Intermediation*, Cambridge: Cambridge University Press.
19. Colin Mayer (1988), 'New Issues in Corporate Finance', *European Economic Review*, 32, 1167–1183.
20. Julian Franks, Colin Mayer, Hideaki Miyajima, and Ryo Ogawa (2022), 'Managing Ownership: The Evidence from Japan', RIETI Discussion Paper.

Chapter 10

1. The four Asian tigers refer to Hong Kong, Singapore, South Korea, and Taiwan, and the East Asian Miracle to Indonesia, Japan, Malaysia, and Thailand in addition. See Jose Campos and Hilton Root (1996), *The Key to the Asian Miracle: Making Shared Growth Credible*, Washington DC: Brookings Institution.
2. This chapter draws on Colin Mayer (2022), 'Inequality, Firms, Ownership and Governance', IFS Deaton Review of Inequalities, https://ifs.org.uk/inequality/ inequality-firms-ownership-and-governance.
3. https://researchbriefings.files.parliament.uk/documents/SN02784/SN02784.pdf
4. Alex Davenport and Ben Zarenko (2020), 'Levelling Up: Where and How', in Carl Emmerson, Christine Farquharson, and Paul Johnson, *IFS Green Budget: October 2020*, 315–371, Institute for Fiscal Studies, London; Luke Raikes, Arianna Giovannini, and Bianca Getzel (2019), 'Divided and Connected: Regional Inequalities in the North, the UK and the Developed World. The State of the North 2019', *Institute for Public Policy North*, November; and Philip McCann (2020), 'Perceptions of Regional Inequality and the Geography of Discontent: Insights from the UK', *Regional Studies*, 54, 256–267.
5. The problem is not just one of regional inequality. Along with the US, the UK has an exceptionally high level of income inequality between the top and bottom deciles of household incomes (see John Burn Murdoch, 'Britain and the US Are Poor Societies with Some Very Rich People', *Financial Times*, 16 September 2022).
6. FCA, Listing Rules (Listing Regime Enhancements) Instrument 2014 (FCA 2014/33). This has recently been amended to allow dual class share structures within premium listings; see https://www.fca.org.uk/publication/policy/ps21-22.pdf.

7. Gareth Campbell, Meeghan Rogers, and John Turner (2016), 'The Rise and Decline of the UK's Provincial Stock Markets, 1869–1929', Working Paper Series, No. 2016–03, Queen's University Centre for Economic History, Belfast.

8. Colin Mayer (2013), *Firm Commitment: Why the Corporation is Failing Us and How to Restore Trust in It*, Oxford: Oxford University Press.

9. Saul Estrin and Adeline Pelletier (2018), 'Privatisation in Developing Countries: What Are the Lessons of Experience?', *The World Bank Research Observer*, 33, 65–102; and Donal Palcic and Eoin Reeves (2019), 'Performance: The Missing "P" in PPP Research', *Annals of Public and Cooperative Economics*, 9, 221–226.

10. See the 2021 Sustainability First report 'Regulation for the Future: The Implications of Public Purpose for Policy and Regulation in Utilities', https://www.sustainabilityfirst.org.uk/publications-project-research-reports/242-regulation-for-the-future.

11. Susanne Frick and Ian Taylor (2022), 'Insights from Resilient Cities: A Research Note', Blavatnik School of Government, University of Oxford: https://www.bsg.ox.ac.uk/sites/default/files/2022-03/2022-03%20Research%20note%20-%20Insights%20from%20Resilient%20Cities_1.pdf.

12. Elinor Ostrom refers to polycentric rather than multi-level governance in complex systems; see Elinor Ostrom (2010), 'Beyond Markets and States: Polycentric Governance of Complex Economic Systems', *American Economic Review*, 100, 641–672.

13. James Hankins (2019), *Virtue Politics: Soulcraft and Statecraft in Renaissance Italy*, Cambridge, MA: Harvard University Press.

14. British Academy (2022), 'Teaching Purposeful Business in UK Business Schools', A Future of the Corporation Briefing Note, https://www.thebritishacademy.ac.uk/documents/4400/Teaching_Purposeful_Business_in_UK_Business_Schools_Future_of_the_Corporation.pdf.

The End

1. https://www.federalreserve.gov/newsevents/speech/powell20220826a.htm.

2. https://www.energy.gov/articles/doe-national-laboratory-makes-history-achieving-fusion-ignition; and https://www.nature.com/articles/d41586-022-04440-7.

3. Thomas Eliot (1942), *Four Quartets: The Little Gidding*, London: Faber and Faber.

4. Milton Friedman (1962), *Capitalism and Freedom*, Chicago: Chicago University Press.

5. Milton Friedman (1962), *Capitalism and Freedom*, Chicago: Chicago University Press.

Index

For the benefit of digital users, indexed terms that span two pages (e.g., 52–53) may, on occasion, appear on only one of those pages.

Introductory Note
References such as '178–179' indicate (not necessarily continuous) discussion of a topic across a range of pages. Wherever possible in the case of topics with many references, these have either been divided into sub-topics or only the most significant discussions of the topic are listed. Because the entire work is about 'capitalism', the use of this term (and certain others which occur constantly throughout the book) as an entry point has been restricted. Information will be found under the corresponding detailed topics.